Media cultures

Media Cultures challenges the elitism and cultural pessimism of much Anglo-American and Continental cultural debate with regard to the role and power of transnational media practices.

In a series of ten innovative essays, an international group of media researchers explores a wide range of cultural practices across national borders and the cultural politics associated with these everyday practices and debates.

Their subjects, ranging from the complex phenomenon of Americanisation, 'Syndicated Wheels of Fortune' and the multi-channel universe, to cult film and the TV fiction of Dennis Potter, provide an innovative response to the all-important question of reconceptualising the theory and practice of transnational media cultures.

The editors Michael Skovmand is Associate Professor of English Literature at the University of Roskilde, Denmark. Kim Christian Schrøder is Associate Professor of English Language at the University of Roskilde, Denmark.

Contributors Ib Bondebjerg, Kirsten Drotner, Jostein Gripsrud, Anne Jerslev, Peter Larsen, David Morley, Graham Murdock, Søren Schou, Kim Christian Schrøder, Michael Skovmand.

Communication and Society
General Editor: James Curran

Media Cultures

Reappraising Transnational Media

edited by
Michael Skovmand
and
Kim Christian Schrøder

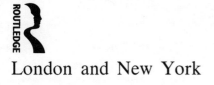

London and New York

First published 1992
by Routledge
11 New Fetter Lane, London EC4P 4EE

Simultaneously published in the USA and Canada
by Routledge
a division of Routledge, Chapman and Hall, Inc.
29 West 35th Street, New York, NY 10001

Phototypeset in 10/12 Times by
Intype, London
Printed in Great Britain by
TJ Press (Padstow) Ltd, Padstow, Cornwall

British Library Cataloguing in Publication Data
Media cultures: reappraising transnational media.
  I. Skovmand, Michael II. Schrøder, Kim Christian
302.234

Library of Congress Cataloging in Publication Data
Media cultures: reappraising transnational media / edited
  by Michael Skovmand and Kim Christian Schrøder.
    p.   cm. — (Communication and society)
    Includes bibliographical references and index.
  1. Mass media. 2. Popular culture. 3. Communication,
International. 4. Intercultural communication.
  I. Skovmand, Michael. II. Schrøder, Kim. III. Series:
Communication and society (New York, N.Y.)
P91.M379 1992
302.23—dc20   91–30422

ISBN 0–415–06384–1
ISBN 0–415–06385–X pbk

Contents

Notes on contributors

Jostein Gripsrud is Professor at the Department of Mass Communication (Humanities Section), University of Bergen, Norway. He has published books on the social history of literature and theatre, and numerous influential articles on film, television and cultural studies in international and Scandinavian journals.

Anne Jerslev is Assistant Professor at the Department of Cinema, Television and Communication, University of Copenhagen, Denmark. She has published widely on film, television and popular culture. Her most recent book is about film director David Lynch: *David Lynch i vore øjne* (David Lynch in Our Eyes), Copenhagen 1991. Her present work deals with Danish female stars.

Peter Larsen is Professor in the Department of Mass Communication, University of Bergen, Norway. He is the editor of the recent Unesco study, *Import/Export: International Flow of Television Fiction*, and has written extensively on mass communication research and semiotics.

David Morley is Lecturer in Communications at Goldsmiths College, London University, UK. He is the author of *The Nationwide Audience* and *Family Television* and of numerous articles on qualitative audience research, cultural theory, and other aspects of mass communication research.

Graham Murdock is Reader in Sociology at the University of Loughborough, UK. He has written widely on the impact of the new communications media and on the political economy of the communications industries. He is the author or co-author of *Demonstrations and Communication* (1970), *Televising 'Terror-*

ism' (1984) and *The Battle for Television: Private Pleasures and Public Goods* (1990).

Søren Schou is Associate Professor of Danish literature at the University of Roskilde, Denmark. He is the author of books on Heinrich Böll (1972) and contemporary Danish writers (1976, 1981), and has contributed to the *History of Danish Literature* (1985) and *History of World Literature* (1991) (both written in Danish). His articles on literature and criticism have appeared in academic periodicals and Danish newspapers.

Kim Christian Schrøder is Associate Professor of English, University of Roskilde, Denmark. He has been Visiting Scholar at the Annenberg School of Communications, USC, Los Angeles. He is co-author of *The Language of Advertising* (Basil Blackwell 1985). The focus of his recent research is on media audiences and their reception of television fiction and corporate advertising.

Michael Skovmand is Associate Professor of English Literature, University of Aarhus, Denmark. He is editor and contributor to *The Angry Young Men* (1976), *George Orwell and 1984* (1984) and *Media Fictions* (1989). His recent work on the mass media, published in Scandinavian journals, has focused on questions of taste and the popular.

Introduction

Kim Christian Schrøder and Michael Skovmand

When people encounter a scholar who devotes his or her entire research interest to Shakespearian drama, Tennyson's poetry, or Orwell's novels, they naturally expect this scholar to show a deep appreciation for the literature which is studied.

When people encounter a scholar who spends time studying women's magazines, advertisements, or television series they equally naturally expect the scholar to look down upon these media and to be motivated by a desire to curtail their pernicious cultural effects.

It is a constituent part of our educational ethos that the teaching of literature should serve to open the pupils' eyes to the greatness of our cultural past and to induce them to lifelong enjoyment of literary art. In the teaching of the contemporary media, on the other hand, the explicit purpose is more often than not to make the pupils aware of their shallowness of vision and ideological seduction, so as to enable them to better resist the lure of these popular cultural forms.

At the bottom of such public and educational discourses lie deep-rooted notions of what constitutes cultural excellence and inferiority, good taste and bad taste, 'quality' and 'trash'. Generally speaking, in our Western culture, very few people would dream of awarding the stamp of quality to any product of the commercial cultural industries. It is one of the aims of this book to intervene critically and creatively in the contemporary cultural and educational debate about these issues in order to promote a less prejudiced understanding of our audio-visual culture.

Besides the paternal-elitist discourses of the various national guardians of culture, the single most coherent body of thought dealing with the negative effects of the cultural industries is that of the so-called Frankfurt School, conceived in the shadow of Fascism in the 1930s and then developed (as its main spokesmen, Theodor Adorno and Max Horkheimer among them, had to flee to the United States) under the impression of American laissez-faire capitalism in material and cultural production.

Ever since, implicitly or explicitly, this theory of the cultural industry as 'mass deception' has dominated the 'critical tradition' of analysis in many European countries and in the United States as well. According to this theory, 'enjoyment' and 'pleasure' are inherently oppressive, because they serve to make people forget the inhumanity of the ruling social order:

> To be pleased means to say Yes, . . . Pleasure always means not to think about anything, to forget suffering even where it is shown. Basically it is helplessness, it is flight; not, as is asserted, flight from a wretched reality, but from the last remaining thought of resistance.
>
> (Adorno and Horkheimer 1944/1977: 367)

The Frankfurters were especially concerned about the conse-quences of the audio-visual media (film and television) because their mode of communication is furthest from the needs of rational man: the sound film thus 'leaves no room for imagination or reflection on the part of the audience' (Adorno and Hork-heimer 1944/1977: 353), just as the then new medium of tele-vision was held to lead to 'the impoverishment of aesthetic matter so drastically that by tomorrow the thinly veiled identity of all industrial culture products can come triumphantly out into the open' (352).

These are obviously voices from the past, but their cultural pessimism is matched, if not surpassed, by quite contemporary contributors to the debate, who have gained an enormous follow-ing among educators. Thus Neil Postman, who received the 1984 George Orwell Award from the US Association of College Eng-lish for his book *Amusing Ourselves to Death*, idealises the role of the printed word in our culture, finding that 'the phrase "serious television" is a contradiction in terms', because 'television speaks in only one persistent voice – the voice of entertainment', and this is a voice which 'short-circuits introspection' (Postman 1987: 81, 105).

Expressing an 'essentialism' akin to that of Adorno and Hork-heimer, Postman argues that every medium, independently of its socio-economic mode of organisation, has a technologically inherent nature, or essence, which predisposes it to certain forms of knowledge. Thus television's epistemology 'is not only inferior to a print-based epistemology but is dangerous and absurdist' (1987: 27), because in this medium 'serious public conversation becomes a form of baby-talk', making the prospect of 'culture-death' imminent (1987: 161).

The wide currency of this vision of contemporary culture as composed of narcotised TV zombies becomes manifest when the press succeeds in disseminating a new popular coinage that labels the average modern individual a 'couch potato'. As defined in a major Danish daily, 'the average American has become a red-eyed couch potato demanding TV entertainment 24 hours a day' (*Politiken*, 5 March 1989). For most of its would-be intellectual readers, however, the couch potato will not be a new phenomenon: it is just a new catchy label for the growing number of modern consumers to which they are fortunate not to belong.

TOWARDS A REHABILITATION OF POPULAR CULTURE

In reading Postman one can at least take comfort from the fact that his credibility as cultural analyst and prophet is somewhat impaired by his striking ignorance of any type of media research over the last twenty years.

The general drift of this research – which the contributors to this book wholly embrace – has been to take popular cultural forms more seriously and, more specifically, to examine what popular audiences are actually doing with the cultural products that they consume in their everyday lives. The basic premise has been to try to understand popular cultural practices as meaningful activities: as part of people's ongoing attempts to make sense of their lives and the specific class, gender, race, and other identities which they inhabit.

Such audience-orientated research has opened up completely new roads of inquiry into the role of the media in society, in particular by refusing to rely on the speculative evidence about audience meaning processes acquired through critical analysis of media products, or 'texts', alone. In exploring empirical methods of inquiry into cultural experiences, so-called reception research has restored the commitment in humanistic media research to studying all stages in the communication process: production, message/text, and consumption, after having for decades turned a blind eye to the strange amputation of the audience dimension from the critical perspective.

The Frankfurters had no qualms about amputating the audience from the study of cultural industry processes, as they quite explicitly regarded consumers as brain-washed accomplices to the cultural industry mass seduction project: 'The attitude of the public, which ostensibly and actually favours the system of the culture industry, is a part of the system and not an excuse for it' (Adorno and Horkheimer 1944/1977: 350).

In other words, 'the deceived masses . . . insist on the very ideology which enslaves them' (Adorno and Horkheimer 1944/1977: 359), for the simple reason that the ideological content is projected directly on to their minds. When consumers expose themselves to cultural industry products, no intellectual effort is necessary to process the meanings, which are imprinted on their consciousness: 'There is nothing left for the consumer to classify. Producers have done it for him' (1944/1977: 352).

Such views on cultural signifying processes permeated cultural analysis until the 1980s, both in semiotically orientated media research and in Lacanian analyses of the way in which texts carry 'subject positions' which readers then must occupy. What empirical reception research into a number of media and genres has discovered over the last ten years has been diametrically opposed to this view. A picture is now beginning to emerge in which popular media audiences are characterised not only by a degree of resilience to the dominant ideological meanings encoded in mainstream cultural products, but also by their cultural connoisseurship, their sensitive and often sophisticated appreciation of the aesthetic creations of the cultural industries (see, for instance, Moores 1990).

Some researchers have recently expressed concern that reception studies are too myopic, as they isolate one moment in the cultural process as being of ultimate significance, ignoring the wider socio-cultural conditions of audience practices (Ang 1990). Ang even suggests that 'what we need is not more ethnographic work on discrete audience groups, but on reception as an integral part of popular cultural practices that articulate both "subjective" and "objective", both "micro" and "macro" processes' (Ang 1990: 244).

We feel that such a call for a stop to research on discrete

audiences is perhaps a bit premature: we need a lot more work on actual decoding processes at the micro level – after all, the published work in this field encompasses no more than, say, a couple of hundred titles (most of them articles), and most of it has been devoted to just one medium (television) and just two genres (soap opera, news).

Nevertheless, we believe that the time has also come to start asking the 'So what?' questions to reception studies: what are the wider social and cultural implications of the increased knowledge we have about audience signifying processes? Two of the contributions discuss this question.

Anne Jerslev analyses the classic and contemporary cult film, not as a textual form, but as a specific relationship between the visual text and an audience drawing on a 'visual encyclopedia'. On the basis of her own empirical work on teenage film and video audiences she then discusses whether the specific form of reception of the cult film genre can be seen as embryonic of more general audience experiences of audio-visual products among future, more aesthetically sophisticated generations.

And taking off from a cross-cultural study of *Dynasty* audiences in the United States and Denmark, Kim Schrøder argues that we must abandon universal and absolute standards of cultural quality and formulate a new, relative concept of quality founded on the audience experiences of audio-visual products, taking into account the diversity of social taste patterns.

THE AMERICAN CONNECTION AND CULTURAL IDENTITY

We live in an increasingly transnational media culture in which access to a multitude of national and transnational TV channels has become an everyday phenomenon for people all over Europe. Each contribution to this book explores different dimensions of this fact, as the authors analyse the media and genres within the transnational circuit, or compare the media cultures of different countries that may be differently involved in this circuit.

It is impossible to discuss contemporary transnational media cultures without facing the spectre of Americanisation, as it is still widely believed that if the European countries do not react forcefully and mobilise their rich and diverse cultural potential, we shall be committing spiritual suicide in a flood of Donald Duck Americanisation.

The fear of being Americanised, dating back to the beginning of the twentieth century, has persistently seen American materialism and vulgarity washing over an authentic, aesthetically sophisticated national cultural heritage. Most recently, the European Community in unison with the Council of Europe has launched its ambitious Audio-visual Eureka Programme, designed to provide an adequate European response to the technological and cultural challenge coming from the American–Japanese audio-visual industries – 'American pictures combined with Japanese technology overwhelming Europe', as François Mitterrand put it in his address to the founding conference (Commission of the European Communities 1989: 16). Insisting that culture forms 'the very cement of Europe', Mitterrand went on to reprimand those who talk of a European community 'as if there were not something that could be called – perhaps the term is a little too broad and demands further thought – a European culture', hastily adding that 'culture is an old issue, one I shall not venture into here. I am not that rash' (13–14). In other words, even among those who are taking the initiatives intended to bolster a 'European culture', one looks in vain for a concrete definition of this very concept.

This pan-European programme is based on the argument that the audio-visual media enter every mind in every home in every country. Therefore, so the argument runs, it is through these media that one must tackle the problem of cultural identity today, by encouraging the diffusion of different cultures and languages, and new forms of aesthetic expression.

First of all, it should be asked whether the label of 'Americanisation' is an adequate description of what is threatening European culture(s). According to recent research it is not: Sepstrup (1989) finds that

> the dominant paradigm among researchers and politicians that West European television is dominated by US-produced programmes is *generally* not very well supported by 'hard' data when the US imports are related to total *supply* and not to total *imports* . . . The fact is that in the EEC countries US television has a minor role compared to West European-produced television.
>
> (Sepstrup 1989: 41)

As Sepstrup also notes, even if the share of American TV fiction on European prime-time screens is not negligible, we know next to nothing about the possible effect on the European, national, social and cultural fabric of exposure to US television. Consequently, some may firmly believe that national identities and traditions are being eroded, while others contend that the central historical element of national cultures will be resistant to the force of Americanisation.

Those of the contributors to this book who discuss Americanisation and other questions of cultural identity refuse to conceptualise the discussion in such simplistic terms. Finding that until now the debates about cultural identity and cultural imperialism have functioned within a largely uninterrogated model of what 'cultural identities' are, David Morley sees cultural identities as a product of structural semiotic oppositions and differences, not as fixed entities that can be separately defined by enumerating their positive characteristics. From this perspective, European culture is constituted through its very oppositions to American culture, Asian culture, Islamic culture, and so on.

This view of cultural identity also means that American culture cannot be regarded as a monolithic entity that impinges on a unified European culture, or unified national cultures. As Søren Schou argues in his chapter, 'Postwar Americanisation and the Revitalisation of European Culture', within each European nation American culture in its diverse mainstream and counter-culture variants unsettles the already existing structural oppositions between the domestic cultures of class, gender, age, and so on. Morley and Schou thus both find, from the respective contexts of British and Danish cultural history, that American cultural products, by breaking away from traditional, class-based notions of good taste, could be absorbed by the actual tastes and desires of large numbers of working-class people.

The consumption and enjoyment of American goods and popular culture thus came to serve for these working-class consumers as a symbolic resistance to the paternalism of the national cultural establishment, as expressed most visibly in everyday life through the public-service broadcasting institutions that until recently commanded the public cultural space in most West European countries.

Moreover, as pointed out by Jostein Gripsrud in his comparative study of the French film *A bout de souffle* and its American version, *Breathless*, the cultural relations between the US and Europe are a two-way street. Notions of the American or the European Other are incorporated and given culturally specific inflections when directors such as Jean-Luc Godard or Jim McBride make concrete sense of them within their specific conditions of production. And what appear as thematic continuities, or straight loans, such as the figure of the melancholy macho, on closer analysis make a different kind of sense, depending on the particular moment to which they are seen to relate. Thus, *A bout de souffle* makes sense primarily in the context of French Modernism/Existentialism, whereas *Breathless* is clearly part of the American melodramatic tradition.

Finally, on the question of Americanisation, we would agree with Silj (1988) that perhaps the main advantage of American television lies in its outstanding production quality – which is not particularly 'American' in the cultural sense of the word:

> Does the merit or demerit of having invented a certain way of producing television belong to the Americans? Or is it just that television works at its best when certain rules are applied, the Americans being the first to have learned and exploited those rules?
>
> (Silj 1988: 204)

In other words, we may see the Americans as merely spearheading, for specific cultural and social reasons, a more general transnational *modernisation process* in the audio-visual field. It may even be, as Søren Schou argues, that American culture has thereby revitalised a European culture that has had very little to offer the majority of the population in post-industrial, urbanised society.

Perhaps revitalisation is also a relevant perspective to adopt for an assessment of the role of transnational news channels in European countries whose populations have been accustomed to just one or two public-service channels. As Peter Larsen observes in his comparative analysis of CNN and Norwegian Broadcasting Corporation News, the recent availability of CNN on Norwegian screens has at least enabled a population previously dependent on the paternal authority of its national public-service channel to discover that there are in fact alternative ways of organising and presenting the news. Basing his analysis on news coverage of the Gulf War, he investigates, among other things, the radically different modes of address, and the accompanying implied viewer positions, employed by the discourses of transnational news channels like CNN and national public-service news programmes.

COMMERCIAL AND PUBLIC-SERVICE BROADCASTING

The chief culprit for the dearth of audio-visual material which ordinary people could perceive as relevant to their hopes and fears has been the traditional European public-service broadcasting institution. Although there has been a lot of whimpering from the intellectual establishment over the assaults on this hallowed phenomenon through deregulation, commercialisation, privatisation and other measures inflicted on them by right-wing governments, sensible defenders of public-service broadcasting are now acknowledging that this institution is indeed in need of revitalisation if it wishes to continue as a major political and cultural forum for national audiences. As Sepstrup (1989) puts it,

> the competition from private broadcasters may be seen as the spur which forces the traditional public service institutions to adopt a new general programming approach and to learn a new television language.
>
> (Sepstrup 1989: 36)

The greatest concern has been expressed over the alleged disappearance of diversity and quality in programming. Often the American situation has been referred to as evidence of the devastating consequences of having a full-blown commercial system in broadcasting. However, only a gross misrepresentation of American broadcasting makes it possible to use it as an example of undiversified cultural production.

In a commercial system two equally strong tendencies are operative: one towards 'common denominator' production, aiming to reach the mainstream taste; the other towards segmented production, targeting the programmes towards well-defined audience groups with specialised needs and interests. In the US, especially in metropolitan areas where minorities have grown to considerable numbers, the broadcasting menu is much more ethnically and culturally diverse than in many European countries, as a comparison between the TV listings of a major US newspaper and those of *The Times* (UK), *Die Welt* (Germany), or *Berlingske Tidende* (Denmark) will demonstrate.

Miège (1987) in his analysis of the logics at work in the new cultural industries sees a strengthening of diversity, because even though 'multimedia corporations . . . are effecting multiproduct business strategies' (Miège 1987: 283), they will have to address all sections of the diverse audience with a range of differentiated products. Especially within the 'flow media', to which broadcasting belongs, programme categories will 'become more specialised and address themselves to more strictly defined audiences' (1987: 276).

It is thus quite likely that a completely market-based system would be able to cater for all or most tastes and interests, though not necessarily in a way that is socially and politically desirable if we wish the media to continue as cohesive forces in our increasingly culturally fragmented societies. There is 'relatively little to be said for a system where minorities simply speak to themselves' (Mulgan 1990: 27). Diversity across channels will thus serve to ghettoise each taste culture within its own narrowcast channel(s).

The real challenge of diversity in broadcasting today, then, consists in creating public-service broadcasting channels which combine diversity of interests, content, and style with a broad cross-cultural appeal to the entire national forum of all citizens – in addition to the presumably vast number of commercial 'common denominator' and special-interest channels available at the local, regional, national, and transnational levels. In his contribution Graham Murdock discusses how in capitalist democracies we can promote a communications system which extends diversity and openness, and thereby provides adequate resources for citizenship. He firmly believes that in spite of the obvious possibilities for narrowcasting, the market cannot deliver the communication resources required for full citizenship in the increasingly multicultural nations of Europe; at the same time, public-service broadcasting institutions have been so over-centralised and unresponsive that it is easy to understand why people are attracted to the dynamism and apparent openness of commercial systems. Murdock therefore argues for 'a new kind of public communicative space, rooted in a constructive engagement with emerging patterns of political and cultural diversity'.

There are some encouraging signs within contemporary media cultures that such a new cultural space is being explored, for instance in new forms of television fiction. As Ib Bondebjerg points out in his analysis of the TV mini-series of Dennis Potter, television is becoming the site of a mixed culture where main-stream meets experiment, and the popular poetic merges with forms of anti-narrative and meta-fiction. Increasingly, as is also demonstrated by the example of the TV series *Twin Peaks*, television is developing into a creative medium in its own right, rather than a repository of genres predating television. And, increasingly, the growth of televisual literacy produces sophisticated audiences who do not identify with the implied naive addressee of traditional television discourse.

The conceptualisation of television as 'flow' rather than as strings of distinct 'texts' further emphasises that such notions as *intertextuality* and *meta-fictionality* are central to any contemporary conceptualisation of what is happening between audiences and television screens.

It is thus becoming increasingly clear that the conventional disparagement of commercial television fare as appealing merely to 'the lowest common denominator', always a highly controversial and superficial metaphor, makes little if any sense when applied to contemporary media cultures. In fact, this type of cultural criticism, as argued by Kirsten Drotner in her chapter on 'Modernity and Media Panics', is part of wider discursive practices orchestrated to contain the culturally unknown: historically, as subaltern classes have gained power and visibility; and repeatedly, as part of the dominant adult generation's attempt to contain the innovative anarchism and vigour of successive youth cultures. However, as Drotner goes on to point out, necessary as it may be to diagnose the repetitive and emotionally charged rhetoric of successive media panics from the time of the French Revolution onwards, this analysis can be no substitute for a broad and culturally committed discussion of the contemporary substance of such terms as cultural quality and the desirability of a shared cultural politics.

A related concern with the relationship between the media and more general cultural practices motivates Michael Skovmand's chapter on the transnational game show *Wheel of Fortune*. He points out that television is not simply a vehicle for the communication of strings of audio-visual material, but should rather be seen as the site of a wide range of cultural practices which may or may not take on televisual forms, and the ramifications of which are part of wider familial, social, and institutional practices and interests. Thus, televisual notions of value and cultural quality are an integral part of the broader formation of these notions as they are transmitted and negotiated in the national and international marketplaces. Much has been made of the trend towards audience segmentation and narrowcasting. In a wider temporal perspective it is perhaps just as important to point to how, for the first time since the Renaissance, virtually the whole range of cultural discourses vie for attention within the same forum. This cultural proximity makes for convergence and cross-referencing, but it also dramatises and accentuates cultural difference and distinction. Hierarchical cultural practices are constantly being undermined by the universal accessibility of the marketplace, which makes the price-tag the primary signifier of quality. Sophisticated processes of exclusion and distinction are continually deployed to maintain the currency of existing cultural capital. By contrast, popular cultural practices of pleasure and participation are continually being circumscribed or colonised by interests of privilege or profitability. Television, struggling for a unitary sense of constituency, attempts to employ the broadest possible modes of address: the gendered mode, the consumerist mode, or the mode of citizenship.

In its deregulated form television is the single most powerful vehicle in the Western world for both direct advertising and for more indirect forms of promoting 'consumer awareness'. It is also the single most powerful forum of public communication, as well as the primary site of the social negotiation of ideas, values, and lifestyles. A major issue of the cultural politics of the nineties will be to what extent television, in what seems to be an increasingly deregulated form, can remain a credible and acceptable forum for all three forms of discourse. In other words, whether public-service broadcasting, in its broadest definition, is to be maintained as a necessary mode of cultural cohesion, or whether it should simply be seen, in retrospect, as a minor transitional aberration.

MEDIA CULTURES: A SYNTHESISING APPROACH

Each in its own way, the contributions to this book are all concerned with illuminating both the role of the audio-visual media in the production of cultural meaning in the 1990s and, self-reflexively, with the changing ways of thinking about and analysing these media. The book is thus part of what Curran

(1990) has recently called 'the new revisionism in mass communication research'.

Writing from the vantage point of cross-fertilised Anglo-American and Continental cultural theories, we wish to offer a politically committed contribution to the ongoing exploration of the media/culture nexus that can 'potentially strengthen the radical tradition of communications research' (Curran 1990: 135), by continuing to regard the media as a site of social and cultural struggle.

In order to understand the complex meaning processes of the contemporary media fully, we would need a synthesising framework that includes all stages in the communication process: production, texts, and audiences, and which explores these processes at all levels from the local to the transnational, asking how the media affect and are affected by existing hierarchies of social and cultural power.

Such a synthesis is too massive a task for anyone to accomplish. We believe, though, that each of the ten essays collected here offers important directions to key elements in the changing understanding of our contemporary media cultures.

REFERENCES

Adorno, T. and Horkheimer, M. (1977) 'The Culture Industry. Enlightenment as Mass Deception', in J. Curran *et al.* (eds), *Mass Communication and Society*, London: Edward Arnold/The Open University (German edn 1944).

Ang, I. (1990) 'Culture and Communication. Towards an Ethnographic Critique of Media Consumption in the Transnational Media System', *European Journal of Communication* 5: 239–60.

Commission of the European Communities (1989) *Assises européennes de l'audiovisuel. Projet EUREKA audiovisuel.*

Curran, J. (1990) 'The New Revisionism in Mass Communication Research. A Reappraisal', *European Journal of Communication* 5: 2–3.

Miège, B. (1987) 'The Logics at Work in the New Cultural Industries', *Media, Culture and Society* 9: 273–89.

Moores, S. (1990) 'Texts, Readers and Contexts of Reading. Developments in the Study of Media Audiences', *Media, Culture and Society* 12: 9–29.

Mulgan, G. (1990) 'Television's Holy Grail: Seven Types of Quality', in G. Mulgan (ed.), *The Question of Quality*, London: British Film Institute.

Postman, N. (1987) *Amusing Ourselves to Death. Public Discourse in the Age of Show Business*, London: Methuen.

Sepstrup, S. (1989) 'Implications of Current Developments in West European Broadcasting', *Media, Culture and Society* 11: 29–54.

Silj, A. (1988) *East of Dallas. The European Challenge to American Television*, London: British Film Institute.

Part I

Media cultures:
the historical process

Chapter 1

Citizens, consumers, and public culture

Graham Murdock

FIGURES IN A LANDSCAPE

For much of the 1980s, talk about social change in advanced capitalist societies centred around questions of consumption. Governments pursued privatisation policies on the promise that they would increase consumer choice. Marketing men set about mapping style communities based on shared tastes, and academics, reading these signs of the times, declared the arrival of the post-modern age in which appearance eclipsed substance and what you saw was all you got. By the beginning of 1989, the figure of the consumer had come to dominate the imaginary landscape of late capitalism.

Elsewhere another movement was gathering momentum. In country after country, from the Philippines to South Korea, people came on to the streets to protest against entrenched centres of political power and demand the rights of citizenship. This movement finally forced its way to the forefront of Western consciousness in 1989, when the pro-democracy movement in China was brutally suppressed and when, in the space of a few weeks in the Autumn, students, professionals, and workers in the major European Communist countries demonstrated against the party's automatic right to rule and called for a genuine competition for power, supported by the right to speak and organise freely. These movements proved unstoppable, and opposition groups were carried to office on a tide of popular acclaim.

Commentators in the West were quick to proclaim a victory for capitalism. In the battle for hearts and minds, America's vision of the future had apparently won a decisive victory. From now on, they argued, societies would aspire to 'liberal democracy in the political sphere combined with easy access to VCRs and stereos in the economic sphere' (Fukuyama 1990: 33). Dissenting voices pointed out that although the Communist dream had clearly failed, the problems of inequality and injustice within capitalism which had produced it remained unresolved (see, for instance, Bobbio 1989: 24). But their warnings were drowned out by the clamour of Western self-congratulation.

By a quirk of historical timing, the dramatic events of the Autumn of 1989 were preceded by the lavish celebrations marking the 200th anniversay of the French Revolution. What linked the events of 1789 with those of 1989 was a shared struggle for full citizenship. The crowds who stormed the Bastille prison and demonstrated in Wenceslas Square were not simply protesting against corrupt regimes, but were claiming the right to participate in shaping public institutions and public culture. They were demanding to be treated as citizens and not as subjects. The language of citizenship was central to all the revolutions in Eastern Europe. 'People had had enough of being mere components in a deliberately atomised society; they wanted to be citizens, individual men and women with dignity and responsibility, with rights but also with duties, freely associating in civil society' (Garton Ash 1990: 148).

In interpreting these demands, the apologists of American capitalism forgot that the French Revolution was waged on behalf of equality and fraternity as well as of liberty. Striking the balance between these three terms has proved enormously problematic, and nowhere more so than in the field of public communications. This difficulty poses particular problems for democracy, since a dynamic and open public communications system is indispensable to the development of full citizenship in complex societies. Consequently, how we organise this system will have profound implications for the quality of public life and popular participation.

The crucial choice is not, as so many commentators suppose, between state licensing and control on the one side and minimally regulated market mechanisms on the other. It is between policies designed to reinvigorate public communications systems which are relatively independent of both the state and the market, and policies which aim to marginalise or eradicate them. Unfortunately, the struggle for a more open and responsive public communications system won't be easy, since existing public cultural institutions are currently in a condition of crisis. To understand why, we need to look more closely at the links between communications and citizenship and to trace the roots of the contemporary situation.

CITIZENS, CONSUMERS, AND COMMUNICATIONS

The growth of the modern communications systems in capitalist societies has been inextricably linked to both the rise of mass democracy and the growth of mass consumption. From the outset, however, commentators of a variety of political hues have pointed to the contradictory relations between capitalist economics and liberal democratic politics, consumerism and citizenship. As the major vehicle for the mass advertising that promoted the new consumer system and the central forum for organising political information and debate in the emerging liberal democratic system based on universal suffrage, the communications system was caught in the centre of this tension.

Whilst the exercise of citizenship presupposes collective action in pursuit of equality and fraternity as well as of individual liberty, the ideology of consumerism encourages people to seek private solutions to public problems by purchasing a commodity. It urges them to buy their way out of trouble rather than pressing for social change and improved social provision. It also redefines the nature of citizenship itself so that it 'becomes less a collective, political activity than an individual, economic activity – the right to pursue one's interests, without hindrance, in the marketplace' (Dietz 1987: 5). This sells people short. The consumer marketplace offers an array of competing products, but it doesn't confer the right to participate in deciding the rules that govern either market transactions or the distribution of wealth and income that allows people to enter the market in the first place. It provides choice at a price, but without empowerment. Before moving on to look at how the tensions between consumption and citizenship have played themselves out in the history of communications, however, we need to define what we mean by citizenship.

THE DIMENSIONS OF CITIZENSHIP

Citizenship must be underwritten by rights in four basic spheres. Firstly, there need to be civil liberties, in the sense of rights that are exercised in the sphere of civil society. These need to be guaranteed by law and free from arbitrary curtailment or suspension by the state. They include: freedom of speech; freedom of movement; freedom of association; and freedom of conscience. Without these basic legal rights to express dissent and to organise opposition, it is impossible to work towards a fully democratic society based on open debate and a genuine competition for power. At the same time, in capitalist societies, civil rights also include the freedom to own and dispose of personal property.

Liberal theorists saw property rights as an essential curb on extensions of state power on the grounds that they supported a plurality of countervailing power centres and ensured that people did not have to depend on government subsidies. But it was soon clear that the unequal distribution of wealth and income under capitalism played a crucial role in regulating access to communicative resources for both producers and consumers. The resulting tension between rights of possession on the one hand and rights of expression on the other has been a major focus of debate ever since.

The second set of rights, and the ones most closely associated with notions of citizenship from classical times onwards, are the political rights to participate in the making and exercise of the laws by which one consents to be governed. In liberal democracies these entail both the right to choose between competing candidates for legislative assemblies, and the right to participate in the application of laws in the courts through the jury system.

Whilst the struggle for civil rights commenced in earnest in the eighteenth century and the long battle for universal adult suffrage in the nineteenth, the institution of the third and fourth sets of rights, social and cultural, is unique to the twentieth. It is based on an extended definition of citizenship as the right to full membership of a social and cultural formation. This implies two things: the right to participate in existing patterns of social and cultural life and the right to challenge these configurations and develop alternative identities and forms of expression.

In a democratic society, however, it is not enough for people simply to possess citizenship rights. They must be able to exercise them, and this requires policies designed to guarantee access to the conditions needed for effective participation. These obviously include the resources secured by welfare policies – a certain amount of 'free' time, a minimum level of health care, and a basic level of disposable income. But they also include the symbolic resources provided by a diverse and open communications system.

CITIZENSHIP AND PUBLIC COMMUNICATIONS

We can identify three important ways in which the communications system is implicated in the constitution of citizenship. First, in order for people to exercise their full rights as citizens, they must have access to the information, advice, and analysis that will enable them to know what their personal rights are and allow them to pursue them effectively. Second, they must have access to the broadest possible range of information, interpretation and debate on areas that involve public political choices, and they must be able to use communications facilities in order to register criticism and propose alternative courses of action. And third, they must be able to recognise themselves and their aspirations in the range of representations on offer within the central communications sectors and be able to contribute to developing and extending these representations.

To meet these criteria, a communications system needs to be both diverse and open. It must enable a society 'to see its questions and puzzles articulated, its uncomfortable contradictions explored, the half truths and absurdities which it is tempted to believe laughed at, its invisible experiences brought into the light, its marginalised groups allowed a voice' (Mepham 1990: 65).

But how should we organise the communications system so as to extend diversity and openness and thereby provide adequate resources for full citizenship? For commentators of a neo-liberal economic persuasion the answer is self-evident. Only free markets can guarantee diversity of expression and open debate. This is an enticing argument, but it takes no account of the history of public communications.

We can identify two formative moments in the development of debates around the connections between communications, commercialism, and citizenship. The first is the period from 1880 to 1918. This saw the beginnings of modern mass democracies, the emergence of the mass consumer system, and the rise of new forms of enterprise in the communications industries, typified by the 'press barons'. The second moment, the 1920s, is dominated by arguments about the proper constitution and purposes of the new medium of broadcasting, and by the struggle to secure a public system which privileged a particular concept of the needs of citizenship over the market's claims to give consumers what they wanted. The legacy of these two moments defines the situation in which we now find ourselves. On the one hand we see a concerted attack on public cultural institutions and a vigorous promotion of market mechanism and the pleasures of consumption. And on the other we see the collapse of public broadcasting's paternalistic project and its inability to respond creatively to the deepening crisis of cultural representation. In this situation, the central question is whether or not it is possible to devise a conception of citizenship – based on a politics of diversity and difference – which can provide a new justification for public communications and offer alternative definitions of empowerment to those promoted by the market. To see why such a rationale is needed, we must first understand why the market cannot deliver the resources required for full citizenship.

THE MOMENT OF THE 'PRESS BARONS': THE LIMITS OF THE MARKET

The market's inability to underwrite citizenship rights was not immediately obvious. On the contrary, the nineteenth-century battle for freedom of the press was more or less universally identified with the struggle against state licensing and government censorship and in favour of the right to compete in the marketplace of ideas restricted only by commercial disciplines and consumer demands.

From this perspective, press freedom was a simple extension of personal freedom of speech and choice. Unfortunately, 'advocates of "liberty of the press" were far too sanguine about the capacity of market competition to ensure universal access of citizens to the media of public communications; they failed to examine the inevitable tension between the free choices of investors and property owners and the freedom of choice of citizens' (Keane 1989: 39). In contrast, the more acute supporters of a commercial press saw very clearly that it would favour the interests of capital, both economically and ideologically. As Milner-Gibson, a leading British campaigner against government controls, pointed out in the mid 1850s, a market system would concentrate the 'cheap press in the hands of men of respectability, and of capital' and give them 'the power of gaining access by newspapers . . . to the minds of the working class' (quoted in Corran and Seaton 1985: 26–7). Subsequent developments bore him out.

In the second half of the century, the increasing professionalisation and scale of newspaper publishing, coupled with the escalating price of new production technologies, made launching a newspaper a more and more expensive proposition. The result was a significant increase in press concentration as less well financed enterprises folded or were taken over by proprietors with deeper pockets. By the century's turn, the age of the press barons had arrived. The fact that a small number of owners could exercise such widespread control over the flow of public information and the organisation of public debate prompted considerable concern among democratically minded observers.

Their other major worry centred on the popular press's growing reliance on advertising finance. As the radical American writer and journalist Upton Sinclair pointed out: 'Financially speaking . . . a newspaper or popular magazine is a device for submitting competitive advertising to the public, the reading-matter being bait to bring the public to the hook' (Sinclair 1919: 282). As critics saw it, this situation presented a three-fold problem. Firstly, dependence on advertising revenue opened newspapers to editorial pressure from large advertisers wishing to promote their corporate interests or prevent the publication of damaging material. Secondly, even if the news was not manipulated, the growth of advertising content privileged the speech of commerce and squeezed the space available to other voices. Thirdly, the advertisers' need for mass sales deformed public debate by pulling the popular press towards sensationalism.

By the early 1900s it was clear to many democrats that organising public communications along purely commerical lines would not provide the cultural resources for universal and substantive citizenship. They had arrived at a paradox. They saw that the press was a major public institution in the sense that it was central to the functioning of a democratic system, but they recognised that private ownership and market dynamics prevented it from performing this function. As the American commentator Delos Wilcox put it in 1900, 'The newspaper, which is pre-eminently a public and not a private institution, the principal organ of society for distributing what we may call working information, ought not to be controlled by irresponsible individuality . . . It is absurd that an intelligent, self-governing community should be the helpless victim of the caprice of newspapers managed solely for individual profit' (Wilcox 1900: 86–9).

Clearly some initiative was needed to square this circle. As the Chicago sociologist Edward Ross argued in 1910, 'Just as the moment came when it was seen that private schools, loan libraries, commerical parks, baths, gymnasia, athletic grounds, and playgrounds would not answer, so the moment is here for recognising that the commercial news-medium does not adequately meet the needs of democratic citizenship' (Ross 1910: 310). Given the deeply ingrained identification of press freedom with freedom from government finance, most commentators ruled out direct public subsidy. As Delos Wilcox lamented: 'The American people must dearly love the freedom of the press, or we should have heard before now much talk of government control or operation of the newspaper' (Wilcox 1900: 90).

One widely canvassed solution to this problem was the idea of endowed papers, funded by public-spirited men and women of wealth, run by boards of trustees drawn from the 'great and the good', and dedicated to rational information and debate. As Ross put it, 'the endowed newspaper would not dramatise crime, or gossip of private affairs: above all, it would not "fake", "doctor", or sensationalise the news . . . it would be a corrective newspaper' (Ross 1910: 311). Because it could not be 'bought, bullied or bludgeoned' by business interests, Ross argued, it would be free to 'blurt out the damning truth' about corporate misdeeds, compensating for the commercial press's failings as a Fourth Estate. He admitted that such a high-minded endeavour 'could not begin to match the commercial press in circulation'; but he felt that it would attract a significant readership among 'teaches, preachers, lecturers and public men, who speak to people eye to eye' and thereby achieve a general impact through the process we now know as two-step flow' (Ross 1910: 311).

This proposal assumed that people of 'moral and intellectual worth', as Ross called them, knew what was best for the 'ordinary' person. It derived from a paternalistic model of capitalist democracy that accepted the ascendency of the market but urged successful professionals and businessmen 'to use their superior judgement and wealth to provide services to the community' which would counter 'the covert dominance of private interests within the public sphere' (Smith 1989: 191).

THE MOMENT OF BROADCASTING: COMMERCE AND CITIZENSHIP

Although endowed newspapers failed to make much headway, the argument that public communication was too important to be left entirely to private enterprise rumbled on, and surfaced again when the future of radio was debated after the First World War.

In the early 1920s, radio in America was very much 'a contested terrain', with corporations wanting to deploy it for commercial purposes and religious groups, intellectuals, educators, professionals, and radicals hoping to use it to further their cultural goals (Kellner 1990: 30–2). The result was a proliferation of signals, which the government was under pressure to regulate. The question was: 'Whose interests should regulation seek to protect?'

In a powerful speech to Congress in 1926, the Secretary of Commerce, Herbert Hoover, argued that radio was 'a public concern impressed with public trust and ought to be considered primarily from the standpoint of public interest' (quoted in Mander 1984: 177). Other commentators revived the idea of endowment and proposed that broadcasting be financed by various mixes of listener subscription, municipal grants and private philanthropy. Champions of commercialism, however, were quick to oppose public subsidy or earmarked taxation. As Senator Dill of Washington put it: 'just as firmly as I believe that the press ought to be kept free and that speech ought to be kept free, I believe the right to use radio ought to be kept free' (quoted in Mander 1984: 180). The 1927 Radio Act attempted to balance this economic logic against the political requirements of mass democracy, and failed. Although it established a Federal Commission to safeguard the 'public interest', the regulators soon adapted to the realities of the emerging advertising-based system. Consequently, 'while talking in terms of public interest, convenience and necessity the Commission actually chose to further the ends of the commerical broadcasters' (Barnouw 1966: 219). The result was a system based around packaging audiences for sale to advertisers.

In contrast, the parallel British debate was resolved by constituting broadcasting as a monopoly, concentrated initially in the hands of a commercial consortium, the British Broadcasting Company, and from the end of 1926 onwards, in a new public body, the British Broadcasting Corporation (the BBC), financed by a compulsory annual licence fee on radio set ownership, overseen by a board appointed by the government, but relatively free to determine its operational goals and programming policies. This very British solution provided the major alternative to the American model of commercial broadcasting and was adopted (with modifications) in a number of countries.

Its relatively easy passage through the British legislative process was due to a combination of factors. In the first place, the public management of essential services during the First World War had fostered a broad political consensus in favour of public corporations as a means of husbanding key resources (Hood 1986). Once the wavebands had been defined as 'a valuable form of public property' by the first official committee on the future of broadcasting (Sykes Committee 1923: 11), it was a short step for the succeeding committee (set up in 1925) to recommend a public corporation system. Secondly, unlike the United States, where broadcasting was viewed primarily as a transportation or transmission system (see Mander 1984: 169), British observers were quick to grasp its immense potential as a cultural agency. They saw it as a valuable addition to the existing network of publicly funded institutions designed to provide cultural resources for citizenship. These included libraries, galleries, concerts, museums, and various initiatives in adult education. The fact that broadcasting could reach the furthest corners of the nation made it a particularly attractive medium for securing cultural hegemony.

To operate effectively in this role, however, the BBC needed a certain measure of autonomy, not only from government interference in day-to-day operations, but equally importantly, from the pressures of advertising finance and profit-seeking. Where commercial broadcasting regarded listeners as consumers of products, the ethos of public service viewed them as citizens of a nation state. It aimed to universalise the provision of the existing public cultural institutions by offering talks, concerts, plays, and readings in a mixed programming service. It reproduced the paternalistic structure of the classical bourgeois family – where father knows best and you don't speak until you are spoken to – at the level of the nation. And by addressing its listeners as families grouped around the radio set, it cemented powerful imaginative links between home and country, father and fatherland.

The new service's essential rationale was set out by the BBC's first Director-General John Reith, in his book *Broadcast Over Britain*, written when the BBC was still a private company. He recognised from the outset that, unlike a newspaper, broadcasting was a public good in the technical sense that its consumption by one person did not preclude its consumption by another. As he noted, 'the broadcast is as universal as the air. There is no limit to the amount which may be drawn off. It does not matter how many thousands there may be listening; there is always enough for others, when they wish to join in' (Reith 1924: 217). But for him broadcasting was also good in a more general, philosophical sense, since its universal reach helped to constitute the audience as members of a unitary public. It was, in his phrase, 'a good thing' that it could be 'shared by all alike, for the same outlay, and to the same extent . . . The genius and the fool, the wealthy and the poor listen simultaneously, and to the same event . . . There need be no first and third class. There is nothing in it which is exclusive to those who pay more' (217–18). The problems arose with the way this unity was constituted.

The BBC's early years were marked by a tension between an impulse towards openness and diversity on the one hand, and moves towards closure around notions of national integration on the other. As Paddy Scannell (1989: 140) has argued, 'The fundamentally democratic thrust of broadcasting lay in the new kind of access to virtually the whole spectrum of public life that radio made available to all.' In the political sphere, this movement was spearheaded by the Talks Department, which set out to develop 'new and direct methods of social reportage: eyewitness, first hand accounts of BBC staff 'observers' of slum conditions; the unemployed themselves at the microphone to describe what it was like living on the dole' (Scannell and Cardiff 1982: 172). In 1935, however, with the Corporation facing mounting criticisms of left-wing bias from Conservative MPs and the Tory press, and with the Charter up for renewal, the Department was abolished, considerably reducing the BBC's openness to non-official voices on political affairs.

There was closure too in the cultural field. Although, potentially, the BBC offered a new and open expressive space, this was commandeered from an early stage by the intelligentsia and the emerging strata of broadcasting professionals. Public broadcasting became one of the principal cultural fields on which the academies and the avant gardes, the established and the outsiders, traditional and organic intellectuals, competed to advance their positions, judgements, and canons of taste. At the same time, the new broadcasting professionals struggled to develop workable definitions of good practice and establish the medium's distinctive aesthetic qualities (see Elliott and Matthews 1987). At the heart of these contests were questions of representation and cultural power: 'Which forms of experience and expression were to be privileged and celebrated and which excluded or condescended to?' 'Who had the right to speak about other people's lives, and what forms of discourse and presentation should be employed?'

For Reith the answer was clear. Broadcasting had to ensure that 'the wisdom of the wise and the amenities of culture are available without discrimination' (1924: 218), and he naturally reserved the right to define what would count as 'wisdom' and 'culture'. His position was unashamedly paternalistic. As he put it in reply to the BBC's early critics: 'It is occasionally indicated to us that we are apparently setting out to give the public what we think they need – and not what they want, but few know what they want, and very few what they need' (1924: 34).

In the area of culture, he followed the traditional intellectuals in identifying legitimate expression with a highly partial selection of approved works which were thought to represent the essential 'spirit' of the nation, and by extension of the Western tradition more generally. The authors, composers, and historical figures who made up this configuration were overwhelmingly white and male, and their words and works were presented in the impeccable accents of the schoolroom and the pulpit.

This selective tradition was defined at the end of the nineteenth century as part of a general invention of tradition designed to create new foci for national unity in a situation where the uneven development of industrial capitalism was creating deep divisions of class and region, and where official religion, in the form of the Church of England, was steadily losing its always slim grip on hearts and minds. Cultural forms that expressed the quintessential qualities of 'Englishness' were central to this project.

In common with compulsory schooling, broadcasting combined the overt promotion of legitimated culture with new rituals of national unity. Reith saw broadcasting the chimes of Big Ben as a particularly potent way of creating a symbolic link between centre and periphery by enabling 'the clock which beats the time over the Houses of Parliament, in the centre of the Empire, [to be] heard echoing in the loneliest cottage in the land' (1924: 220). The symbolic community of the nation was further cemented by broadcast relays of state ceremonies and the monarch's Christmas address to the people, which began in 1932 (see Scannell and Cardiff 1982).

Beneath the often sentimental rhetoric, however, there was a coercive edge to Reithian paternalism. It aimed to dislodge existing allegiances and tastes and replace them with a common culture based around approved definitions of 'Englishness'. As Reith argued in his autobiography, 'It is not insistent autocracy but wisdom that suggests a policy of broadcasting carefully and persistently on the basis of giving people what one believes they should like and will come to like' (Reith 1949: 133). In pursuit of this aim, public broadcasting marginalised or repressed the situated cultural formations generated by labour, ethnicity, and locality.

Between 1922 and 1924, when the BBC first began broadcasting as a commercial company, the network comprised a station in London, a number of relay stations in other parts of the country, and nine local stations outside the capital producing most of their own programmes and offering a distinctively 'local public service, rooted in the community' (Scannell and Cardiff 1982: 166). Reith disliked this loose arrangement and set about centralising the system, creating a National Programme service, based in London, supplemented by five regional production centres. These centres continued to champion diversity, often in defiance of edicts from head office, as when the Northern Region broadcast a concert by unemployed musicians in preference to a recital by Pablo Casals, fed from London. But overall, the effect of reorganisation was 'to replace local variety and difference by a standard conception of culture and manners' (Scannell and

Cardiff 1982: 166). Definitions of culture as a whole way of life gave way to Reith's promotion of a particular selective tradition. Dealing with the culture of the mass entertainment industry remained problematic, however.

The BBC started life as a commercial concern whose 'stated function' was providing entertainment (Reith 1924: 147). This requirement remained central when it became a public corporation, since as a monopoly it was obliged to cater for the whole range of listeners' tastes. Reith responded by redefining entertainment as rational recreation, arguing that 'To entertain means to occupy agreeably. Would it be urged that this is only to be effected by the broadcasting of jazz bands and popular music, or of sketches by humorists?' (1924: 18). Reith championed wholesomeness. Nothing raucous, risqué, combative or critical of authority was allowed.

There was a strong streak of anti-Americanism in this stance. Reith resented the growing colonisation of mass entertainment by Hollywood and tin-pan alley and took every opportunity to lament the popularity of jazz and 'the picture house'. By 1929 this concern had prompted an internal inquiry in to the 'ramifications of the Transatlantic octopus' and the possibility 'that the national outlook and, with it, character, is gradually becoming Americanised' (quoted in Frith 1983: 103). This hostility to American culture played a key role in the BBC's cultural mission in the sense that the distinctive qualities of 'national culture' were largely defined negatively, as what separated 'us' from 'them'.

Many of the struggles that have taken place within public broadcasting since Reith's day have been about prising open the terms of the couplet, firstly by challenging prevailing definitions of 'Englishness' and winning space for vernacular cultures, and secondly, by promoting a more positive image of American culture. This process has entailed a gradual opening up of public broadcasting both to the populism of transatlantic cultural forms and to the experiences and voices of groups who were marginalised or excluded by the Reithian project – the working class, young people, regional interests, ethnic groups, and women.

The first major break with Reithian paternalism came in 1954, with the arrival of commercial television. Although it was financed by spot advertising, the ITV system remained bound by the basic tenets of 'public service', but interpreted these terms somewhat differently from the BBC. Its structure as a federation of regionally based companies reduced the central pull of the metropolis and enlarged the space for local programming. Its populist ethos was far less deferential to authority and much more willing to engage with vernacular cultures and popular pleasures, including those made in the USA. Critics saw this as a triumph for trivialisation and Transatlantic culture. The Pilkington Committee on broadcasting, who reported in 1962, for example, were in no doubt that 'The effect on the British way of life of much American material – especially during peak time – is to be condemned' (*Report of the Committee on Broadcasting* 1962: para. 333). But this was only part of the story. Alongside the inevitable game shows, the imported American shows, and the tilt towards consumerism, the new populism produced a commitment to contemporary realist drama, new styles of documentary reportage, more aggressive and independent political interviews, and new modes of audience feedback. In response, the BBC adapted its own practices. Nevertheless, the question of representation remained highly problematic.

Despite the greater pluralism of public broadcasting in the 1960s and 1970s 'ordinary' people were still spoken about far more often than they spoke for themselves. And when they did speak, what they had to say was carefully framed or edited to fit the prevailing formats constructed by broadcasting professionals. These unequal power relations have continued down to the present. Whereas people are allowed to articulate their views, the right to analyse, judge and extrapolate is monopolised by experts, public figures, and broadcasting professionals. Although 'the subjects of documentary are entitled to opinions about their experience, and may be invited to express them, those opinions have only subjective force. They lack the generalising power of the opinions of public persons' (Scannell 1989: 162). Increasing dissatisfaction with this state of affairs, and with public broadcasting's failure to keep pace with the proliferation of political and social discourses, has produced a crisis in the relations between public broadcasting and the viewer-as-citizen. This crisis in representation is exacerbated by the increasing tension between broadcasters, state agencies, and government.

Public broadcasting's relation to the 'nation' and particularly to notions of the 'national interest' has been a focus of dispute from the outset. Reith was quite clear that the BBC had a key role to play in providing the information people required to exercise their political rights as citizens, arguing that: 'it is a serious menace to the country that suffrage be exercised without first-hand and personal knowledge. An extension of the scope of broadcasting will mean a more intelligent and enlightened electorate' (1924: 113).

In the event, the BBC's ability to mediate between citizens and politicians was severely limited. Reith's original plan to broadcast parliamentary proceedings was scotched; up to the mid-1930s, news bulletins were restricted to relaying material taken from the wire services; and debates on controversial issues were hedged around by a thicket of restrictions. Faced with these pressures, the BBC operated less as an open space for public debate, and more, as Reith later put it, as 'the integrator of democracy' (Reith 1949: 136).

This consensual role was reinforced by continual pressure from state and government, and by the Corporation's own definitions of impartiality and balance in the coverage of political affairs. Although the BBC was formally independent in editorial matters, it was, and still is, open to a variety of pressures from Whitehall and Westminster. These range from the manipulation of the licence fee level and appointments to the Board of Governors to the use of the Charter's reserve powers to ban certain kinds of broadcast. As a result, in a number of key instances, from the General Strike of 1926 to the current conflict in Northern Ireland, debate on the issues at stake has not been as open or as diverse as the ideals of full citizenship require.

In an effort to widen its sphere of autonomy, the BBC developed its own rules for covering political affairs. As Charles Lewis, the first Organiser of Programmes, explained in 1924: 'Although under Government licence, broadcasting is not Governmental, it would be fatal for it to become the catspaw of any political policy. It must establish itself as an independent public body, willing to receive any point of view in debate against its adversary. Its unique position gives the public an opportunity they have never had before of hearing both sides of a question expounded by experts. This is of great general utility, for it enables the 'man in the street' to take an active interest in his country's affairs' (quoted in Smith 1974: 43). This statement neatly encapsulates the contradictory nature of public broadcasting's relation to the political rights of citizenship. On the one hand it is supposed to operate as an idealised public sphere in which 'any point of view' can 'debate against its adversary'. On the other, this openness is qualified by three professional assumptions: that there are only two main sides to any argument; that these positions are best expounded by 'experts'; and that the broadcaster's role is to act as an impartial umpire holding the middle ground. Although these canons have been strongly challenged by alternative notions of 'good' journalistic practice based on greater partisanship or increased popular participation, they have proved remarkably resilient.

Looking back over public broadcasting's development, we can see that it played four key roles in organising the new system of representation that emerged to service the extension of citizenship rights in the first half of the century. Firstly, it provided a public forum within which the platforms of the major political parties and legitimated interest groups were presented and packaged for general consumption. Secondly, its probes into popular thinking provided a new source of surveillance and feedback for power-holders. Thirdly, the fact that it was predominantly a national service helped to cement the association between the ideals of citizenship and dominant definitions of the nation and its culture. Fourthly, and perhaps most importantly, it redrew the line between the public and private spheres, creating new connections between domesticity and the wider life of the modern city. It broke the link between participation and physical mobility and introduced a range of public events into every home. It also brought about a 'domestication of public utterance' as speakers at the microphone learnt to address listeners as individuals rather than crowds (see Scannell 1989: 148). Nor was the traffic between public and private spheres entirely one way. Despite the many limitations, radio, and later television, offered a new kind of space, in which ordinary people could speak about their experiences, air their views, and question their elected representatives.

Even so, there is a considerable gap between public broadcasting's current system of representation and the complexities of contemporary social life. As a result, its institutions and practices are under increasing attack as both a system of social delegation and a system of expressive forms. More and more people are challenging the broadcasters' right to organise the nation's conversation with itself according to their definitions of professionalism and expertise, and raising questions about the ways that established programme formats continue to marginalise, trivialise, or objectify substantial areas of social and cultural activity.

THE QUESTION OF REPRESENTATION

The primary causes of this growing crisis of confidence are to be found in the revival and emergence of movements which undermine traditional definitions of national culture and provide new points of identity and mobilisation. In the first place, there has been a marked revival of sub-national movements in areas that were subjugated to a central national authority but which were never completely colonised culturally. In Britain, these movements are concentrated in the Celtic periphery of Wales, Scotland, and Ireland. At the same time, England is having to negotiate the move from being a colonial power to becoming a multicultural society. This has profound implications for entrenched notions of national culture, since historically, so many elements of Englishness have been defined in terms of distinctions between the colonisers and the colonised, the civilised and the savage. With large-scale immigration and settlement from the ex-colonies, 'they' are no longer 'out there', at a distance, on another part of the map. They are here among 'us' with full citizenship rights, including the right to participate in defining the future of the national culture. In this new situation the mental scaffolding supporting traditional cultural formations and identities is rendered increasingly precarious and unstable.

The revival of sub-national movements and the new politics of of multiculturalism are characteristic not only of Britain, but of contemporary Europe more generally, in both the East and the West. Indeed, the tensions caused by ethnic, religious, and nationalist movements are most acute in the former Communist states and in the Soviet Union. Consequently, all the countries of greater Europe are now faced with developing a public communications system capable of responding to the new politics of division and difference and of providing the full range of resources for citizenship that this emerging situation demands.

To add to the difficulties facing this project, it is clear that the problems of public communication can no longer be solved exclusively within the boundaries of individual nation states. The new cultural formations of nationalism, ethnicity, and post-colonialism operate across frontiers. The collapse of Communist power in Eastern Europe is extending this process, as the nations within nations declare independence and set out to measure their similarities and differences as members of greater Europe. Post-colonialism too is endemically transnational. Mass migration has installed a permanent Third World presence at the heart of major European metropolises, and introduced new cultural formations and points of identity rooted outside Europe. The rise of militant Islam is the most obvious example.

Given this situation, it is clear that any policy for public communications in the 1990s must address the new cultural politics at the level of Europe as a whole as well as at the level of individual nation states.

MARKETS AND PUBLIC SPACES: MULTIPLICITY, DIVERSITY, AND DIFFERENCE

The best-publicised and best-financed response to this situation has come for the new entrepreneurs of the moving image, aided and abetted by government enthusiasm for privatisation policies which have allowed them to expand their activities and enter new markets with the minimum of public-interest constraints. The new commercial television industries of video, cable, and direct satellite broadcasting are being sold on the promise that they will by-pass the centralised, paternalistic, and outmoded structures of public broadcasting and deliver a range of new and different services, more in tune with the emerging needs of viewers. This promise is underwritten by two technological features of this new system.

Firstly, satellite distribution releases broadcasters from the technical limits of national terrestrial transmission systems and enables programming to be distributed transnationally, with viewers receiving the signals either directly, through a personal dish antenna, or indirectly, through a link to a local cable television company.

Secondly, the shortage of channels on traditional national systems has obliged broadcasters to offer a mixed menu of programmes in which the various interests of viewers are spread rather thinly across the schedule, or not represented at all. The greater capacity of the new delivery systems allows for narrow-casting, with specialist channels devoted to particular interests. These can range from channels for sports fans or film enthusiasts to channels for children or ethnic minorities. The result, it is claimed, is greatly increased choice for the viewer.

This vision of increased plurality and openness is immensely enticing, but if we look more closely at what is actually happening, we can see that the new television industries will not deliver the informational and cultural resources needed for effective citizenship in the new Europe. On the contrary, the limitations identified by early critics of commercially organised communications systems are even more prominent in the present system.

Multiplicity does not guarantee diversity. More does not always mean different. It can equally well mean more of the same or the same basic cultural form being circulated in a variety of markets and packages. The major area of expansion within the moving image industries over the last decade has been in distribution channels, not in original production. Consequently, the bulk of material available on video, cable, and satellite are re-releases of feature films or reruns of old broadcast programmes. This suits the new multimedia moguls very well. Their optimum economic strategy is to exploit the original material they make or own to the maximum by selling it in as many markets as possible and by using it as a basis for a range of ancillary products. You can watch *Batman* on video and cable as well as in the cinema, and you can buy the record of the soundtrack, the novel of the script, and a whole range of Batman merchandise, from toys to T-shirts, but it is still the same basic cultural form. As Mel Harris, head of the television group at Paramount Pictures, recently put it: 'When you are in the business of building myths and icons you want to exploit them in as many ways as possible' (Brasier 1990).

Within this emerging system, advertisers have more cultural power than ever before. Even where the established institutions allow a certain amount of spot advertising, national broadcasting networks are far from ideal from an advertising point of view. Slots are relatively scarce and increasingly expensive, and advertisers are faced with a number of regulations limiting what they can and can't promote. They have relatively little control over the programming environment which surrounds their messages, and with the rise of remote control consoles, audiences can avoid the ads altogether by flicking from channel to channel. The solution is to integrate the advertising message into the programmes themselves. Options include: sponsoring a sporting or cultural event for television in return for screen credits; financing original programme production; underwriting the purchase of a package of programmes which will be named after your company or product; paying to have products displayed or used 'naturally' in a feature film or television drama; constructing whole programme strands or even channels around promotional material such as rock videos; and developing home shopping shows, where viewers can telephone orders for goods displayed on the screen immediately after seeing them. Taken together, these initiatives ensure that the public spaces provided by the new television channels are substantially colonised by commercial speech and the discourse of consumerism.

This movement is reinforced by the fact that access to the new television services depends on viewers' ability to pay for both the new hardware and the new programming. Whereas public broadcasting is a public good, equally available to all, the new services are commodities produced for sale. Those who cannot afford the prices charged are excluded.

Paradoxically, many of those least able to buy into the new services are most in need of a television system that speaks for them and their aspirations. Because people living in peripheral regions and members of the new ethnic communities suffer disproportionately from unemployment and low wages, they are permanently disadvantaged within a cultural system where participation depends on cash payments (see Murdock and Golding 1989). Even if they could afford the entry price, the system would not meet their needs, since it is overwhelmingly orientated to addressing people in their personae as consumers. Consequently, the future of public broadcasting remains central to the future development of full and effective citizenship.

Even ardent supporters of a 'free' market system recognise this. As the Peacock Committee argued, in the report which paved the way for the partial deregulation of British commercial television, there 'will always be a need to supplement the direct consumer market by public finance for programmes of a public service kind supported by people in their capacity as citizens and voters but unlikely to be commercially self-supporting in the view of broadcasting entrepreneurs' (Home Office 1986: para 133).

Faced with over-centralised public institutions, it is easy to see why people are attracted by the dynamism and apparent openness of commercial systems. This is particularly so in Eastern

Europe, where public enterprise is identified with the authoritarian rule of the party-state. In reaction to this we currently see two movements. Firstly, there is a rapid reinvention of civil society and the demand for constitutional rights to freedom of belief and conscience, freedom of speech, freedom of movement, and freedom of association, together with demands for political enfranchisement and the right to choose between genuinely competitive parties in free elections for legislative bodies. At the same time, there is an equally rapid move to reintroduce commercial enterprise, market dynamics, and private property rights. These initiatives have generated a visible contradiction between expression and possession as the familiar dynamics of capitalist economics reimpose themselves. It is already clear that a public communications system organised on commercial lines cannot guarantee the cultural resources for effective citizenship, and that more and more people are denied access to the information and analysis they need by the poverty produced by unemployment and massive economic dislocation. Here again, the restructuring of public broadcasting will be central.

In thinking about the future of public broadcasting, we need to develop policies at both the national and international levels. But the first requirement must be for a production base in each European country strong enough to address the full diversity of social activity, political debate, and cultural identity that makes up the life of the nation. Rather than liquidating significant differences in the interests of creating a unitary 'national culture', we should aim to explore them in the hope of forging new accommodations and similarities based on mutual understanding and respect. Organisationally, one of the most interesting possible models for achieving this is provided by Channel 4 in Britain.

The channel was set up to extend the diversity of broadcast output by paying particular attention to the needs of ethnic and other minority groups and by actively encouraging experiments with programme forms. Instead of centralising most of its production in-house, it commissions its programming from independent producers. Not only do they tap into currents in national life that mainstream broadcasting has marginalised or ignored, they often present familiar themes in an unexpected light. Because they often have closer relations to the communities and movements they make programmes about, they have access to experiences and people that conventional programming often misses or treats only superficially or stereotypically. Unlike the narrowcasting strategies of cable entrepreneurs, which cater for minority interests with dedicated channels (often on a subscription basis), Channel 4 continues public broadcasting's core commitment to accommodate diversity within a mixed programming schedule, available to everyone without extra payment. This is essential, since a positive response to diversity depends on a collective exploration of difference, not the perpetuation of separate spheres. This requires a communicative system that sets 'local languages of identity alongside a public language of collective aspiration' (Sacks 1991: 9).

By challenging the dominant viewpoints and procedures of mainstream production, Channel 4, at its best, has demonstrated how public broadcasting can respond creatively to the new politics of culture and the demands of contemporary citizenship. Defending and extending these gains will be far from easy in the current climate, where across Europe, public broadcasting's capacity to support open debate and expressive diversity is being eroded by varying mixes of commercialism and renewed governmental interest in policing representations.

In addition to enlarging the diversity of national production, we also need to develop new mechanisms for making and distributing programmes based on this strategy within Europe as a whole. This can be done through bilateral arrangements, through consortia, and more ambitiously via satellite. But here again we need to have a clear grasp of the ways in which these initiatives can contribute to the vitality and openness of public culture. Collaborative ventures in programme production and exchange can extend cultural diversity in three main ways. Firstly, programmes which show 'us' as we appear to others or which offer alternative perspectives on familiar national events and issues can play a valuable role in challenging ethnocentric attitudes. Secondly, programmes which articulate other nations' experience from the inside rather than from 'our' vantage point can help to dislodge national stereotypes and open up new possibilities for empathy and understanding. Thirdly, as the ecology movement has demonstrated so forcefully, national policies have international ramifications. The implications of acid rain, the chemical pollution of the Rhine, and the dumping of toxic waste in the North Sea can only be understood through programming which brings the widest possible range of information, contextualisation and argument to bear on them.

It is clear that neither the new commercially based television industries nor the traditional institutions of public broadcasting can meet the challenge posed by the new formations of culture and citizenship, either nationally or internationally. To achieve this we need to develop a new kind of public communicative space, rooted in a constructive engagement with emerging patterns of political and cultural diversity. We must reject all attempts to shore up political and symbolic hierarchies which are visibly crumbling and embrace a philosophy of public communication based on the recognition of difference and the toleration of dissent. But above all, the continuing struggle against the obstacles to open debate must take place 'in the context of that march towards a society which recognises our equal dignity' (Lee 1990: 140). In the words of Vaclav Havel (1989: 153–4): 'We must not be ashamed that we are capable of . . . solidarity, sympathy and tolerance, but just the opposite: we must set these fundamental dimensions of our humanity free from their 'private' exile and accept them as the only genuine starting point of meaningful human community.'

REFERENCES

Barnouw, Erik (1966) *A Tower in Babel*, New York: Oxford University Press.

Bobbio, N. (1989) 'After the Barbarians', *New Statesman and Society*, 24 November: 24.

Brasier, M. (1990) 'The New Sun Also Rises on Hollywood', *The Guardian*, 26 March.

Curran, James and Seaton, Jean (1985) *Power Without Responsibility*, London: Methuen.

Dietz, M. G. (1987) 'Context is All. Feminism and Theories of Citizenship', *Daedalus*, Fall: 1–24.

Elliott, Philip and Matthews, Geoff (1987) 'Broadcasting Culture. Innovation, Accommodation and Routinization in the Early BBC', in James Curran *et al.* (eds), *Impacts and Influences: Essays on Media Power in the Twentieth Century*, London: Methuen: 235–58.

Frith, Simon (1983) 'The Pleasures of the Hearth. The Making of BBC Light Entertainment', in Tony Bennett *et al.* (eds), *Formations of Pleasure*, London: Routledge: 101–23.

Fukuyama, F. (1990) 'Are We at the End of History?', *Fortune*, 15 January: 33–6.

Garton Ash, T. (1990) *We the People. The Revolution of '89 Witnessed in Warsaw, Budapest, Berlin and Prague*, Cambridge: Granta Books.
Havel, Vaclav (1989) *Living in Truth*, London: Faber & Faber.
Home Office (1986) *Report of the Committee on Financing the BBC*, London: HMSO, Cmnd. 9824.
Hood, Stuart (1986) 'Broadcasting and the Public Interest. From Consensus to Crisis', in Peter Golding *et al.* (eds), *Communicating Politics*, Leicester: Leicester University Press: 55–66.
Keane, John (1989) 'Liberty of the Press' in the 1990s', *New Formations* 8: 35–53.
Kellner, Douglas (1990) *Television and the Crisis of Democracy*, Oxford: Westview Press.
Lee, Simon (1990) *The Cost of Free Speech*, London: Faber & Faber.
Mander, Mary (1984) 'The Public Debate about Broadcasting in the Twenties. An Interpretive History', *Journal of Broadcasting* 28. 2: 167–85.
Mepham, John (1990) 'The Ethics of Quality Television', in Geoff Mulgan (ed.), *The Question of Quality*, London: British Film Institute Publishing: 56–72.
Murdock, Graham and Golding, Peter (1989) 'Information Poverty and Political Inequality. Citizenship in the Age of Privatised Communications', *Journal of Communication* 39. 3: 180–95.
Reith, J. C. W. (1924) *Broadcast Over Britain*, London: Hodder & Stoughton.
—— (1949) *Into the Wind*, London: Hodder & Stoughton.
Report of the Committee on Broadcasting (The Pilkington Report) (1962), London: HMSO, Cmnd. 1753.
Ross, E. A. (1910) 'The Suppression of Important News', *Atlantic Monthly* 105: 303–11.
Sacks, Jonathan (1991) 'A Community of Communities', *The Listener*, 3 January: 8–10.
Scannell, Paddy (1989) 'Public Broadcasting and Modern Public Life', *Media Culture and Society* 11. 2: 135–66.
Scannell, Paddy and Cardiff, David (1982) 'Serving the Nation. Public Service Broadcasting before the War', in Bernard Waites *et al.* (eds), *Popular Culture, Past and Present*, London: Croom Helm: 161–88.
Sinclair, V. (1919) *The Brass Check: A Study of American Journalism*, Pasadena, California. Published privately by the author.
Smith, A. (1974) *British Broadcasting*, Newton Abbot: David & Charles.
Smith, Dennis (1989) *Capitalist Democracy on Trial*, London: Routledge.
Sykes Committee (1923) *Broadcasting Committee Report*, London: HMSO, Cmnd. 1951.
Wilcox, D. F. (1900) 'The American Newspaper. A Study in Social Psychology', *Annals of the American Academy of Political and Social Science*, July: 56–92.

Chapter 2

Modernity and media panics

Kirsten Drotner

In the early 1980s, most industrialised countries entered the VCR age. In Scandinavia, this entry was accompanied by a rapid transformation (some would say disintegration) of the public-service media institutions, a transformation that was hastened by the advent of cable and satellite television. Together, these developments sent shock waves through the public mind. In Denmark, one specific youth programme triggered the public conscience. Emulating a Swedish enterprise, the Danish Broadcasting Corporation showed excerpts from popular video nasties interspersed by interviews with young video enthusiasts, i.e. boys in their teens.

Should censorship be imposed on videos for private use? Can video distribution be curbed? How can we protect the young from visual excrescences? These and similar questions became hotly debated in the press, and they were soon followed by a number of professional conferences and political hearings on video violence. At the same time, the VCR market exploded (from 35,000 to 170,000 VCRs between 1980 and 1981 among a population of 5 million), publishers' youth lists plummeted, and book prices soared. Library loans were relatively unaffected. Prompted by key publishing directors, the initial focus on video was widened to encompass the entire relation between visual and print media, a relation that was almost unanimously envisaged as an opposition. By the mid-eighties, video retailers had imposed a certain self-censorship, media education was somewhat strengthened, the discussion died out – and the VCR sales kept increasing.

Viewed in isolation, the reaction to video is a somewhat banal phenomenon. The context, however, is rather more intriguing.

For the Danish situation has close parallels in most other industrialised countries at the time. The demand for censorship may
vary according to national traditions: in Europe, Britain and
Sweden offer some of the most vigorous proponents of censorship (Barlow and Hill 1985; Våldsskildringsutredningen 1987,
1988). But the arguments brought forward in the debates, the
professions of the contestants, and the very course of the reactions are strikingly similar across the map.

Not only that. The reaction to video has clear historical ante-
cedents. From the advent of mass-circulation fiction and magazines to film and television, comics and cartoons, the introduction
of a new mass medium causes strong public reactions whose
repetitiveness is as predictable as the fervour with which they
are brought forward. Adult experts – teachers and social
workers, cultural critics and politicians – define the new mass
medium as a social, psychological, or moral threat to the young
(or mixtures of the three), and appoint themselves as public
trouble shooters. Legal and educational measures are then
imposed, and the interest lessens – until the advent of a new
mass medium reopens public discussion. That spiralling motion
characterises a *media panic*. The very repetitiveness and lack of
nuanced analysis have kept me and most other critics of popular
culture from seriously engaging with the history of media panics
in any sustained way. Yet, over the years I have been struck by
the similarity of the debates, and not only their standard forms
of argumentation, but even their choice of words: what makes
media panics so *persistent* across national and historical differences? Why are *children and young people* focal to the panics?
Why are the reactions so *strong*? Let me share some of my
answers with you.

'A UNITY OF DISUNITY': MODERNITY AND CULTURAL ANALYSIS

One of the first people to chart the course of a public panic was
the British sociologist Stanley Cohen. In 1972, he brought out
Folk Devils and Moral Panics (Cohen 1972). Influenced by the
American Howard Becker's work on deviance, Cohen uses the
conflicts in the early 1960s between the British youth groups
Mods and Rockers to analyse how the mass media in general
and the press in particular may create a negative group image

that fuels back into public debate as stigma and back into the self-image of the groups concerned as guidelines for further action. The police, teachers, and social workers get involved and we have what Cohen defines as a moral panic. It is rooted in 'conflicts of interests – at community and societal levels – and the presence of power differentials which leave some groups vulnerable to such attacks' (Cohen 1972: 198).

Cohen's analysis is pertinent also to the issue of media panics for two reasons: he demonstrates how young people become symbols of larger social contradictions, and he analyses how these contradictions are basically power struggles. Moral panics, according to Cohen, serve as ideological safety valves whose effect it is to restore social equilibrium. These aspects are important to media panics, as we shall see. But because Cohen largely limits his sources to press clippings and similar media sources, it is difficult to gauge to what extent other factors play a part in the panics: it seems as if the press itself orchestrates public opinion. In media panics, the mass media are both the source and the medium of public reaction. We must therefore seek an analytical space beyond the media if we are to understand the deeper problems involved in the panics. We must also enlarge our time perspective.

The development of the mass media and the reactions upon them must be understood in relation to the wider parameters of *modernity*. The economic and social upheavals of industrialisation, urbanisation, and secularisation have as their corollary profound transformations of cultural symbols, experiences, and expressions. Following Marshall Berman, we may define these transformations of culture and consciousness as the foundation of modernity. It is 'a paradoxical unity, a unity of disunity: it pours us all into a maelstrom of perpetual disintegration and renewal, of struggle and contradiction, of ambiguity and anguish' (Berman 1988: 15).

Berman follows a tradition of equating modernity with novelty and change, a tradition that dates back at least to Charles Baudelaire, and may be critiqued for ignoring its gender bias (Wolff 1985). While agreeing with Berman that modernity is a set of related representations and historical instances, I would follow feminist researchers in stressing the heterogeneity of its development: it is not merely change, it is equally continuity, not only transformations of public pace and place, but also relocations of private forms of signification. Modernity was always inscribed in intricate gender and age relations, and so any analysis of modern culture must be equally sensitive to contradictions, in relation both to our objects of analysis and to the process of analysis.

The constant transformation of traditions and relations has two important analytical implications. On the one hand, the cultural dynamic inherent in modernity facilitates a temporal and spatial perspective on cultural processes, so that we may analyse them as changing historical processes rather than as acts of God or fate. Modernity facilitates cultural *analysis*. On the other hand, this very dynamic undermines established norms, social networks, and fixed standards of experience: it is impossible to find an analytical space beyond the objects under investigation. Modernity precludes any objective cultural *critique*. We are always implicated in our investigations whether we like it or not. While we analyse others, we define ourselves, not as a result of a moral obligation but as a social condition.

This paradox is in my opinion the contradictory, but necessary, basis of cultural investigation, including an investigation of media panics. Consequently, I will discuss the panics within the parameters of modernity and the discourses that they throw into relief. While I make no attempt to situate the panics within the intricate development of actual media, I shall emphasise two media panics that are often left to analytical oblivion, namely popular fiction and film. Bearing in mind that the cross-cultural context is central to answering my initial questions, I shall focus on the panics that these media create in Scandinavia, Britain, and Germany.

'POISON FLOWING': PANIC HISTORIES

In the history of mass communication, print media naturally offer the first examples of media panics. Perhaps best known is the so-called comics campaign that swept many European countries as well as North America in the 1950s. The American psychiatrist Frederic Wertham's *Seduction of the Innocent* (Wertham 1954) has gone down as the archetypal reaction to a new mass medium. The title indicates Wertham's view of the comics as morally contagious and sexually dangerous. It also expresses his view of children as vulnerable creatures whose innocence must be protected by conscientious adults. The contents of the book confirm the cultural perspective shown in its title, and Wertham's form of argumentation, as well as his strategy of selecting the most extreme examples taken out of context, is entirely typical of other panics. *Seduction of the Innocent* became enormously influential and was used in countries as diverse as Italy, Sweden, and Britain as proof of the detrimental effects caused by comics (Barker 1984). But although Wertham is often singled out as the prime media adversary, he merely follows a tradition whose formation is even more revealing.

In 1795, when the French Revolution was a hotly contested social issue all over Europe, a group of evangelical philanthropists in Britain launched a zealous campaign against what they termed 'the poison continually flowing thro' the channel of vulgar and licentious publications' (quoted in Neuburg 1977: 255). As an antidote, the group started to publish a series of so-called cheap repository tracts. These were strongly didactic religious tales and songs that were decked out as traditional ballads and broadsides with their coarse paper, crude woodcuts, and bad print. The tracts were often given away as prizes in the newly established Sunday schools and other places of moral reform. Traditional popular fiction, the emotionally charged and politically subversive tales, should be beaten by serious moral edification that soon included religious magazines as well (Drotner 1988, chs. 2–4).

I mention this example for two reasons: first I find it important to stress that media panics are no simple side-effects of commercial mass production or technological innovation. Britain may offer the earliest examples of panics leading directly to cultural counteraction simply because, very early on, literary production, both entertaining and educative, was highly developed there: after all, Britain was the first industrialised and urbanised country in the world. But around the same time, we find concerned educationalists in Germany, such as Friedrich Gedike, warning against an enormous growth in juvenile literature whose mental nourishment, he says, is like 'unwholesome and insipid fruit' (quoted in Furuland and Ørvig 1986: 251).

Second, the immediate aftermath of the French Revolution highlights how the contradictions of modernity are deeply politically implicated: literacy means access to Bible-reading and so it is a good thing, right-minded people would claim. But if one can read the Bible, one may also lay eyes on Tom Paine's radical pamphlet *The Rights of Man* or the thrilling tales of broadsides and chapbooks. So literacy can also be a dangerous liberty. In a developing capitalist society, the spreading of general skills such as literacy is an economic asset, while the regulation of these qualifications is a political liability. Economic and social modernisation highlights the contradictions inherent in any media development, and the French Revolution throws these contradictions into sharp political relief. All later media panics are based on such political, social, and cultural discourses of power. But the strategies employed change.

In the nineteenth century, media panics focus on print media for very obvious reasons. The 1870s and 1880s see an unprecedented growth in cheap, commercial periodicals whose success is sustained by groups of apprentices, clerks, and maids, i.e. urban adolescents beyond adult educational authority. They have both time and money on their hands, and with them direct censorship of reading-matter is a difficult endeavour. But this difficulty only makes the moral propagators more intent. That their efforts often serve to conceal social ills that are even harder to combat (poor housing and low educational standards, for example) does not diminish the seriousness of the moralists' concern. But it influences their measures. From the 1880s on, media panics focus less on banning what seems bad literature, more on promoting what seems good literature. Again, Britain and Germany are among the first to propagate 'quality' books as a means of social elevation.

In 1888, the young British journalist Edward Salmon published what to my knowledge is the first investigation of children's reading interests: inexpensive periodicals, penny-part novels and serialised romances top his young informants' list of priorities. His findings so appalled him that he spoke of juvenile reading as a 'disease [that] once fairly afoot holds its ground, and carries on its mental destruction for years – for a lifetime' (p. 193). Like Wertham almost seventy years later, Salmon is particularly enraged by the mediocre taste displayed by middle-class children, whose parents are supposed to pass on a higher moral stance than are working-class parents. And like Wertham, Salmon locates popular reading as *the* source of juvenile delinquency:

> a clerk who had devoted his leisure to a study of Harrison Ainsworth's novels [the author who, from 1834 on, popular-

ised stories of highwaymen with his serial about Dick Turpin]
tried to induce his master to leave his bedroom by mewing
like a cat at his door, and awaited his exit with a handkerchief
charged with chloroform. Having rendered his employer insen-
sible, it was his object to steal the cashbox. His plan failed,
and he was taken into custody.

(Salmon 1888: 190)

Germany was modernised later and at a much faster pace than
Britain and France, for example. The German state only emerges
in the 1870s, of course, and civil servants and intellectuals com-
prise the greater part of the middle classes. Outside direct contact
with economic production, these groups are focal in the public
evaluation of modernisation, and their general verdict is as
intense as it is negative: modernity brings about a loss of individuality, a severing of 'natural' bonds, and an atomised lifestyle.
(The sociologist Ferdinand Tönnies' classic separation of a traditional, organic *Gemeinschaft* and modern, mechanic *Gesell-
schaft* immediately springs to mind here, along with the cultural
critic Oswald Spengler's *The Decline of the West*). The German
media panics must be understood within this perspective.

A few years after Salmon's investigation in England, the
German teacher Heinrich Wolgast published *Das Elend unserer
Jugendliteratur: ein Beitrag zur künstlerischen Erziehung* (1896).
In this widely influential book (the seventh edition appeared in
1950), Wolgast claims that modernisation's only redemption is
that it brings about new aesthetic potentials: in particular,
children's appreciation of proper books may create a wholeness
of being that is undermined in other areas of life. Wolgast was
important in the contemporary German reform movement of
aesthetic education that sought to counteract the ill-effects of
modernity through an elevation of cultural taste, and his book
was influential in the formation of a literary movement whose
participants put up an earnest struggle against the so-called
'unworthy literature' (*unwertige Literatur*). Wolgast's organicist
ideas were later transplanted into Sweden, for example.

In Scandinavia real media panics were born with this century,
and they follow well-trodden paths. Educationalists and librarians
attempt to remedy the perceived criminal effects of popular reading by more positive measures. By this time, popular literature
means pulp magazines, often imported from Germany (or from

the US via German translations) from around 1908. *Buffalo Bill* and *Nick Carter* are the most popular among the thirty or so weeklies available, and the magazines have enormous impact, not least with adolescent boys. In Denmark, Nick Carter gets his own anti-Carter societies. And in Sweden, an entire campaign against the pulps is named after the detective hero (Boethius 1989). Here, the author and teacher Marie Louise Gagner is a prominent advocate of giving, as she says in 1909, 'our youth good literature; then it will be less tempted to illicit acquisitions of the bad variety' (quoted in Furuland and Ørvig 1986: 256). Gagner's parallel in Denmark is Niels K. Kristensen, a teacher from Copenhagen, whose express aim it is to offer his own prolific writings as superior alternatives to the periodicals. By being introduced to 'planned and selective leisure reading [children] around the age of 14 may reach the cultural level of an adult' (Kristensen 1903: 24).

The various strategies of using 'quality' culture as a means of moral, and by implication social, elevation forms a stable element in media panics throughout this century. The campaigns, moreover, are gradually institutionalised. The concept of social elevation through moral edification originates in bourgeois ideas of enlightenment, as we shall see. But it resonates widely with working-class groups and it becomes central to the cultural policies promoted by the Social Democrats in Scandinavia as elsewhere. For example, it is no coincidence that the first time children are mentioned in any Danish cultural legislation is in a library Act in the 1930s. Public libraries become cornerstones in the interwar attempts to extend Culture to the people. Similarly, the Social Democrats' youth organisation, Socialdemokratisk Ungdom, is among the groups carrying on a spirited fight against pulp literature between the wars, but it is an uphill struggle. In 1936, various religious and political groups succeed in having a few weeklies banned, but the success is short-lived. It needs the ideological warfare of the Second World War to recreate a successful literary panic. The result of this is seen in the various comics campaigns of the 1950s.

From the First World War on, new popular media vie for adult attention as potential threats to the young: first film, then radio, and records promoting dance music and jazz. Unlike popular literature, these new media do not share their means of expression with a medium blue-printed as art (i.e. the book).

This makes criticism of these media rather more difficult, less standardised, and in many ways more interesting. As already mentioned, the discourse of the panics is basically a discourse of power whose stakes are the right to define cultural norms and social qualifications. Such a discourse is clearly complicated when the new media demand and nurture competences that cannot be controlled institutionally like reading. The abilities to listen, watch, and move rhythmically can be developed beyond the confines of formal training – and they are (Williams 1981: 94). Such differences between print, visual, and auditory media naturally influence the panics over them.

Of the three new media, radio, film, and records, radio is the most intimate – it enters people's homes directly – and hence some parental supervision of its use can be expected. (Only the transistor radio of the 1960s serves to break that pattern.) Moreover, in most European countries, radio is a public-service medium, and so, from the outset, the radio bears the marks of middle-class values and principles of selection: for example, in the early days of the BBC in Britain programmes are punctuated with silences for reflection, and in Norway broadcasters themselves urge people to use the new medium selectively (Frith 1983: 107; Dahl 1975).

For young people, however, reflection is not the most alluring aspect of the new media. Going to the cinema or to public dances are activities that are less open to adult control than is the case with home reading and listening to the radio (or records). Like the dance hall, the cinema is a public place of recreation, and offers more unalloyed forms of pleasure and more American versions of entertainment. This challenging combination does not go unopposed. Like popular fiction, film is accused of causing crime, violence, and sexual depravity. But unlike most print media, film is part of public recreation, its impact is more visible, and so the threat seems greater. In Britain, for example, the first inquiry into film was set up in 1917 by the National Council of Public Morals. Its report, *The Cinema in Education* (1925), far from validates the accusations. Thus, the council states in its conclusion: 'it certainly has not been proved that the increase in juvenile crime generally has been consequent on the cinema, or has been independent of other factors more conducive to wrongdoing' (quoted in Richards 1984: 71). Even so, the allegations of delinquency continue unabated. Similarly, the claim that films induce sexual seduction is vigorously voiced, especially by religious groups whose fear of the perceived immoralities in the dark are not limited to the screen.

As Hollywood gains superiority as the international film industry, the panics over film are increasingly inflected by nationalist, even racialist, overtones. In Britain, perhaps the most extreme example is *The Devil's Camera*, written in 1932 by two journalists, R. G. Burnett and E. D. Martell. The authors object to the cinemas' 'sex-mad and cynical financiers', who are identified as 'mainly Jewish'. They go on to profess that

> It is unimaginably tragic that at [this] time the cinemas should be revelling in squandermania, promiscuity, crime and idleness. Our national strength is being sapped, our capacity to triumph over adversity undermined.
>
> (Quoted in Richards 1984: 55, 56)

In German film panics, the nationalist overtones are coupled with a more direct anti-Americanism. The dual development of rapid modernisation and inflation after the First World War impoverishes the academic and administrative middle classes as well as many self-employed people. As the cultural elite loses its social stronghold, its opposition to new cultural artifacts intensifies. A film critic, Herbert Jhering, writing in 1926, is typical of the response:

> The number of people who see films and never read books is in the millions. They are all co-opted by American taste; they are made equal, made uniform . . . The American film is the new world militarism approaching. It's more dangerous than Prussian militarism. It doesn't devour individuals, it devours masses.
>
> (Quoted in Kaes 1987: 21)

With a curious historical irony given the contemporary strengthening of the Nazi movement, film is linked here with seduction of the masses. Crucially, this 'fear of the mob' is projected on to the USA as the combined embodiment of industrialisation and commercialisation. This mixture of capitalist and nationalist reasoning recurs in later panics such as the European comics campaign of the 1950s.

'A COMMUNAL SOFTENING OF THE BRAIN': COMMON ASSUMPTIONS

What changes of strategy stand out from these junctures in the history of the media panics? There is a change in panic discourse over the years from what we might call a pessimist elitism towards a more optimistic pluralism. The emphasis in the early panics on censorship and direct social regulation of the masses in general, and the young in particular, gradually gives way to more tacit paternalistic measures that promote good literature as a means of moral elevation. In recent years, even this norm of moral elevation is being challenged by an ideal of democratic choice: children know cultural quality when they see it.

The historical development of the panics from elitism to pluralism is paralleled within cultural politics by a move away from democratising Culture towards increased cultural democratisation. Unquestioned cultural elitism has indeed been somewhat undermined in both cultural criticism and cultural politics. Democracy has undoubtedly gained by this process. Also, there are important internal contradictions within the various discourses: between political and religious groups, between cultural conservatives and cultural liberals – not to mention the shifts which occur within the overall majority, whose voices are never heard in the panics. These contradictions influence public strategies (censorship, education) as well as the cultural spaces left for the young at any given time.

Still, the similarities of the panics tend to overshadow their differences. All panics are united by a firm belief in rational argumentation: if people only know about the dangers of the media, if only their tastes are elevated, or if the media mechanisms are properly revealed, then they will change their cultural preferences. But this belief is facilitated by, indeed founded on, an intrinsic *historical amnesia*. Every new panic develops as if it were the first time such issues were debated in public, and yet the debates are strikingly similar.

This amnesia is closely related to another common characteristic of the panics: their *historical incorporation*. The intense preoccupation with the latest media fad immediately relegates older media to the shadows of acceptance. Thus, the trends towards cultural democratisation are chiefly seen with media that we have grown accustomed to, media that have proved their

innocence, so to speak. So, today comics can be hailed in safety:
Mickey Mouse and Donald Duck have been appropriated by pop
artists such as Roy Lichtenstein and Andy Warhol, the ICA in
London and other renowned museums promote cultural cross-
overs as gallery pieces, and even the comic figure Tin-Tin has
his own museum. But the new media, such as home videos in
the 1980s, still conjure up anxieties that are very similar to those
expressed over periodicals a hundred years ago.

Crucially, these similarities are rooted in three basic assumptions underlying all panics. The first of these assumptions is
concerned with *culture*. The media are bracketed as part of
popular culture, they are defined in opposition to high culture
or art, and they are found wanting. The dichotomy of high and
low culture is defined as a hierarchy of values. Let me list some
of the familiar oppositions that are usually associated with this
dichotomy: art versus entertainment, innovation versus tradition,
authenticity versus imitation, distanciation versus involvement,
rationalism versus emotionalism, critique versus acceptance. In
this list of associations, we begin by an opposition between artifacts based on formal differences of production (the individual
artistic *œuvre* versus the mass-produced media output), but we
end up with an opposition between people based on their different modes of reception (critical insight gained by book-reading
versus useless daydreaming in front of the box). Thus, the cultural hierarchy based on differences of production almost imper-
ceptibly turns into a social and psychological distinction of use.

That the media have an immediate impact is part of the second
general assumption, which deals with *social psychology*. Most
stage managers of media panics offer very simplified notions of
what is involved in cultural interpretation. On this basis, media
experience and social action are directly linked: if we see violence
on the screen, we become criminals. Or, according to others, if
we are exposed to media violence, our senses are dulled, so that
we accept a higher degree of 'real' violence. While nineteenth-
century panics emphasised the social evils resulting from mass-
circulating fiction, today media opposition centres on psychological ill-effects. Arguments are being internalised as the media
penetrate deeper into our social lives.

The refinement of textual theory – from reception studies and
feminism to deconstruction – that has marked media research
over the last fifteen years does not seem to revoke the Pavlovian

ideas. Part of the reason for this may be that textual theories do not readily lend themselves to empirical investigation, and few of them are sensitive to psychological development. Moreover, the methodological difficulties involved in empirical studies are in inverse proportion to the age of the recipients (see critique in Drotner 1988: chap. 1). But is part of the reason also that panics cannot bear nuancing?

Children and young people are continually defined as victims in the panics. This leads to the third assumption, which deals with the *relation* between culture and social psychology. According to this assumption, cultural development and human development are aspects of one and the same process. Children's cultural edification is part of, indeed proof of, their social elevation. Therefore their cultural fare must be guarded, watched over, and protected, because its composition is vital for their mental growth. Following this logic, if we as adults watch soap operas every afternoon, then our humaneness is gradually undermined. But if children watch soap operas every afternoon, then they never even get a chance to develop this humaneness. This type of reasoning is deeply ingrained in most Western societies, and is also found amongst supporters of the media. Thus, John Buchan, director of British Instructional Films between the wars and a professed advocate of film, declared in Parliament that

> The really vicious film is not very common; it is very rare. What we have to complain of much more is silliness and vulgarity . . . vulgarity may be a real danger, if it results in a general degradation of the public taste and a communal softening of the brain.
>
> (Quoted in Richards 1984: 54)

Cultural and mental development, according to this belief, are two sides of the same coin. The coin is called enlightenment. As we have seen, this concept lies at the core of the emphasis upon rational argumentation underlying all panics, just as it is the foundation of dominant cultural policies with liberals and social democrats. Historically, this dominant position is shaped by the fundamental importance of enlightenment in the development of modernity.

As mentioned at the beginning of this chapter, modernisation is a dynamic process founded on a capitalist competition for profit. Some traditions and qualifications are rendered obsolete, others become increasingly important, and people are constantly engaged in interpreting this complex constellation of continuity and change. While actual experiences naturally vary according to age, sex, race and region, everybody must learn the fundamental lesson of modernity: the need to live with the possibility of social, cultural, and psychological change. *Modernity fosters individuality as a social norm.*

Now, how can we all develop an individuality that is socially determined? Obviously we cannot. Modernity is founded on a paradox. Paradoxes cannot be resolved, but their contradictions may be tackled and possibly mediated. Modernity facilitates the creation of difference (gendered individuality), while at the same time it nurtures the ramifications of difference (the social norm). The term nurture is important. For the inherent contradictions of the paradox are negotiated through the concept of *enlightenment*. Upbringing is seen as the locus of enlightenment, and childhood is defined in terms of development: the child can and must develop – i.e. be 'brought *up*' – to the norms governing adult life (this often equals middle-class norms, as we have seen).

So, human and cultural development become equivalent in the dominant discourse of modernity. They are united by a shared opposition to non-enlightenment that is normatively defined as barbarism and lack of culture. A main result of this opposition is the hierarchy of taste as expressed in the dichotomy of art and entertainment. Within this discursive context, it is understandable why pedagogical and cultural debates become so important in modernity and why they are often conflated, as in the case of media panics. Through the panics, adults seek to redefine the parameters of enlightenment, parameters that are shaken and possibly undermined by the advent of every new mass medium: what do our children need? What should be the norms of a good life? How can we accommodate these aims to new cultural developments (and vice versa)? Because these questions are fundamental to our everyday interpretation of modernity, they resonate widely across the social scale uniting teachers, politicians, and parents around common cultural aims, despite important differences in the means employed. Through the panics, people attempt to overcome the paradox of enlightenment, which, however, cannot be 'overcome'. And so the panic activists continue their Sisyphean struggle. This explains the first of our introductory questions concerning the persistence of the panics. But why do they focus on children and young people? And why are many media reactions so adamant that they deserve the name panics?

THE DARK SIDE OF THE MOON: UNDERLYING REASONS

In modernity, children and young people have always occupied a pioneering cultural position. The formation of modern childhood and youth, in which new generations are brought up within the parameters of family and school, coincides with an unprecedented commodification of culture. As children and later adolescents lose social and economic power in the world of work, they gain cultural power in the world of commercial leisure.

From the mid-nineteenth century on, the young have been unrivalled consumers of weeklies, and from the infancy of film in the 1900s, they have constituted a major film audience. That many commercial media are fundamentally, if not exclusively, media for the *young* is a fact that often escapes researchers of popular culture. Here, the discussion is generally limited to a social discussion of elitist art as opposed to the entertainment of the masses. But the youthfulness of the media public has not escaped adult attention in the public debate. Indeed, it is what actually fuels the panics. For the social claims and cultural competences that the young often gain as spin-offs of their media use pose a potential threat to existing power relations in social as well in cultural and psychological terms. Today, many young people express sophisticated abilities in deciphering visual symbols, abilities that they often express in action rather than talk (Drotner 1989). Furthermore, many of these competences become very visible to the public. Thus, film-going, visits to discos and attending concerts are social events that all imply a youthful occupation of public space, today as before.

The media contents often emphasise emotional involvement and bodily expressiveness and experimentation. This hedonistic letting go is in tune with the promises of consumption, but is sharply opposed to the norms governing employment and school relations. The media uses of the young perspectivise with particular clarity contradictions that are intrinsic to modernity itself. These contradictions are defined and confined as 'problems' within the dominant discourse of enlightenment.

On a *social level*, media panics basically attempt to re-establish a generational status quo that the youthful pioneers seem to undermine. This tacit generational struggle is demonstrated in the adult strategy of externalising the problem: it is the *young* and their media uses that are targeted as evils. Nowhere is this more evident than in the panics over violence: while a single splatter movie may harm an adolescent for life, any number of killings are tolerated on television news (these are facts) or in ordinary gangster films (these are fads).

On a *cultural level*, the panics are part of a cultural struggle. The gradual undermining through this century of the cultural elite as a critical force serves to reinforce the generational conflict already described. Those who have invested most in gaining an accepted cultural capital are also the principal victims if this capital loses its currency.

Not surprisingly, then, librarians, teachers, and cultural critics have been instrumental in staging media panics. Again, we see the process of externalisation in operation, this time in terms of culture. The focus is exclusively on children's use of *media*, while it is 'forgotten' that most children's cultural practices are characterised by diversity of use more than by rigid divisions of form.

Media panics, then, can be understood as tacit or explicit means of social regulation. This explanation corroborates Stanley Cohen's 'safety valve' theory of the moral panic, while it emphasises that the social regulation is performed through a cultural enlightenment of the young. The media panics focus on the young precisely because, within the discourse of enlightenment, their development is the most decisive and the most vulnerable. Sociological and cultural analysis, then, may assist us in explaining the persistence of the panics as well as their focus on the young. But what about our third question: why are the reactions so strong? An answer to this cannot be captured through these approaches, and yet this question indicates perhaps the most fundamental conundrum of the panics: *the panic instigators speak in the name of reason, but their language is that of the emotions.* This opposition between form and content is found in all media panics. To understand it, we must turn to *psychological analysis*. To test the panic language, consider the above quotations and especially the metaphors. They centre on three symbolic registers, namely *food* ('poison', 'insipid fruit'), *hygiene/health* ('pollute', 'disease'), and *sexuality* ('licentious', 'indecent', 'seduction', 'promiscuity'). These registers immediately associate themselves with the oral, the anal, and the genital phases of psychological development.

The recurrent symbolism, spanning two hundred years, is revealing not so much by what it explicitly says as by what it tacitly assumes: popular culture in general and the mass media in particular are associated with bodily functions that in most societies are socially and culturally regulated. Furthermore, within the perspective of modernity, these associations are heavily invested in gender and generational terms. The registers of (anal) hygiene/health and (genital) sexuality suggest that the media undermine our self-control and are very similar to a prostitute: not only do they entice us, so that we lose our senses, their proprietors are also in it only for the money. And many people need to go back. The whore, the *femme fatale*, these images of explicit female desire are conjured up in the denigration of the media.

According to the literary critic Andreas Huyssen, the denigration of the popular is concomitant with an elevation of modernism from the end of the previous century on: it is the historical moment of the high/low divide in cultural criticism. The denigration is explained as a way for middle-class, male intellectuals of coming to terms with their own precarious position by externalising to women, and hence exterminating within themselves, dangerous aspects of their own personality, namely desire and emotionality (Huyssen 1986). This connection, I think, is very revealing if we wish to understand the vehemence governing media panics. The feminine/popular comes to operate as a hidden Other of male modernism, high culture, or art. Like the dark side of the moon, the invisibility of the feminine/popular serves to delineate and define high culture. But through this invisibility, the feminine/popular also points to its own absence in the critical discourse.

Still, the male–female opposition is an opposition that adults are forced to negotiate all the time. So this intricate connection appears as a tangible field of tension both in cultural criticism and in the discourses that inscribe everyday life. But to this dualism, I want to propose adding a third factor that equally operates as a defining principle in the media panics (and perhaps in the art/entertainment dichotomy at large). This principle is even more submerged than that of the feminine, and that is perhaps why it has received no critical attention. But it does surface in the metaphors used in the above quotations. For along with the symbols of anal and genital sexuality associated with femininity, there is the register of food. (In Scandinavia, we speak of junk, Coke, or burger culture.) This register refers to an even earlier stage, namely the oral phase, during which the infant makes no distinction between self and other. The prominence in the panics of references to this phase points to the *childlike* as perhaps the most important undercurrent in the debates: it equals self-forgetting involvement, abandonment, spontaneity.

Children and young people, I would argue, are prime objects of the media panics not merely because they are often media pioneers; not merely because they challenge social and cultural power relations, nor because they symbolise ideological rifts. They are panic targets just as much because they inevitably represent experiences and emotions that are irrevocably lost to adults: one cannot go back in time and become a child again. Perhaps this common human condition becomes a particularly painful realisation in modernity because modernity is based precisely on evolution and a linear progression of time. To modern adults, children become captive symbols of what is lost not only in an individual sense, but in a social sense. The male–female opposition is malleable: it may be negotiated and confronted. But the child–adult opposition is not open to the same kind of options: childhood becomes a 'paradise lost'.

In his *Passagen-Werk*, Walter Benjamin links the development of the child and of modernity. In both cases, the realisation of loss is a fundamental experience (Benjamin speaks about awakening – see Buck-Morss 1983). Loss may be mourned because it is past, or it may be a source of inspiration because it can be recalled as loss. I think Benjamin's analysis is pertinent to my discussion of the childlike as an undercurrent governing media panics. For just as one may evaluate loss in positive or negative terms, so adults living in a dynamic society attempt to negotiate the concept of the lost paradise of childhood in two opposite ways: one may emphasise the *loss* more than the paradise and evaluate childhood negatively as the phase resulting in adult division and disintegration; or one may stress the *paradisial* unity more than the loss, and then childhood becomes a positive proof

that change is still a personal option in modernity. In the media
panics, the childlike is primarily negative: the media threaten to
poison or choke us (an association with the infant's fear of
the all-powerful mother?), or they lead to social and mental
destruction. The positive associations with the childlike are found
in the views on cultural selection, according to which children
have an 'instinct' for cultual quality.

The media panics do not tell us much about actual media.
But as cultural seismographs, they reveal broader problems of
modernity. If it is true, as I claim, that the panics are one way
of addressing and trying to balance an inherent modern paradox,
then it is perhaps in line with the irony of history that the panics
themselves feed on a paradox: they are based on one or more
Others that – through their very absence – remain central sources
of renewed attacks. It is impossible to speak 'about' these
Others. On the other hand, without them it is impossible to
speak at all.

DISCURSIVE LIMITS

The psychological insights point to the limits of panic history
both as discourse and as analytical category. Panic activists
repeatedly apply the emotions in their struggle for rationality
and common sense. But not only that. They equally struggle
against emotions within themselves. Thus, one cannot argue with
panic proponents, and it is no good trying to prove irrationalities
or logical flaws. *Panic discourses cannot be countered discursively.*
That is ultimately why film opponents between the wars continue
their allegations of crime despite commission reports and other
evidence to the contrary. That is also why Pavlovian explanations
of media effects retain their currency in the panics despite theoretical developments. The emotional undercurrents of the panics
are determining factors in selecting what can surface and what
must remain hidden in the discourse.

This process, in turn, enforces analytical self-reflection: why
do some of us become professionally engaged with media panics?
Do we react on panics with ridicule, disgust, or indifference?
Through our deconstruction of the panic discourse, we reveal
our own anxieties, preferences, and concerns. We are part of
the discourse too. Media panics tackle central questions about
cultural quality, personal development and social change under

the rubric of enlightenment. Whether we like it or not, we are part of that discourse, if only because many of us occupy positions of interpretation and evaluation as teachers, researchers, or media professionals. The media panics may escape our attention, but their basic problematics affect us nevertheless.

Analysis provides no neat recipes to enter or, indeed, close the panics. But it may clarify the basis of discourse and our own position in it. We may realise that we are deeply implicated in complex ethical questions, but we may equally find that we hold a stake in the possible answers. Such self-reflection, in my opinion, is central to any analysis of cultural signification. In the case of panics, their history even holds the key to cultural action.

REFERENCES

Barker, M. (1984) *A Haunt of Fears: The Strange History of the British Horror Comics Campaign*, London, Sydney: Pluto Press.

Barlow, G. and Hill, A. (eds) (1985) *Video Violence and Children*, London: Hodder & Stoughton.

Berman, M. (1988) *All that is Solid Melts into Air: The Experience of Modernity*, Harmondsworth: Penguin (first published 1982).

Boethius, U. (1989) *När Nick Carter drevs på flykten*, Stockholm: Gidlunds förlag.

Buck-Morss, S. (1983) 'Benjamin's Passagen-Werk: Redeeming Mass Culture for the Revolution', *New German Critique* 29: 211–40.

Cohen, S. (1972) *Folk Devils and Moral Panics*, London: MacGibbon & Kee.

Dahl, H. F. (1975) *Hallo, Hallo! Kringkastingen i Norge, 1920–1940*, Oslo: J. W. Cappelen.

Drotner, K. (1988) *English Children and their Magazines, 1751–1945*, New Haven: Yale University Press.

—— (1989) 'Girl Meets Boy: Aesthetic Production, Reception, and Gender Identity', *Cultural Studies* 3, 2.

Frith, S. (1983) ' "The Pleasures of the Hearth": The Making of BBC Light Entertainment', in T. Bennett *et al.* (eds), *Formations of Pleasure*, London: Routledge & Kegan Paul.

Furuland, L. and Ørvig, M. (1986) *Utblick över barn- och ungdomslitteraturen: debatt och analys*, Stockholm: Rabén & Sjögren.

Huyssen, A. (1986) 'Mass Culture as Woman: Modernism's Other', in T. Modleski (ed.), *Studies in Entertainment: Critical Approaches to Mass Culture*, Bloomington, Indiana: Indiana University Press: 188–207.

Kaes, A. (1987) 'The Debate about Cinema: Charting a Controversy (1909–29)', *New German Critique* 40: 7–33.

Kristensen, N. K. (1903) 'Morskabslæsning som Opdragelsesmiddel for Børn', in R. C. Mortensen (ed.), *Det pædagogiske Selskabs*

Aarsberetning 1902–03 [enclosed with *Vor Ungdom*], Copenhagen: Nielsen & Lydiche: 23–32.

Neuburg, V. E. (1977) *Popular Literature: A History and Guide*, Harmondsworth: Penguin.

Richards, J. (1984) *The Age of the Dream Palace: Cinema and Society in Britain, 1930–1939*, London: Routledge & Kegan Paul.

Salmon, E. (1888) *Juvenile Literature as it is*, London: Drane.

Våldsskildringsutredningen (1987, 1988) *Videovåld, I, II*, Stockholm: Almänna Förlaget.

Wertham, F. (1954) *Seduction of the Innocent*, New York: Rinehart.

Williams, R. (1981) *Culture*, Glasgow: Fontana.

Wolff, J. (1985) 'The Invisible Flaneuse: Women and the Literature of Modernity', *Theory, Culture & Society* 2, 3: 37–46.

Part II

National and transnational media cultures

Chapter 3

Electronic communities and domestic rituals
Cultural consumption and the production of European cultural identities

David Morley

Contemporary technological developments, and particularly the emergence of satellite television, have given a new urgency to the question of information flows. Thus Collins (1988b: 6) has noted the greater difficulty, for national states, of policing the circulation of electronic products, precisely because they assume no material form (unlike films or books) with which a customs post can deal more easily. Similarly, Schlesinger (1986: 126) has noted that satellite broadcasting threatens to undermine the very basis of present policies for the policing of national space. Collins has pointed to the possibility that satellite television may presage the generalisation of the 'Canadian experience' of subservience to American cultural interests (Collins 1988b: 13), and has observed elsewhere that satellite television may indeed be seen to herald what he calls the 'Canadianisation of European television' (1988a: 20). Thus, these new technologies have been argued to have worryingly negative consequences for established national (and indeed continental) identities, and, at the same time, to have potentially unpoliceable and thus 'disturbing' effects, not only in disaggregating established audiences/communities, but also in creating new ones across national boundaries. Against these fears, various writers have also noted the limitations on the exportability of American culture, both in the sense of the limitations imposed in principle (by language/culture) on the export of information products as opposed to material goods, and in the empirical sense that European fears about being swamped by American culture can be argued to be, to some extent, contradicted by empirical evidence of continuing audience preferences for 'home' products (see Mills 1985).

THE CONSTRUCTION OF CULTURAL IDENTITIES

Up to the present the debates surrounding the questions of cultural identity and cultural imperialism have functioned with a lagely uninterrogated model of what 'cultural identities' are. On the whole, the question has been posed (with varying degrees of technological determinism) as one of the potential impact of a 'new technology' (for example satellite broadcasting) on a set of pre-given objects: 'national (or cultural) identities'.

Formulations (and assumptions) of this type seem to underlie many of the EC debates (and indeed some EC policy) surrounding these issues. Thus, it is often assumed, for instance, that the integrity and continued existence of communities and their political institutions depend crucially on their 'communications sovereignty' and that if a community consumes 'too much' (unspecified) exogenous information, 'the legitimacy of the native political institutions will come under threat and the community will ultimately cease to exist' (Banks and Collins 1989: 2). It is in this light that we can perhaps best understand much current EC policy which, in response to the perceived threat of 'cocacolonisation', is concerned to promote and develop a sense of European identity, in which unity is the goal and information/culture (which is perceived to have 'homogenising' effects – cf. Schlesinger 1987: 220) is the means to achieve it. Or, as Jean Monnet put it, 'if we were beginning the EC all over again, we should begin with culture' (quoted in Schlesinger 1987: 222).

From this perspective, current debates, such as those over the potential 'de-nationalisation' of Italy (since Italy is seen to incur the danger of becoming an area of 'pure consumption', because of the weakness of its production base – Schlesinger 1986: 137) acquire a different significance. Schlesinger argues (and rightly in my view) that 'collective identity and its constitution is a problem, not something that may be presumed to exist as a prior condition of political agency' (Schlesinger 1987: 240). From this angle, culture has to be seen as a site of perpetual contestation (both inter- and intra-nationally), and we cannot view the 'achievement' of a national culture as some kind of one-off task which, having been 'completed', could equally be 'undone'. Rather it is, necessarily, a continuous and continuously problematic process (cf. Gramsci 1971, on hegemony as a continuous movement between unstable equilibria). In similar vein, Donald argues that we might usefully focus on

> the apparatuses of discourse, technologies and institutions (print capitalism, education, mass media and so forth) which produced what is generally recognised as 'the national culture' . . . the nation is an effect of these cultural technologies, not their origin. A nation does not express itself through its culture: it is cultural apparatuses that produce 'the nation'. What is produced is not an identity or a single consciousness . . . but (hierarchically organised) values, dispositions and differences. This cultural and social heterogeneity is given a certain fixity by the articulating principle of 'the nation'. 'The national' defines the culture's unity by differentiating it from other cultures, by marking its boundaries; a fictional unity, of course, because the 'us' on the inside is itself always differentiated.
>
> (Donald 1988: 32)

IDENTITY AS DIFFERENCE: CONSTITUTIVE RELATIONS

In his classic study of linguistics, Saussure (1974) argues that within the realm of language, there are only differences, with no positive terms. Thus, when he analyses the problem of identity in language (when two linguistic units are to count as instances of the same category), he concludes that identity is wholly a function of differences within a system. Thus, as he argues, we must approach the problem from within the fundamental recognition that the 'units' of language which we wish to understand are 'purely differential and defined not by their positive content but negatively, by their relations with the other terms of the system. Their most precise characteristic is in being what the others are not' (Saussure 1974: 117).

I wish to argue that this same principle should be applied in the analysis of cultural identities: that is, rather than analysing cultural or (national) identities one by one and then subsequently (as an optional move) thinking about how they are related to each other (through relations of alliance or opposition, domination or subordination), we must grasp how these 'identities', in Saussure's terms, are only constituted in and through their

relations to each other. Thus, to make the argument more concrete, it is inappropriate to start by trying to define 'European
culture', for example, and then analysing its relations to other
cultural identities. Rather, from this perspective, 'European culture' is seen to be constituted precisely through its distinctions
from oppositions to American culture, Asian culture, Islamic
culture, and so on. Thus, difference is constitutive of identity.
Again Schlesinger offers a useful formulation:

> identity is as much about exclusion as it is about inclusion
> and the critical factor for defining the ethnic group therefore
> becomes the social *boundary* which defines the group with
> respect to other groups . . . not the cultural reality within
> those borders.

(Schlesinger 1987: 235)

Schlesinger's argument is that, viewed in this way, collective
identity is based on the (selective) processes of 'memory' so that
a given group recognises itself through its memory of a common
past. Thus, he argues, we can develop a dynamic view of identity,
focusing on the ability of ethnic groups to recompose and redefine their boundaries continually (1987: 230).

The argument, so far, has been pitched at the level of socio-
cultural analysis. However, there is another dimension to the
problem, which is well developed by Donald in his recent analysis
of the constitution of English culture, where he also addresses the
psychic processes involved in the constitution and maintenance of
identity and difference. In pursuit of this argument, Donald asks
why there are so many grotesque foreign villains (for instance
Fu Manchu, Dr No) in popular fiction, and why the problem of
identity is so often played out by its projection on to 'dangerous
women' in popular films (for example film noir).

Donald's point is that these popular fictions speak to fundamental psychic processes, and attention to them can help us to
make sense of what he calls the 'paranoid strand in popular
culture, the clinging to familiar polarities and the horror of difference' (Donald 1988: 44).

As he puts it,

> Manifest in racism, its violent misogyny, and its phobias about
> alien culture, alien ideologies and 'enemies within' is the terror
> that without the known boundaries, everything will collapse

in undifferentiated, miasmic chaos; that identity will disintegrate, that the 'I' will be suffocated or swamped.

(Donald 1988: 44)

This is the fear at the heart of the question of 'identity', whether posed at the level of the individual or of the nation. Driven by such fears, as the Mattelarts have noted, the defence of a given 'cultural identity' easily slips into the most hackneyed nationalism, or even racism, and the nationalist affirmation of the superiority of one group over another (Mattelart *et al.* 1984). The question is not abstract: it is a matter of the relative power of different groups to define national identity, and their abilities to mobilise their definitions through their control of cultural institutions. Here we enter the terrain of what Hobsbawn and Ranger (1983) have referred to as the 'invention of tradition'. Tradition is not a matter of a fixed or given set of beliefs or practices which are handed down or accepted passively. Rather, as Wright (1985) has argued, tradition is very much a matter of present-day politics and of the way in which powerful institutions function to select particular values from the past, and to mobilise them in contemporary practices (cf. Mrs Thatcher's support for the return to 'Victorian values' in the UK). Through such mechanisms of cultural reproduction, a particular version of the 'collective memory' and thus a particular sense of national identity is produced.

A PARTICULAR CASE: THE CONSTRUCTION OF BRITISH NATIONAL IDENTITY

Various commentators (see, inter alia, Ascherson 1988 and Glenny 1988) have pointed to the re-emergence of nationalist movements in recent years (not least in Eastern Europe as the constraints of Soviet hegemony are loosened) and also to the politically contradictory character of their demands for national autonomy (perhaps most clearly expressed in the use of traditionally nationalist symbols by the Hungarian underground rock band the Galloping Pathologists). Clearly the issues at stake here are pertinent right across Western (witness also the Basque and Breton movements, and so forth) and Eastern Europe. However, being English, I shall attempt to pursue the point by means of an analysis which focuses on a cultural process with which I am more familiar and in which I am, necessarily, implicated more directly.

Both Hood (1988) and Samuels (1988) argue that the key cultural process in play in contemporary British politics is one in which a romantically sanitised version of the British past is being busily recreated: a quite reactionary vision of pastoral England/Albion. Samuels describes this process as the creation of a 'born again cultural nationalism' which operates across a number of fields. Thus we see the boom in the conservation/ 'heritage' movement; the re-evaluation of English landscape painting; educational reforms aimed at returning to 'traditional standards' in English and History, as core components of the educational curriculum; in the realm of fashion we see a return to 'fashionable old-fashioned' styles; and in the realm of architecture and design a return to the use of 'traditional materials', as Habitat replaces its Scandinavian pine with 'traditional English kitchen furniture' and Covent Garden's new shopping piazza is recreated as a (Dickensian) walk down England's memory lane, past 'shoppes' offering 'traditional fare' in a picturesque nightmare of time undone. Samuels cuttingly defines this overall tendency as operating within the context of a 'defence of national tradition against European intellectual history . . . a kind of (upper) class revenge for the "modernisations" [read "Europeanisation"] of the 1960s' (Samuels 1988).

Clearly, there is more at stake here than the question of whether one likes 'traditional paisley patterns'. What else is at stake is the question of race; because the 'England' being reconstructed in this way is being reconstructed around a tradition which is unproblematically white: which Britain's population is not. In his study of British racism, *There Ain't no Black in the Union Jack*, Gilroy (1986) puts the point simply, characterising all of this as a 'morbid celebration of England and Englishness from which blacks are systematically excluded' (Gilroy, quoted in Donald 1988: 31).

In taking up this argument Hall rightly points out that

> ethnicity, in the form of a culturally-contrasted sense of Englishness and a particularly closed, exclusive and regressive form of English national identity, is one of the core characteristics of British racism today.

(Hall 1989: 29)

He argues for the need to 'decouple ethnicity . . . from its equiv-
alence with nationalism, imperialism, racism and the state, which
are the points of attachment around which a distinctive British,
(or more accurately English) ethnicity has been constructed' and
for the need 'to develop a new cultural politics and a new conception of ethnicity . . . which engages rather than suppresses difference'.

The point, I believe, would hold equally well in the context
of debates around what it means to be 'European'. As Robins
puts it,

> European identity can no longer be, simply and unproblemati-
> cally, a matter of Western intellectual and cultural traditions.
> As a consequence of its belligerent, imperialistic, and colonial-
> ist history, Europe now contains a rich diversity of cultures
> and identities. The question is whether ethnic (and also gen-
> dered) differences are disavowed and repressed, or whether
> they can be accepted, and accepted, moreover in their differ-
> ence.
>
> (Robins 1989: 28)

'US' AND 'THEM': EUROPE VERSUS AMERICA

In this section I aim to explore the dynamics of the debate about
American culture in Europe, from the point of view of the
structuralist perspective outlined above. I shall argue that anti-
Americanism usually has a suppressed class content, which means
that it also functions as a defence of dominant class definitions
of the national culture in question.

It is worth noting that all of this has a very long pedigree. If
President Mitterrand's nightmare – of the day when a European
can be defined as someone who watches American soap opera
on a Japanese television – is of relatively recent provenance, we
can find much the same sentiment being expressed in the British
context in 1945 by Lord Keynes, then Chairman of the Arts
Council:

> How satisfactory it would be if different parts of the citizenry
> would again walk their several ways as they once did. Let
> every part of Merry England be merry in its own way. Death
> to Hollywood!
>
> (Quoted in Donald 1988: 32)

We should, of course, also remember Mattelart's warning that

> the idea of a monolithic, triumphant imperialism, wiping out
> all diversity and homogenising all cultures is absurd . . . The
> idea that imperialism invades different sectors of a society in
> a uniform way must be abandoned. What must be substituted
> is the demand for an analysis that illuminates the particular
> milieux that favour [or hinder] this penetration.
>
> (Mattelart 1979: 61)

This is not simply an academic perspective: the same recognition
of the continuing pertinence of 'national differences' has
informed the recognition of many American companies that they
will need to develop 'national variants' of their products (and
adverts) for different national markets within Europe, rather
than relying on 'Eurobrands'. In a similar way, Collins has noted
the retreat of many of the satellite companies, away from their
original pan-European ambitions, towards a revised perspective
which accepts the limitations and divisions of separate language/
cultural markets in Europe (Collins 1988b).

Here the experience of the Howard Johnson hotel/restaurant
chain in the early 1970s seems to be repeated. In 1972 their
chairman announced their withdrawal from the overall Euro-
market, saying 'we are too Americanised to make it in
Europe . . . [in the general leisure market] our company is now
drawing up plans for a new chain of more European-style
motels . . . looking for market areas where the cultural differences between America and Europe are less marked and will
pose less problems, eg. business travel and hotels' (quoted in
Bigsby 1975).

So, on some things, at least, the Marxists and the businessmen
can agree. However, the problems at issue here are, in fact, more
complex still. The chairman of Howard Johnson's comments find
an interesting parallel in Collins' analysis of the differential 'cultural discount' for various types of products, in a range of markets, where cultural differences function to 'discount' or limit
the range of the 'exportability' of a given product. But 'cultural
discount' is no simple matter of geographical proximity. Collins
goes on to quote a 'World Film News' survey from the 1930s,
which reported that film exhibitors in working-class areas were

on the whole satisfied with the more vigorous American

films . . . (but) practically unanimous in regarding the majority
of British films as unsuitable for their audiences. British films,
one Scottish exhibitor writes, should rather be called English
films, in a particularly parochial sense; they are more 'foreign'
to his audience than the products of Hollywood over 6000
miles away.

(Quoted in Collins 1988a: 7)

'DALLAS WITH TAILFINS': THE VULGAR POLITICS OF TASTE

I have argued earlier that when the defence of cultural identity
gets confused with the defence of a fixed past, it runs the risk
of playing a strictly conservative role, quite apart from the difficulties of establishing any definition of the 'authentic'/national
culture being 'defended', which will inevitably contain elements
which were originally 'foreign'.

Over the last decade *Dallas* has functioned as the most obvious
'hate symbol' of cultural emasculation, as immortalised in
Alastair Milne's (ex-Director-General of the BBC) fear that deregulation would lead to the 'threat of wall-to-wall *Dallas*'. As
Ien Ang put it, *Dallas*' international popularity was frequently
offered as knock-down 'evidence of the threat posed by US
style commercial culture to all authentic national cultures and
identities' (Ang 1985: 2). Thankfully, as a result of Ang's own
work and that of Katz and Liebes (1989) in their multi-national
study of differential 'decodings' of the programme, the debate
has moved on a little, as we have seen the quite varied ways in
which audiences from different cultural backgrounds use, perceive, and interpret the programme in the light of the cultural
resources and 'filters' at their disposal.

I want to suggest that these debates need to be seen in the
context of the long gestation of anti-Americanism in European
culture, and that, specifically, the present debate about the
impact of commercial American television programmes, in a
Europe still dominated in many countries by a very traditional
form of public-service programming, can usefully be informed
by consideration of the debates surrounding the introduction of
commercial television in Britain in the 1950s.

Up to that time the BBC had a monopoly of British television.
That monopoly was originally granted at a time when the British

cultural elite saw its position undermined by the seemingly unstoppable flow of American popular culture, Hollywood, tin-pan alley, 'cheap American fiction', and so on. The role of the BBC was to maintain (under Lord Reith's stewardship) national standards in the face of this threat to the Great English Cultural Tradition (see Mulgan and Worpole 1985).

The problem was that, as soon as ITV was launched in the 1950s, offering new cultural forms based on elements of working-class and regional cultures (melodramas, irreverent presenters, non-standard accents, and the like), the working-class audience deserted the BBC in droves. As Mulgan and Worpole put it: 'the BBC . . . by its refusal to engage with anything other than the cultural tradition of the Southern upper class, left a vast, vacant, cultural space which the early entrepreneurs of ITV were only too happy to fill' (1985: 41).

The cultural significance of this development has been the subject of considerable debate in the UK over the last few years (summarised in articles by Connell 1983 and Garnham 1983). In that context Connell argues that the key factor was that the commercial channel, ITV, 'led the way in making connections with and expressing popular structures of feeling and taste. By its very logic a commercial TV station is bound to attempt to meet the tastes and needs of its audience' (Connell 1983). The BBC quickly learnt that, if it was to survive, it had to emulate ITV's success in this respect, which it was only able to do by itself producing more material which directly connected with working-class patterns of taste and cultural preferences.

Traditionally, the left and its anti-American allies have explained the dominance of American programmes in the inter-national television market by reference to the considerable econ-omic advantages accruing to American producers, as a result of the huge scale of their domestic market. These advantages are, of course, considerable; but what if there is also something intrin-sic to the products, which constitutes the basis of their appeal to working-class audiences in other countries? In his investigation of literary tastes among the British working class, Worpole inter-views a number of men who recall their pleasure in discovering American detective fiction writing in the 1930s. Here is an ex-docker explaining why, for him, this American literature had a greater appeal than the writers of the English literary tradition:

I read the English writers, H. G. Wells, Arnold Bennett . . .
but they weren't my kind of people [sic]. You always had the
edge of class there . . . What intrigued me about the American
writers was they were talking the way we talked.

(Worpole 1983: 30)

I shall return to this point at the end of this section: for the
moment, let me just note the importance of the vernacular language in constituting the appeal of these American forms of
popular culture.

The idea that English or European 'high culture' is in danger
of being swamped by a relentless deluge of 'Americana' is not
new. Dick Hebdige (1988) traces these fears back to at least the
1930s, when writers as different as the Conservative Evelyn
Waugh and the Socialist George Orwell were united by a fascinated loathing for modern architecture, holiday camps, advertising, fast food, plastics, and (later) chewing-gum. To both Waugh
and Orwell, these were the images of the 'soft', enervating, 'easy
life' which threatened to smother British cultural identity. By the
1950s, the battle lines in this debate were drawn, with 'real
culture' quality and taste on one side; and the ersatz blandish-
ment of soft disposable commodities, stream-lined cars, rock and
roll, crime and promiscuity on the other. As Hebdige says, when
anything American was sighted, it tended to be interpreted (at
least by those working in the context of education or professional
cultural criticism) as the 'beginning of the end'. Hebdige
describes how the images of crime, disaffected youth, urban
crisis, and spiritual drift became 'anchored together around popular American commodities, fixing a chain of associations which
has become thoroughly sedimented in British common-sense'
(Hebdige 1988: 57). Thus, in particular, American food became
a standard metaphor for declining standards. The very notion of
the Americanisation of television stands for a whole series of
associations to do with commercialisation, banality, and the
destruction of traditional values.

The debate which Dick Hebdige opens up here goes back to
Richard Hoggart's work, *The Uses of Literacy*. Hoggart's (1958)
book is a detailed appreciation of traditional working-class community life, coupled with a critique of the 'homogenising' impact
of American culture on working-class life, which he saw as being
destroyed by the 'hollow brightness', the 'shiny barbarism', and

'spiritual decay' of imported American culture, which was leading
to an 'aesthetic breakdown' in which traditional values were
undermined and replaced by a 'Candy Floss World' of 'easy
thrills and cheap fiction'.

This lamentation of the deleterious effects of Americanisation
was, and continues to be, advanced from the left just as much
as from the right of the political spectrum. However, Hebdige's
central point is that these 'vulgar' American products, stream-
lined, plastic, and glamorous, were precisely those which
appealed to a substantial section of the British working class (cf.
my earlier comments on the popularity of ITV with its working-
class audience). While, from the paternalistic point of view of the
upolders of 'traditional British values', these American imported
products constituted a 'chromium hoard bearing down on us',
for a popular audience, Hebdige argues, they constituted a space
in which oppositional meanings (in relation to dominent traditions of British culture) could be negotiated and expressed.

In passing, I would also like to add one more twist to the
story. The images which Orwell and Hoggart use to characterise
the damaging effects of American popular culture have a recurring theme: the 'feminisation' of the authentic muscle and masculinity of the British industrial working class, which they saw as
under attack from an excess of Americana, characterised essentially by passivity, leisure and domesticity, warm baths, sun-
bathing and the 'easy life'. When the discussion of American
programming is combined with the discussion of programming in
the form of soap opera, principally understood as a feminine
form in itself, we are clearly, from Hoggart or Orwell's position,
dealing with the lowest of the low, or as Charlotte Brunsdon
(1986) has characterised it, what is seen as 'the trashiest trash'
(cf. Huyssen 1988).

As Bigsby put it some time ago, in a world where the 'modern'
experience has often been equated with an 'Imaginary America'
(cf. Webster 1988),

> opposition to popular culture and complaints about American-
> isation have often amounted to little more than laments over
> a changing world . . . where 'Americanisation' frequently
> means little more than the incidence of change, and change,
> especially in new cultural forms, provokes established patterns
> of negative reaction. The new is characterised as brash, crude,

unsubtle, mindless and (as Matthew Arnold insisted) destructive of taste and tradition. 'America' is thus mobilised as the paradigm of the traditionless, the land of the *material* counterposed to the *'cultural'* [i.e. 'Europe'].

(Bigsby 1975: 6)

In her contribution to the British debate about American popular culture, Cora Kaplan usefully points towards an approach which is sensitive to the different meanings which the same products can have in different national contexts, thus moving us away from the unhelpfully 'essentialist' terms in which many of these debates have, thus far, been couched. She notes that in their 'home' context, in the 1950s and 1960s,

> American thrillers/westerns etc. were seen as somehow 'essentially' right-wing, in some ideological sense . . . [however] in Britain the genres and narratives of American popular culture acted as a kind of wedge, forcing into the open, by contrast . . . a recognition of the class-bound complacency of the 'Great Tradition' of British Culture.

(Kaplan, quoted in Webster 1988: 179)

As Hebdige argues, in Britain the debate about popular culture, in the key period of the 1950s and 1960s, condensed around the question of the design/style of 'modern' American products and, especially, their 'streamlining', which was seen as 'vulgar' ('in bad taste') by reference to the established canons of European design. These 'streamlined' products (especially American cars), which were so (regrettably) popular among working-class consumers, were decried as decadent, decorative, and 'excessive'. These things were seen as 'vulgar', in the strict sense of the 'vulgate': 'of, pertaining to the common people'. These American products were scorned by British cultural elite as being 'the jazz of the drawing board . . . products of a short-term, low-rent, chromium utopia'. And worst of all was the ever-popular Cadillac, whose tailfins were described as representing 'the Vietnam of product design' (Hebidge 1988: 65–6).

The problem for these critics was, of course, that the popularity of these products, while it might be decried and regretted, could not be wished away. By breaking away from traditional, class-based notions of 'good taste', these products did make genuine connections with the actual tastes and desires of large numbers of working-class people. For those consumers, these products represented positive symbols of a massive improvement in the material quality of their lives. For them 'America' was a very positive symbol functioning largely by opposition (see Saussure, quoted earlier) to what they perceived as the dead hand of traditional English culture, as defined by the cultural elite.

I argued earlier that identity is always as much a question of differences as it is of similarities and that what matters is to understand who is being differentiated from whom. For Europeans, 'America' has long provided the negative pole against which 'we' have defined ourselves, the image of what 'we' are not, or that which 'we' do not wish to imagine ourselves to be, or that which, it is feared, 'we' are about to become. But the terms of this debate have now acquired a certain historical fixity, which is (cf. Althusser 1972) relatively autonomous of their material basis. Because now, as Ang and I put it elsewhere,

> while the European nations still wrangle over their respective attempts to protect their cultural sovereignty from this 'American invasion' the terms are shifting yet again, as we approach the point at which Spanish becomes the first language of all the Americas and as the United States begins to face the consequences of having become the world's largest debtor nation.
>
> As the pivot of the world economy swings from the Atlantic to the Pacific basin a fundamental modification in the balance of economic power is taking place, whose impacts have begun to make themselves felt in the cultural sphere as well. Sony's purchase of CBS presages what may yet turn out to be a fundamental realignment of international cultural forces, and the old cultural ramparts along Europe's Atlantic coast may well turn out to be facing in quite the wrong direction. In fact, European nations may now face the prospect of a different form of marginalisation from the world stage, a prospect that throws the threat of 'Americanisation' into quite a new perspective.
>
> (Ang and Morley 1989: 140)

DOMESTIC VIEWING AS NATIONAL RITUAL: FAMILY, TELEVISION, NATION

I have spent some time engaging with the debates about cultural identity, new technologies, and the 'transnationalisation of culture' in the terms in which they are customarily posed, i.e. from the point of view of production economics, the changing technologies of distribution, and their potential cutural effects on the media audience. Given that my own interest in these matters arises directly from my involvement in media audience research, I now want to reverse the terms of the argument, and look at the question from the point of view of the domestic users/audiences of these 'new technologies', as they function in the context of household/family cultures. I want to suggest that the question to be asked is how the new patterns of supply of programming will be filtered and mediated by the processes of domestic consumption. The key issues, I suggest, concern the role of these technologies in disrupting established boundaries (at the national and domestic levels, simultaneously) and in rearticulating the private and public spheres in new ways. My argument is that analysis of the processes of creation of new 'image spaces' and 'cultural identities' needs to be grounded in the analysis of the everyday practices and domestic rituals through which contemporary 'electronic communities' are conducted and reconstituted (at both micro- and macro-levels) on a daily basis.

Scannell (1988) has usefully analysed what he calls the 'unobtrusive ways in which broadcasting sustains the lives, and routines, from one day to the next, year in, year out, of whole populations'. This is, in effect, to pay attention to the role of the media in the very structuring of time. Scannell's focus is on the role of national broadcasting media as central agents of national culture, in the organising of the involvement of the population in the calendar of national life. Similarly, he analyses the way in which broadcast media constitute a cultural resource 'shared by millions', and the way in which, for instance, long-running popular serials provide a 'past in common' to whole populations. Here we move beyond the study of the isolated text and at the same time beyond any abstract notion of the study of television as an undifferentiated 'flow'.

How might we conceive of this articulation between the domestic and the national? Some years ago Ellis referred, somewhat gnomically, to television as 'the private life of the nation-state' (Ellis 1982: 5). His comment can be seen as a parallel to the argument in Brunsdon and Morley (1978) about the way in which certain forms of current affairs television in Britain are concerned to construct an image of the national 'we' as composed precisely of an 'us' whose constituent elements are 'ordinary families'. This, as we argued in that context, frequently provides the very basis of the broadcasters' claims to 'represent' their audience, and of their implicit appeals for various forms of audience 'identi-fication' with the programme presenters. In the same way, John Hartley has argued that 'television is one of the prime sites upon which a given nation is constructed for its members' (Hartley 1987: 124), drawing, like many others, on Benedict Anderson's concept of the nation as an 'imagined community', the construct of particular discourses. As Anderson puts it: 'An American will never meet, or even know the names of more than a handful of his fellow Americans. He has no idea of what they are up to at any one time. But he has complete confidence in their steady, anonymous, simultaneous activity' (Anderson 1983: 31).

Wherein lies this 'simultaneity'? Among other sources we can perhaps look to the regulation of simultaneous experience through TV broadcast schedules. Where does this 'confidence' come from? Among other sources, Anderson points to the news-paper as a mechanism for providing imaginary links between the members of a nation. As Hartley puts it, newspapers are 'at one and the same time the ultimate fiction, since they construct the imagined community, and the basis of a mass ritual or ceremony that millions engage in every day' (Hartley 1987: 124).

In his paper 'Media, Technology and Everyday Life' Herman Bausinger (1984) develops the point about the newspaper as a linking mechanism between the rituals of the domestic, the organisation of the schedules of everyday life, and the construc-tion of the 'imagined community' of the nation. Bausinger com-ments on the nature of the 'disruption' caused when a morning edition of a newspaper fails to appear. His point concerns that which is missed. As he puts it: 'Is it a question of the missing content of the paper? Because the newspaper is part of it [a constitutive part of the ritual of breakfast for many people], reading it proves that the breakfast time world is still in order' (Bausinger 1984: 344).

And of course, vice versa. A similar point, and indeed a

stronger one, given the necessary simultaneity of broadcast TV viewing, could be made in relation to the watching of an evening news broadcast for many viewers, where the fact of watching and engaging in a joint ritual with millions of others can be argued to be at least as important as any informational content gained from the broadcast.

The further point, inevitably, concerns the significance of these arguments in the context of current and prospective changes in the structure of broadcasting. The proliferation of broadcast channels, cable, and satellite is likely to move us towards a more fragmented social world than that of traditional national broadcast television. These new forms of communication may in fact play a significant part in deconstructing national cultures, and the 'rescheduling' potentialities of video and other new communications technologies may disrupt our assumptions of any 'necessary simultaneity' of 'broadcast' experience.

There is a substantial body of evidence that broadcast television constitutes a significant cultural resource on which large numbers of people depend, to a greater or lesser extent, for supplying their needs both for information and for entertainment. There is further evidence that television plays a significant role (both at a calendrical and at a quotidien level) in organising (literally scheduling – see Paterson 1980) our participation in public life, in the realms both of politics and leisure activities. The arrival of satellite television is bringing about significant changes both in the extent and the nature of the supply of programming (directly, through its own programme strategies, and indirectly, through the responses which existing broadcast institutions are making in order to compete with their new rivals). Given these circumstances, the need is clear for the cultural impact of these changes in programme supply to be closely monitored during this key period of broadcasting history, in which established patterns of consumption may be expected to fragment in a number of directions. The key issue concerns the role of the 'new technologies' in offering a changed (and varying) 'menu' of cultural resources, from and by means of which we will all be constructing our senses of 'self-identify'. In analysing those processes we must attend closely to how 'cultural identities' are produced, both at the macro- and micro-levels, and ask what role the various media play in our construction of our sense of ourselves, as individuals and as 'members' of communities at various levels, whether as members of families, regions, nations, or communities of other types.

REFERENCES

Althusser, L. (1972) *For Marx*, London: Penguin.
Anderson, B. (1983) *Imagined Communities*, London: Verso.
Ang, I. (1985) *Watching Dallas*, London: Methuen.
Ang, I. and Morley, D. (1989) 'Mayonnaise Culture and Other European Follies', *Cultural Studies* 3. 2.
Ascherson, N. (1988) 'Below Stairs in Europe's House', *Observer*, 11 December.
Banks, M. and Collins, R. (1989) 'Tradeable Information and the Transnational Market', research paper, CCIS, Polytechnic of Central London.
Bausinger, H. (1984) 'Media, Technology and Everyday Life', *Media, Culture and Society* 6. 4.
Bigsby, C. (ed.) (1975) *Superculture: American Popular Culture and Europe*, London: Elek Books.
Brunsdon, C. (1986) 'Women Watching TV', paper presented to the Women and the Electronic Media Conference, Copenhagen, April.
Brunsdon, C. and Morley, D. (1978) *Everyday Television: Nationwide*, London: British Film Institute.
Collins, R. (1988a) 'National Culture: A Contradiction in Terms?', paper presented to the International Television Studies Conference, London, July 1988.
——(1988b) 'The Peculiarities of English Satellite TV in W. Europe', paper presented to the Programme on Information and Communication Technology Conference, Brunel University, May 1988.
Connell, I. (1983) 'Commercial Broadcasting and the British Left', *Screen* 24. 6.
Donald, J. (1988) 'How English is it?' *New Formations* 6.
Ellis, J. (1982) *Visible Fictions*, London: Routledge.
Frith, S. (1983) 'The Pleasures of the Hearth', in J. Donald *et al.* (eds), *Formations of Pleasure*, London: Routledge.
Garnham, N. (1983) 'Public Service versus the Market', *Screen* 24. 1.
Gilroy, P. (1986) *There Ain't no Black in the Union Jack*, London: Hutchinson.
Glenny, M. (1988) 'The Rise in Spirit: Cultural Identities in E. Europe', *Guardian*, 15 December.
Gramsci, A. (1971) *Prison Notebooks*, London: Lawrence & Wishart.
Hall, S. (1989) 'New Ethnicities', in K. Mercer (ed.), *Black Film, British Cinema*, London: ICA.
Hartley, J. (1987) 'Invisible Fictions', in *Textual Practice* 12.
Hebdige, D. (1988) 'Towards a Cartography of Taste', in D. Hebdige, *Hiding in the Light*, London: Comedia/Routledge.
Hobsbawm, E. and Ranger, T. (eds) (1983) *The Invention of Tradition*, Cambridge: Cambridge University Press.

Hoggart, R. (1958) *The Uses of Literacy*, London: Penguin.
Hood, S. (1988) 'The Couthy Feeling', *New Statesman and Society*, 12 August.
Huyssen, A. (1988) 'Mass Culture as Woman: Modernism's Other', in T. Modleski (ed.) *Studies in Entertainment*, Bloomington, Indiana: Indiana University Press.
Kaplan, C. (1986) 'The Culture Crossover', *New Socialist* 41 (September).
Katz, E. and Liebes, T. (1989) 'On the Critical Ability of TV Viewers', in E. Seiter *et al.* (eds), *Remote Control*, London: Routledge.
Mattelart, A. (1979) 'For a Class Analysis of Communications', in A. Mattelart and S. Sieglaub (eds), *Communication and Class Struggle*, vol. 1, New York: International General.
Mattelart, A., Delcourt, X., and Mattelart, M. (1984) *International Image Markets*, London: Comedia.
Mills, P. (1985) 'An International Audience?', *Media, Culture and Society* 7.
Mulgan, G. and Worpole, K. (1985) *Saturday Night or Sunday Morning*, London: Comedia.
Paterson, R. (1980) 'The Art of the TV Schedule', *Screen Education* 35.
Robins, K. (1989) 'Reimagined Communities: European Image Spaces, Beyond Fordism', *Cultural Studies* 3. 2.
Samuels, R. (1988) 'Little Englandism Today', *New Statesman and Society*, 21 October.
Saussure, F. de (1974) *Course in General Linguistics*, London: Fontana.
Scannell, P. (1988) 'Radio Times', in P. Drummond and R. Paterson (eds), *TV and its Audience*, London: British Film Institute.
Schlesinger, P. (1986) 'Any Chance of Fabricating Eurofiction?', review article, *Media Culture and Society* 8.
—— (1987) 'On National Identity', *Social Science Information* 26. 2.
Webster, D. (1988) *Looka Yonder: The Imaginary America of Populist Culture*, London: Comedia/Routledge.
Worpole, K. (1983) *Dockers and Detectives*, London: Verso.
Wright, P. (1985) *On Living in an Old Country*, London: Verso.

Chapter 4

Barbarous TV international
Syndicated *Wheels of Fortune*

Michael Skovmand

Since the beginning of regular radio broadcasts, game shows have been a habitual and popular part of the media fare in our part of the world. Generations of listeners and viewers have spent hours and hours participating in games testing their memory, intelligence, and specialised or general knowledge. And yet, it seems to me, very little research, or scholarly debate, has been devoted to this particular branch of the media. I would suggest that there are historical and institutional reasons for this.

One obvious reason for this neglect is that game shows have simply not been found worthy of sustained scholarly attention. Generically, TV game shows are a carry-over from radio shows, whose concepts, in turn, were borrowed from or inspired by a variety of parlour games. So, as a genre, game shows seem not innovative at all, but part of an unbroken and unproblematic historical continuum of cultural practices.[1]

Another reason is that game shows are generally perceived as culturally insignificant and/or politically innocuous. Unlike such genres as news, documentaries, or drama, game shows are unlikely vehicles for contemporary commentary or debate. Consequently, they have not been the focus of the discussion of novel or disruptive issues, nor have they been seen to be the site of particular social or institutional bias. Although the famous quiz scandals in US television in the fifties brought TV prize games into temporary disrepute, game shows as a genre continued in modified forms – or, as in the case of *The $64,000 Question*, were resumed after a suitable pause. Game shows may have been looked upon as a contributing factor in the 'narcotising dysfunction' of TV in general, or as a part of the 'waste land' of Western or Westernised broadcasting, but they are hardly ever singled out for particular mention, or reviewed, except perhaps as the backdrop for the antics of some glamorous TV personality. Game shows form a continuing series: they are part of the televisual furniture (Welch 1958).

Mike Clarke, in his book *Teaching Popular Television*, makes some interesting comments on the status of the game show. One of the reasons why the game show ranks even lower than soap opera and crime series, according to Clarke, is 'that it has no ready equivalent in literature or on the stage'. Practitioners of television criticism are habitually recruited from the Humanities departments of universities. They are intellectuals steeped in traditions of literary analysis, who find it difficult to recognise game shows, indeed the whole range of non-fictional 'live' entertainment, as 'texts for analysis'.

TEXT OR CULTURAL PRACTICE?

There are good reasons why intellectuals find it so difficult to perceive game shows as 'texts for analysis'. To use a rather appropriate metaphor, game shows are 'hard to pin down' – in the sense that they are not inert matter, like a dead insect. They keep wriggling.

Game shows foreground the fact that they are a *cultural practice* rather than a 'text'. Unlike a 'text', a cultural practice is not 'authored'. There is no authority, no *auteur*, whose personal/ institutional choices have organised the production of the text. Instead, there are rules and conventions, traditionally accepted by the participants, and roles, provisionally distributed.

What is more, game shows are 'live', or rather, they function as live television. Although they are made in bundles of between three and five a day, and have been recorded weeks in advance of the actual screening, they are presented as live, and are so for all practical intents and purposes, in the sense that the game component as such is almost 100 per cent unedited, with ad breaks and presentation of prizes as the only post-production inserts. It is, in other words, time-shifted, but functionally live, and tell-tale references to current or seasonal events are carefully avoided to maintain that sense of liveness.

This notion of liveness again militates against the idea of its being a 'text for analysis'. There is no 'central consciousness' or organising perspective. There is no stable role distribution. There is, on the contrary, an element of surprise and improvisation which makes the actualised narrative structure unpredictable – always, of course, within the given game format. One programme may chronicle the fortunes of the heroic failure, another the lucky streak of the mediocre contestant. There is no telling in advance, because neither an absent *auteur* nor the host of the show wields a determining influence on the course of events.

The study of 'participatory' forms of television radicalises the discussion about television as a social and cultural site, or forum. This is why any approach to a show like *Wheel of Fortune*, and to TV game and quiz shows in general should be a two-pronged one: on the one hand, these shows should be seen as part of the category of 'live' television entertainment, that is to say as part of the wider category of popular television programming. On the other hand, game and quiz shows should be seen as part of a field of *cultural practices* which are not necessarily communicated by way of television at all, a field of practices which include parlour games, bingo, fairs, and gossip.

In an interview from 1984 (Modleski 1986), Raymond Williams points in a similar direction, towards an overlooked interface between popular culture in general and popular television programming:

> Popular culture now sometimes means to some of its practitioners that which represents a certain kind of interest or experience, as against the modes of an established culture or against a power . . . But the other meaning, in which I've been particularly interested lately, takes up a whole range which never got recognized as culture at all within an old dispensation: that of a very active world of everyday conversation and exchange. Jokes, idioms, characteristic forms not just of everyday dress but occasional dress, people consciously having a party, making a do, marking an occasion. I think this area has been very seriously under-valued, and it isn't only that it is undervalued in itself. We're not yet clear about the relation of those things to certain widely successful television forms.
>
> (Modleski 1986: 5)

In recent decades, it is probably the divergent attitudes to 'mass

culture' among intellectuals which have drawn the most irreduc-
ible dividing lines within the intellectual community.

The two major instances, the people and the major means
of communication, seemed poles apart, and in particular the
reductionist rhetoric of structuralist analysis of the 1970s seemed
incapable of moving beyond stating what appeared to be the
obvious: that the mass media were a major reproductive agency
of dominant ideas, most insidiously at work in their 'popular'
guises. John Tulloch's analysis of British TV quizzes, 'Gradgrind's Heirs' (1976), is no exception:

> One programming form that explicitly concerns itself with
> 'knowledge' whilst claiming at the same time the status of
> 'entertainment' is the television quiz. Bearing in mind Mur-
> dock and Golding's dictum that 'it is not sufficient simply to
> assert that the mass media are part of the ideological apparatus
> of the state, it is also necessary to demonstrate how ideology
> is produced in concrete practice', I will attempt to indicate
> how that ideology is reproduced in two current quiz pro-
> grammes. My principal assumption is that even seemingly triv-
> ial broadcast forms – forms that invite and depend on us
> taking them for granted – play an important part in structuring
> consciousness and thereby ensuring the continued repro-
> duction of social contradiction.
>
> (Tulloch 1976: 3)

Media analysis of popular television programming in the early
and mid-seventies would typically set out with intentions similar
to Tulloch's, i.e. they would be 'demonstrations of how ideology
is reproduced in concrete practice', and the result would almost
inevitably demonstrate 'the continued reproduction of social
contradiction'.

John Fiske, in his *Television Culture* (1987), manages to
combine the determinacy of this position with an extremely
voluntarist notion of audience. As he puts it,

> Quiz shows, like advertising, are undoubtedly part of com-
> modity capitalism, and use many of the similar cultural
> strategies. For instance, glamorous models are used to display
> the prizes and thus associate commodities with sexuality, ther-
> eby linking buying with sexual desire and satisfaction . . .

But, he goes on to say,

the motivations of producers of quiz shows that determine the main characteristics of the genre do not necessarily determine the ways that they are read or used by the viewers . . . quiz shows produce particularly active, participatory viewers. Their mini-narratives are structured around the hermeneutic code which poses and then resolves enigmas. But unlike typical narratives, quiz shows are not presented as enacted fiction, but as live events.

(Fiske 1987: 272)

Fiske sums up his position by appropriating a version of Stuart Hall's concept of 'articulation':

So, while quiz shows may articulate (speak) consumerism as they carry the voice of their producer, they may also articulate (speak) responses to that consumerism in accents that speak the interests of the consumer.

(Fiske 1987: 273–4)

In my view, the challenge to any analysis of popular television lies not simply in pointing to these abstract contradictions, but in demonstrating through theoretically informed concrete studies just how these contradictions are negotiated as part of a much more complex and historically specific communicative practice. The following analysis of game shows in general and *Wheel of Fortune* in particular is an attempt in this direction.

GAMES OF DISTINCTION AND GAMES OF PARTICIPATION

In *Television Culture*, John Fiske presents a useful 'hierarchy of quiz shows', organised in relation to the social and cultural currency accorded to the various competences required for participants in the shows, either directly as contestants, or vicariously, as audience. At the top, Fiske places extreme demonstrations of factual knowledge, as we know it from quizzes such as *Mastermind* or *The $64,000 Question*. Below that is the transitional category of 'everyday knowledge', displayed in such shows as *The Price is Right* and *Wheel of Fortune*. As we move downwards in the hierarchy, we pass into the category of what Fiske calls 'human knowledge', involving knowledge of people in general (*Family Feud*), and, at the bottom of the hierarchy, the competences involved concern knowledge of specific people, for example between spouses (*The Newlywed Game, Mr and Mrs*).

Fiske's hierarchy is based on the relative social value attached to the competences displayed in the shows. In this, he draws on Pierre Bourdieu's concept of cultural capital, as competences acquired through education and upbringing which are in a complex, but ultimately subordinate, relation to economic capital. However, just as rewarding in this context are Bourdieu's *dynamic* concepts of distinction and participation (Bourdieu 1984). Games like *Mastermind* and *Trivial Pursuit* are essentially games of distinction, in which the successful contestant distinguishes themselves by displaying valued competences to the exclusion of others.[2] Games of distinction are a complex phenomenon: they are deliberately distanced from sordid notions of direct material gain, and yet socially or culturally profitable, i.e., ultimately, 'work' by other means. Games of participation, by contrast, are seen as vulgar and barbarous in their direct relation to tangible sentiment, or gain, and scandalous because they are culturally and socially unprofitable, 'a waste of time'.

Games like *The Newlywed Game* and *Wheel of Fortune* are games of participation, in which the display of competences include the other contestants in playful interaction. If we look beyond television, Bingo, simple card games, and children's games are cultural practices which are inclusive rather than exclusive. They are basically games in which distinction is not conferred upon the individual as a recognition of the possession of a permanent competence of marketable cultural value. Luck, chance, or a provisional role distribution include the contestants in a sense of collectivity and participation, as opposed to the games of distinction, in which individuality and exclusiveness are at a premium.

It should be emphasised, however, that Bourdieu's categories are not categories defining essences. Most games are capable of being transformed from distinctive into participatory games, or vice versa. Arguments over ball games or card games are typically of this nature – contestants are accused of not 'taking the game seriously', i.e. trying to turn a 'distinguishing' game into a participatory one, or vice versa.

Wheel of Fortune is tendentially a participatory game. It is underscored by the hosts that it is the kind of game in which 'everybody wins'. (In the Danish and Scandinavian versions, for instance, contestants without winnings are given an inexpensive watch in order to underline the idea that nobody leaves the game empty-handed.) The added appeal of popular 'audience participation' shows lies in the extra bonus of simply appearing on television. The prevalence of this philosophy is substantiated by several sources.[3]

This basic participatory quality of the show is demonstrated most clearly in limited cases in which this atmosphere is challenged by contestants who appear exceptionally clever and/or too greedy, thereby upsetting the delicate balance of comradeship and exciting competitiveness. It is then the role of the otherwise low-key host to step in and attempt to correct this by bringing the culprit in line with the other contestants.

THE INVENTION OF THE *WHEEL*

The history of the success of *Wheel of Fortune* is interesting in its own right, and in addition underscores some general points about the genre and its position within mainstream popular TV production.

The game was invented by Merv Griffin, the American singer and TV host. He modelled it on the traditional game of 'Hangman', but gave it a less morbid form, and combined the wordgame with the roulette-like feature of the spinning wheel of fortune. It was launched in 1973 by Merv Griffin as a daytime show for NBC, syndicated since 1983 by King World Productions; syndication rights had been bought in 1982 for $50,000. In 1986 Griffin sold the show to the Coca-Cola Company for $250 million, a sensational price at that end of the business. The production price per episode is remarkably cheap and entirely predictable, and is said to be about $25,000 (Pollan 1986: 24). Actually, the chances are that it is appreciably less, since the advertising value of providing prizes for the show would be more than sufficient to sponsor the production. Four or five episodes are produced consecutively in daily production runs, adding up to 195 episodes per year plus 65 reruns (Pollan 1986: 24). At present, the show is produced under contract in eight European countries.

There has been no shortage of attempts to explain the spectacular success of *Wheel of Fortune* in the United States. Like most other successes, it seems to hinge on a combination of external and internal factors.

The Cinderella story of Vanna White, the mute, wildly applauding cheerleader hostess whose presence on the show propelled her from total anonymity to superstardom overnight, was a consequence of the success of the show, but the Vanna White story in turn increased the show's momentum. For Pat Sajak, the male host of the show, *Wheel of Fortune* has also been a career-maker. So far, his success on the *Wheel* has earned him a talkshow of his own.

Generally, in the choice of hosts, participants, prizes, and decor, it is the emphasis on relative ordinariness which characterises the show. The aggressive competitiveness of other comparable game or quiz shows is virtually non-existent on the *Wheel*. Instead, there is a laid back, relaxed atmosphere of friendliness and mutual supportiveness. Institutionally, the unusual move to place a game show like *Wheel of Fortune* in the prime-time access slot (the legally stipulated non-network period preceding network prime time) proved to be an important factor in making it take off. Awakening from twelve years of daytime doldrums, within two years it had a following of 43 million viewers in that slot (as opposed to 8 million in the daytime). Success within the US media system creates its own momentum. Once a show demonstrates exceptional attractiveness, its market value is further increased because of its usefulness as a lead-in or lead-out to boost the ratings of neighbouring shows. The profitability of local stations depends less on the size of their prime time audience than on the two hours that precede prime-time, i.e. 'early fringe' and 'prime-time access', and there are several examples showing how the *Wheel of Fortune* has been decisive in boosting the flagging economy of local stations (Pollan 1986: 24). The *Wheel* was increasingly bought not only by minor local stations, but by stations in the major US markets owned and operated by the networks, functioning specifically, and very effectively, as a lead-in or lead-out to what was coming into increasing prominence: their local news bulletins.

The demographic appeal of *Wheel of Fortune* is remarkably similar in Europe and the US: it has a broad, generally lower-middle-class appeal, with a bias towards the demographically interesting target group of women between 25 and 54. The Achilles' heel, however, of a show like the *Wheel* tends to be the (slight) age bias of its audience, which may make it vulnerable in a media system like the American one, in which there is a premium not just on ratings, but on the purchasing power of the audience. Nevertheless, it remains the most successful syndicated game show in recent US TV history,[4] having been consistently at the top of the polls of syndicated shows since the mid-eighties. Its success, followed up by the successes of *Jeopardy* (a highly competitive quiz show) and *The Oprah Winfrey Show* (a talk show with a dynamic black hostess), has turned King World Productions into one of the major players in the syndication business.

The success of *Wheel of Fortune* was exported during the 1980s, to Britain, France, Germany, and Scandinavia, among other countries. The varied reception of the *Wheel* reflects the differences of the existing media systems and traditions. The Danish experience is a case in point.

In Denmark, the *Wheel* was used as part of the launching, in October 1988, of the second Danish channel, a public-service channel partly financed by advertising, partly by licence fees. The *Wheel* came to signify a more brash, populist, and Americanised approach to live entertainment, contrasting strongly with the staid, paternalist stance of Channel 1. Within weeks the *Wheel* became a hit with the Danish audience, consistently scoring rating points of 30 per cent or more. Furthermore, the *Wheel* became a pawn in a hostile game of competitive scheduling of the main evening news bulletin between the two channels. The popularity of the *Wheel* meant that it could be placed practically anywhere without significant loss of rating points: it could even challenge the long-established success of the main evening news on Channel 1. So, as in the US, it was not only the intrinsic qualities of the *Wheel*, but also its usefulness as a scheduling pawn which made it so attractive a purchase.

But what are the intrinsic qualities of *Wheel of Fortune*? It is important to point out that the *Wheel* is not a stable entity. In the US and elsewhere it has been modified over time, and there are important national variations between, say, the American, the German, and the Danish versions. Nevertheless, the contracting producers of the *Wheel* are under an obligation to present a fairly homogeneous product, and there is indeed a shared structure and a shared visual aesthetic, as well as a shared sense of mood and tone, for all the national variations.

The sets share a basic design: a large, flashy vertical display board bearing blank tiles behind which the letters of the word puzzle are hidden, plus a large, multi-coloured roulette-like wheel with wedges, all marked with numbers except two which say 'Bankrupt' and 'Lose a Turn'.

The wheel indicates the rewards earned by picking a correct letter, and the person who solves the word puzzle is allowed to spend his accumulated winnings by 'going shopping' among a range of commodities, ranging from necklaces and expensive kitchen utensils to VCRs and cruises. The 'shopping' is done in identical fashion in all versions of the *Wheel*: the face of the winner is inserted in the corner of the frame, making choices of commodities, while the camera glides lovingly up and down the glittering display of wares. (The shopping element has been reduced considerably in recent years in the US version, in favour of straight cash winnings.[5]) After the choices have been made, an off-screen melodious male voice gives a brief characterisation of the goods chosen, including their price, while the camera again caresses the merchandise.[6] The top scorer goes on to a bonus round which offers prizes such as cars, cruises, and luxury stereos.

The serial character of the show is emphasised by having the winner appear on some of the following shows, for instance for a maximum of three in a row (the US), or by having a final play-off among the week's winners (Denmark).

There are, in other words, two distinct phases in the show: the game phase and the consumer phase. The game phase is structured by its two components, the board and the wheel, signifying the two elements of the game: skill and luck. Arguably one of the secrets of the success of the *Wheel* is precisely the balance struck between skill and luck. American critics have argued that one of the main appeals of the US *Wheel* is that it is precisely pitched at a level of difficulty at which the majority of its audience will enjoy the sense of superiority of being just a fraction quicker than the contestants at solving the word puzzle. Admittedly, the US version appears considerably easier to solve than most European versions. The US version uses longer phrases (which means fewer misses) and assists its contestants by supplying extra letters. This is in harmony with other features in the US version which emphasise the show's lack of competitiveness: the way contestants root for each other – it is everybody together against the wheel and the puzzle – and the way in which everybody is made a winner, since everybody keeps the amounts they have won, even from the rounds where they did not earn the right to go shopping.

The *Wheel*, like other serialised formats, has a core constituency, but unlike soap operas, with their narrative continuity, the audience figures are volatile, because a relatively large proportion of the *Wheel* audience is easily affected by the offerings of competing channels. Obviously, this is explainable by the fact that watching the *Wheel* is an everyday, low-key type of practice which can easily be missed now and then without detriment to the viewing experience. Interestingly, as Danish audience figures document, this means that the smaller the *Wheel* audience, the *higher* the quality assessment (on a scale from 1 to 5) given by the audience.[7] Indeed, this notion of low-intensity viewing applies also to the viewing of any individual episode of the *Wheel*. It is no coincidence that a programme like the *Wheel* has a majority of women viewers, because although the programme *may* be watched with rapt attention, the chopped-up structure and the low intensity of the show *accommodates* the kind of distracted, peripheral viewing of the majority of women, to whom the home is not only the site of the TV set, but their actual place of work.[8]

FOUR *WHEELS* COMPARED

Wheel of Fortune is produced in many countries outside the United States under contract with King World Productions. To what extent is this show a stable entity when produced outside the United States? How well does it travel? Alongside the American version, I have taken a closer look at three *Wheels*, produced under very different circumstances from the US version: the German *Glücksrad*, produced by Sat1, *Lyckohjulet*, produced by pan-Scandinavian TV3, and *Lykkehjulet*, broadcast by TV2, the second Danish channel.

Glücksrad is broadcast by the pan-German commercial satellite station Sat1, owned by German media mogul Leo Kirsch, whose footprint covers a good deal of Central and Northern Europe. The game show is broadcast at 7 p.m. on weekdays only.

Lyckohjulet, (7 p.m. on weekdays) is broadcast by the satellite station TV3, catering for the Scandinavian region and alternating between Swedish, Norwegian and Danish, although Swedish is the predominant language, which reflects the fact that the station is owned by the Sweden-based international media conglomerate Kinnevik. Like Sat1, it is a commercial channel whose revenue is based on the sale of advertising time.

Lykkehjulet is broadcast seven days a week, at 6.30 p.m. on weekdays and at 7.30 p.m. on weekends. It is produced by Nordisk Film for TV2, the terrestrial second Danish channel, a semi-independent TV station whose revenue derives partly from licence fees shared with the Danish Channel 1, partly from limited block advertising and sponsoring agreements. Unlike the three other *Wheels* mentioned, this version is uninterrupted by advertising breaks. I am deliberately refraining from quoting audience figures for the four shows, because it would be almost impossible to treat these figures on a par. Suffice it to say that the US and Danish versions are exceptionally successful game shows, while the German and Scandinavian versions are an integral part of the programming of two satellite channels which are trying to get established with a multinational and extremely heterogeneous audience.

The following thumbnail sketch of the four versions attempts to answer the following question: is a game show like *Wheel of Fortune* exported wholesale, or is it remodelled substantially to accord with the local broadcasting culture?

My characterisation of the four shows is based on (1) a comparison of four distinctive variables within the invariable format, plus (2) a quantitative assessment of the relative weight given to four narrative categories of the show. The four distinctive features I have singled out are:

(a) the participation/non-participation of the studio audience
(b) the applause/non-applause of the hostess and contestants
(c) the participation/non-participation of the hostess
(d) the décor of the set

The participation of the audience

The American *Wheel* is characterised by a high degree of involvement on the part of the studio audience, which includes family members of the contestants. The cheering of the audience is a marked feature throughout the game, and contestants are frequently, by gesture or gaze, in contact with family members in the audience. After the winner has emerged, family and friends spill on to the set to participate in the celebration.

The *Glücksrad* and *Lyckohjulet* both signal the presence of a studio audience through a token initial pan, but other than that there is little interaction except unobtrusive audience applause. There is no trespassing by the audience on to the set.

The Danish *Lykkehjulet* has no visual representation of its audience (which is very small because of the cramped studio conditions of Nordisk Film) either before, during, or after the show, and its reactions are audibly reinforced by synthetic means.

The applause of the hostess and contestants

The supportive applause of Vanna White and all the contestants when the wheel is spun is a kind of 'cheerleader' enthusiasm which appears slightly odd to European audiences, I would suggest. Neither *Glücksrad* nor *Lykkehjulet* has adopted this practice. *Lyckohjulet*, however, practises a very low-key version of the American way of applauding, carried out by the contestants with visible unease. This is compounded by the fact that *Lyckohjulet*, unlike any other version known to me, is essentially a two-person confrontation: it has two initial 'national' rounds with two contestants of the same nationality in each round, whereupon two contestants of different nationalities meet in the final.

The participation of the hostess

The relative 'competence' given to the hostess is a particularly interesting feature, which signals variant notions about gender and equality. Vanna White remains mute throughout the show, a representation of femininity which seems quaint even in the US media context, but which is adopted by *Glücksrad's* hostess, whereas both Scandinavian hostesses exercise the faculty of speech. A mute hostess would probably, in a Scandinavian context, be taken as a controversial sexist feature, particularly in combination with a male host.[9] The Swedish hostess of *Lyckohjulet* engages in a brief pre-game chat with the Norwegian host, and announces the phrase categories. The Danish hostess goes even further than this, in that during the show there is occasional bantering between host and hostess, in which even the disembodied voice of the announcer of prizes is involved from time to time.

The décor of the set

The variation in décor seems to be in striking accordance with the crudest national stereotypes: the US *Wheel* décor spells gaudy, glittery vulgarity; the German décor is matter-of-fact, with contestants performing on a background of steely grey; the pan-Scandinavian *Lyckohjulet* is done in tasteful matching light blue and pink pastels; and the décor of the Danish *Lykkehjulet* is a rather child-like set of circles and staircases, done in feel-good primary colours.

The quantitative analysis, based on random sampling between November 1989 and May 1990, attempts to quantify the narrative constituents of the four variants, in four rough-and-ready categories: (1) the actual game component; (2) talk, including introductions and continuity within the show; (3) 'shopping', i.e. the phase in which the contestants spend their hard-won money on the merchandise, and where the merchandise is portrayed by camera and voice-over; and (4) the interruptions made by advertising breaks.

The percentages are given with and without the ad sections included, in order that the Danish version (which has no ad breaks) may be comparable.

Quantitative analysis

Wheel of Fortune (USA)

				minus ad blocks
game:	13 mins	38 secs	48.20%	65.23%
talk:	5 mins	24 secs	19.09%	25.84%
shopping:	1 min	52 secs	6.60%	8.93%
ad blocks:	7 mins	23 secs	26.10%	
total:	28 mins	17 secs		

Lyckohjulet (TV3, Scandinavia)

game:	15 mins	27 secs	49.41%	56.11%
talk:	6 mins	47 secs	21.70%	24.64%
shopping:	5 mins	18 secs	16.95%	19.25%
ads:	4 mins	44 secs	15.14%	
total:	32 mins	16 secs		

Glücksrad (Sat1, Northern Europe)

game:	9 mins	43 secs	31.67%	45.33%
talk:	5 mins	18 secs	17.27%	24.73%
shopping:	6 mins	25 secs	20.91%	29.94%
ads:	9 mins	15 secs	30.15%	
total:	30 mins	41 secs		

Lykkehjulet (TV2, Denmark)

game:	14 mins	15 secs	57%
talk/continuity:	5 mins	15 secs	21%
shopping/prizes:	5 mins	30 secs	22%
total:	25 mins		

The above figures, while open to many kinds of interpretation, seem to point towards the following conclusions, which are in part substantiated by my more qualitative analysis.

The US *Wheel* is the most game-orientated and participatory version among the four under examination, with the Danish *Lykkehjulet* in second place, and *Glücksrad* decidedly at the bottom. The 'talk' component is remarkably stable across the board. The 'shopping' component, which competes for time with the game part, is lowest in the US version, and indisputably highest in the German satellite version. In fact, *Glücksrad* comes across as saturated with commodities – if you add the 'shopping' component, three quarters of which have an occasional *Werbung* (=advertisement) sign flashing, indicating that this is technically an ad, to the genuine ad block, you will find that more than fifty per cent of your half-hour game show consists of undisguised advertising! This compares with slightly less than 33 per cent in the US and pan-Scandinavian versions.

At the risk of oversimplification, I will venture the following conclusion, based on the above: *Wheel of Fortune* is a game show in which popular/participatory and consumerist modes of address compete. A popular/participatory game show requires a genuine sense of constituency for the show to work. There is that sense of constituency in the practice of the US and Danish versions. In the case of *Glücksrad* there does not seem to be such a sense, and consequently the show relies on its consumerist address and appears as primarily a vehicle for advertising. In the case of the pan-Scandinavian *Lyckohjulet* there is an attempt to create a 'Scandinavian' sense of constituency and mode of address, but given the lack of cohesiveness of its actual satellite audience, the game show comes across as simply a slightly more up-market version of *Glücksrad*.[10]

THE *WHEEL*: RAMPANT ADVERTORIALISM?

The hybrid 'advertorialism' is an attempt to describe the erosion of the barriers in print and electronic media alike between editorial matter and advertising. In the 1980s, MTV was perhaps the most obvious example of how these barriers virtually disappeared: on MTV, video clips, shown as 'editorial' programming, function as advertisements for themselves, for the records, the artists, their concerts, and so on. The 'sweet deal' between the television company and the advertisers, i.e. video producers, by which programming content is delivered free of charge in exchange for airtime, also exists, to an unknown extent, in the production of a programme like *Wheel of Fortune*.

Regardless of the amount of legal restrictions attempting to prevent programme producers from making unauthorised agreements with the companies delivering the prizes, the heart of the matter is that the commercial value of having one's wares exhibited on a show as successful as *Wheel of Fortune* is so enormous that it cannot be ignored, especially not by TV executives on the lookout for overall improvement in profitability. In a sense, this is a temptation lurking in the shadows of any major media production. The provision of cars and clothes for *Miami Vice*, the selection of the location for the next James Bond movie, the brand choice of whisky for a major feature film like *The Great Gatsby* all involve potential conflicts between 'editorial' and financial considerations. There is nothing extraordinary in that, since this conflict exists abundantly already. However, in the case of 'public', if not public-service media, such as daily newspapers and broadcast television, the threat to the integrity of the medium as a 'forum' of public exchange is a real one when and if the audience find it impossible to determine the boundary lines between editorial and advertising content. The optimistic libertarianism of John Fiske (in *Television Culture*) would maintain that the problem does not exist, because however treacherous the producers of programmes may be, the active audience will generally make their own, perhaps alternative, sense of the programme. This argument, however, does not do away with the problem that the programme makers may have to accept undue commercial interference with the programme, precisely because the commodities are an integral part of the editorial content. One of the litmus tests of such potential interference could be to ask the following questions: could Jack (the off-screen male voice presenting the prizes) actually make fun of the goods without breaking the (perhaps tacit) consensus between programmers and purveyors? Would it be permissible for contestants openly to express displeasure with certain prizes? If not, why not?

CONCLUSION

Anyone attempting to draw bombastic, heavy-handed conclusions about an 'interactive' game show like *Wheel of Fortune*, or indeed any genre of popular television, should recall the extreme caution of a study such as McQuail *et al*. (1972). One of the main conclusions of their study, which included quizzes, a radio serial, a TV soap opera, two TV action series, and TV news programmes, was quite simply that

> people can look to quite different kinds of material for essentially the same gratification and, correlatively, find alternative satisfactions in the same televised material.
>
> (1972: 153)[11]

Does this view not coincide perfectly with that of John Fiske, who sees no contradiction between doing an ideological critique of the producers of popular television, while at the same time celebrating the 'openness' of 'the popular text' and the active independence of its audience? I do not think so. On the contrary, my attempt at a comparative analysis of national versions of a game show like *Wheel of Fortune* is making the rather anti-essentialist point that 'popular television' is not a stable entity, geographically or over time. It also draws conclusions about live, interactive programmes such as *Wheel of Fortune* which cannot be applied to popular fictional programming such as soaps or sitcom, which are not remade under contract, but exported wholesale. In fact, one conclusion of the above analysis might be that one should be extremely wary of operating with a general concept such as 'the popular text': any programming, but certainly live participatory programming, should always be seen as relative to the way in which the broadcasting system in point relates to its actual and imaginary audience, and relative to the range of other popular cultural practices which may or may not take on televisual forms.[12]

NOTES

1 See, for example, Johan Huizinga's broadly anthropological approach to man as a 'playing animal' in *Homo Ludens* (1944).

2 One should, however, be aware of gradations of competences involved and the way they are displayed. There are differences of cultural valuation ascribed to, for instance, the demonstration of encyclopedic knowledge of the complete works of Shakespeare and, say, the autistic total recall of telephone directories. And even the wizard contestants on game shows like *Mastermind* are still just clever amateurs compared to those really in the know who host the show, make up the questions, and sit in judgement.

3 In January 1990, I had an opportunity to witness the briefing session before the daily production run of the three episodes of the Danish version of *Wheel of Fortune*. It was repeatedly emphasised by the Danish host that the contestants should stop worrying about prizes: they were already winners in having been selected for the show. Everything else, including prizes, should be enjoyed simply as a 'bonus'. And in actual fact, this attitude, from my experience with contestants, seems to be the prevailing one. A quite similar finding is reported by Alexander Cockburn in *American Film* (Cockburn 1986: 26).

4 In its heyday in the mid-1980s, *Wheel of Fortune* consistently scored a rating of 20 per cent or more. In 1989–90 it dropped to between 14 and 15 per cent, which still leaves it at the top of the polls for bartered series of shows. Of course, with the advent of new networks, plus the proliferation of additional offerings on cable or satellite, ratings are not what they used to be. By comparison, the quiz show *The $64,000 Question*, in July 1955, within a month of its introduction, scored a Nielsen rating of 41.1, the highest in the nation, equalling an audience of 13,423,000 households.

5 In fact, one should be cautious of static forms of analysis of popular serial forms, as there are real shifts in emphasis taking place over time, within each individual show and across the range of, for example, quiz and game shows. Gary Whannel makes that point in his discussion of the changes taking place in British television in the eighties, between early and late Thatcherist populism (Whannel 1990: 107).

6 Within the last couple of years, the US version has done away with the extended and time-consuming shopping spree and restricted itself to money prizes and a few luxury items such as cruises and kitchens, plus of course the final bonus, usually a car.

7 See AIM TV-Undersøgelser (Danish TV Audience Research Institute), for the period November 1989 to May 1990.
8 For a much more detailed development of this argument, see Morley 1986.
9 In an interview with me, Bent Burg, the Danish host of *Lykkehjulet*, pointed out that they wanted a blonde, but not a dumb blonde, as hostess, as this went against 'Danish mentality'.
10 The rather vague term 'sense of constituency' is indebted to Newcomb and Hirsch's idea of TV as a 'cultural forum' (Newcomb and Hirsch 1986).
11 This finding is supported and sophisticated by much subsequent research, most recently by Wernblad *et al.* (1990), whose reception analysis of the Danish version of *Wheel of Fortune* focuses on 'ideal types' among the Danish audience, whose relations with the show are analysed in parallel to the gratification patterns demonstrated by McQuail *et al.* (1972), i.e. 'self-rating appeal', 'basis for social interaction', 'excitement' (the fourth category, 'educational appeal', is more relevant to the quiz shows than to a game show like *Wheel of Fortune*, although a whole generation of Americans claim to have learnt how to spell from watching the *Wheel*).
12 Charlotte Brunsdon makes a similar point very succinctly in her essay 'Text and Audience':

> The need to specify context and mode of viewing in any textual discussion, and the awareness that these factors may be more determining of the experience of a text than any textual feature, do not, in and of themselves, either eliminate the text as a meaningful category, or render all texts the same . . . The recognition of the creativity of the audience must, I think, be mobilized back in relation to the television text, and the demands that are made on program makers for a diverse and plural programming which is adequate to the needs, desires and pleasures of the audience. Otherwise, however well intentioned, our work reproduces and elaborates the dominant paradigm in which the popular is the devalued term.
>
> (Brunsdon 1989: 125–6)

REFERENCES

Bourdieu, P. (1984) *Distinction*, London and New York: Routledge.
Brunsdon, C. (1989) 'Text and Audience', in Ellen Seiter *et al.* (eds), *Remote Control*, London: Routledge.
Clarke, M. (1987) *Teaching Popular Television*, London: Comedia.
Cockburn, A. (1986) 'The Money Pit', *American Film*, July/August.
Fiske, J. (1987) *Television Culture*, London: Routledge.
Grossberger, L. (1986) 'Triumph of the Wheel', *Rolling Stone*, 4 December.
Huizinga, J. (1944) *Homo Ludens*, Basel: Pantheon.
McQuail, D., Blumler, J., and Brown, R. (1972) 'The Television

Audience, A Revised Perspective', in D. McQuail (ed.), *The Sociology of Mass Communications*, Harmondsworth: Penguin.

Modleski, T. (ed.) (1986) *Studies in Entertainment*, Bloomington, Indiana: Indiana University Press.

Morley, D. (1986) *Family Television: Cultural Power and Domestic Leisure*, London: Comedia.

Newcomb, H. M. and Hirsch, P. M. (1986) 'Television as a Cultural Forum: Implications for Research', in W. D. Rowland and B. Watkins (eds), *Interpreting Television*, London: Sage Publications.

Pollan, M. (1986) 'Jackpot', *Channels*, 22 June.

Seiter, E. *et al.* (eds) (1989) *Remote Control: Television, Audiences and Cultural Power*, London: Routledge.

Tulloch, J. (1976) 'Gradgrind's Heirs – The Quiz and the Presentation of Knowledge by British Television', *Screen Education*, Summer.

Welch, P. E. (1958) 'The Quiz Program: A Network Television Staple', *Journal of Broadcasting* 2. 4.

Wernblad, G. *et al.* (1990) 'Der skal også vuære noget for de små i samfundet – en receptionsanalyse af Lykkehjulet', Institut for Informations- og Medievidenskab, Aarhus Universitet.

Whannel, G. (1990) 'Winner Takes All: Competition', in A. Goodwin and G. Whannel (eds), *Understanding Television*, London: Routledge.

Chapter 5

French-American connection
A bout de souffle, Breathless, and the melancholy macho

Jostein Gripsrud

INTRODUCTION

In Jean-Luc Godard's first feature film, *A bout de souffle* (1960), there is a crucial scene in which the hero, played by Jean-Paul Belmondo, stops in front of a poster advertising a Humphrey Bogart film. We get a close up of a Bogart star portrait, held for several seconds, then an equally long close up of Belmondo, stroking his lips with his thumb – a gesture Bogart is known for.

The film and this scene thus bring together at least two closely related discursive oppositions: 'French' versus 'American' and 'art' versus 'mass culture'. In the international codification of national cultures, 'France' tends to represent high culture, and 'the US' low culture. But the particular scene I just described shows French 'art cinema' of the late fifties and early sixties paying tribute to the epitome of international mass culture: Hollywood. There is no obvious irony in the scene, even if it may produce ironic smiles in the audience.

These smiles may be seen as smiles of (ironic) recognition: the scene shows a diegetically 'real' character demonstrating his intimate and imitating relationship to a star persona of the cinema. The scene thus thematises the relationship between filmic 'heroes' and their audiences, specifically the relationship between a certain male (type of) Hollywood hero and a mostly male European audience: well educated, art-oriented, possibly more or less politically radical.

This scene, and actually the whole of *A bout de souffle*, thus points towards a highly important and interesting process of international and 'intersocial' cultural exchange: the 'appropriation' of Hollywood low-culture genres, signs, and styles by

European high-culture producers and audiences since the fifties. This chapter is devoted to a tentative discussion of what actually happens in a certain case of this process. What gets lost on the way, and what is added? To what extent and in what sense is the old saying 'the translator is a traitor' true here?

I will concentrate on the relations between *A bout de souffle* and its relatively recent American remake, Jim McBride's *Breathless* (1983). McBride's film is very different from Godard's, even if the storyline remains largely the same. It differs from the French original in specific, significant ways, which, as I will try to show, illuminate the cultural exchange under scrutiny. It may seem as if Godard's 'translation' of American filmic impulses gets 'retranslated' (back) to an American 'original' version. McBride's film may thus be seen by some people as a very 'postmodern' phenomenon: it is an 'original' which appears more than twenty years after a 'copy' – but both chronologically and otherwise it is still the other way around . . .[1]

Since the two films basically tell the same story, they may be said also to share a theme or problematic: that of 'maleness' or masculinity in a modern society. My discussion of the films will centre on the question of how the two films allow this problematic to be presented. Since *A bout de souffle*, and consequently also *Breathless*, are 'derived' from earlier Hollywood films, particularly those associated with Humphrey Bogart's persona, I will also include some perspectives on these predecessors, particularly those pertaining to the issues of melodrama and a certain male character type, which I call the 'melancholy macho'.

It seems reasonable to start by giving a summary of the story-line of the two films – noting on the way some of the points on which they differ.

THE STORY

A small-time crook – Michel (Jean-Paul Belmondo) in the French version, Jesse (Richard Gere) in the American – steals a car in the opening scene: Michel steals an American car in Nice, Jesse a European (Porsche) in Las Vegas. Both do it with the help of a good-looking young woman. They both find a gun in the car.

Reckless driving – Michel listening to jazz, Jesse to Jerry Lee Lewis' rock and roll – attracts the attention of traffic police, and after a chase both heroes shoot and kill a policeman. The killing is portrayed very differently in the two films: Michel's shooting seems deliberate, and he is not shown having a look at the victim before he runs off. Jesse, on the other hand, gets stuck in the desert sand after trying to avoid crushing a rabbit (!), then seems to kill by accident, and leaves his jacket under the wounded policeman's head (while uttering sounds of shock and despair) before running away.

They then get to Paris and Los Angeles respectively, where they have two things to do: get paid for a previous criminal job and, not least, look up a woman with whom they want to run off to Italy and Mexico respectively. Michel first visits another female friend and steals money from her purse while she has her back turned. This scene is missing in the American version. Michel then meets the woman he has come to find, Patricia (Jean Seberg), in the street, where she sells the *New York Herald Tribune*. She tells him she can't come with him to Italy, because she wants to be a student at the Sorbonne – also because her parents will stop supporting her if she doesn't study. Jesse finds the woman he is looking for, the French Monica (Valerie Kaprisky), at a university (recognisable as UCLA), where she is in the middle of an oral exam, part of her finals in architecture study. She turns down Jesse's suggestion that they should go to Mexico together, because she is to pursue a career as an architect.

Michel and Jesse take the respective women to a restaurant/café, without having the money to pay for anything, but resolutely go to the toilet to steal the money needed from a guest. Michel is markedly more brutal than Jesse in this scene.

Monica is helped in getting started on a career by one of her professors, who invites her to dinner and spends the night with her – then sets up a meeting for her with a famous European architect. The professor is in many ways a caricature. In Godard's film, Patricia is given the opportunity to work as a journalist on the newspaper she was selling on the street after spending the night with an editor who buys her lunch. Her first assignment is to attend a press conference with a famous American film director.

Meanwhile, the male hero tries to get his money, but only succeeds in getting a cheque he can't cash since he is now known from the media (newspapers in Godard's film, also television in McBride's) as a cop-killer. The hero goes to bed with the woman.

Monica tells him she may be pregnant (as a result of their previous encounter in Las Vegas). Jesse happily accepts these prospects. Michel's reaction to similar information from Patricia is that she should have been careful – otherwise he has no comments. The police are now really closing in on the hero, who takes the woman, in another stolen car, to her press conference/meeting with the film director/architect.

While the women are busy at these meetings, Jesse and Michel try to raise money by selling the stolen car to a used car dealer. But the dealer knows that the police are chasing our hero, and refuses to give him money – but still keeps the car. Jesse/Michel gets into a fight with the dealer, and takes some money to get away in a taxi. Michel takes a taxi and goes back to the city to meet Patricia, while Jesse meets Monica in Venice (LA), where the meeting with the architect took place.

The two films now develop in quite different ways. Jesse is chased by the police in Venice. Monica is confronted by the police, and tells them Jesse has gone to San Francisco. Monica is shadowed while walking around in Venice. The part hyper-realist, part surrealist murals of Venice become a dominating element of the mise-en-scène in these sequences. Jesse steals yet another car, Monica joins him, and they talk about a possible life in Mexico – with a baby. In downtown LA, they meet with Berruti, the gangster who owes money to our hero, at a strange discothèque. Berruti says he can't come up with the money until the next day, and they barely escape the police in some well-done but quite conventional chase-scenes. Such scenes are missing in *A bout de souffle*. The next day, Monica calls the police to inform them where to find Jesse. When she tells Jesse about this, she signals – while answering negatively to Jesse's direct question – that she loves him. This final discussion between the two is very different in *A bout de souffle* (see below). Jesse happily runs to meet Berruti and collect the money. As in the French version, he gets his money, refuses to flee, and turns down a gun offered to him by Berruti, who still throws it after our hero.

When the police come, Michel holds the gun in his hand, without aiming to shoot, and is immediately shot in the back. He runs, staggering, down the street before collapsing at the end of the block. Patricia runs towards him with little emotion showing on her face. Michel lies on his back, with a cigarette in his mouth, still wearing his sunglasses. He grimaces in a way he has done earlier in the film, and then says: 'Tu es vraiment une dégueulasse.' Patricia asks bystanders what Michel said, and they repeat it. She then asks 'Qu'est-ce que c'est, "dégueulasse"?', strokes her lip in the Bogart way, and fades into black.

Jesse, on the other hand, hears Monica calling his name, and looks towards her with a little smile on his lips while the police line up with their guns in the background. The final sequence is an astonishing montage. Monica's romantic leitmotif (by Philip Glass) is mixed with Jesse's (Jerry Lee Lewis' 'Breathless'), so that the two pieces take turns in dominating. Jesse, standing with the gun on the ground between his legs, turns around to face the police while 'banging' (at the beat of his boogie music) at an imaginary fence or window around him, and gets into a brief, frenzied rock and roll dance. He then stops, stretching his arms towards Monica, who is suddenly shown running towards him while shouting 'Jesse, I love you!' – even if in the actual scene she is supposed to be standing still. Jesse sings with greatly exaggerated gestures 'you, you leave me – ahhh! – breathless!', then suddenly bends to pick up the gun and turns to shoot at the police. Freeze frame – and a wild, punk-rock version of 'Breathless' starts, which also accompanies the end titles.

A BOUT DE SOUFFLE AND THE FRENCH NEW WAVE: THE MEANINGS OF STORY AND STYLE

As known from film history textbooks, *A bout de souffle* was one of several French films appearing in the early sixties which are now collectively known as 'the New Wave'. François Truffaut had the original idea for the film, and Claude Chabrol is listed in the credits as adviser. These are, along with Godard himself, central directors in the 'New Wave' generation, who started as film critics in the journal *Cahiers du cinéma*.

As critics they developed the tendency in film criticism now known as 'auteurism'. The central idea here was that 'great' directors could be regarded as 'authors' of their films, since, it was claimed, they managed to leave their personal stamp on them, even if they were produced within very strict industrial and generic confines. Certain directors working in Hollywood were especially popular as examples of this.

The critical position developed in *Cahiers du cinéma* was not

politically radical. It was formed in accordance with two main
objectives. First, there was an interest in the establishment of
the director as a creative subject comparable to the author in
literature or the painter, sculptor, and so on in the visual arts.
In this way, even the collectively or industrially produced film
could – in some cases at least – conform to modern, romantic
notions of art, and film directors would improve their status
within the cultural field. As Godard triumphantly expressed it
after Truffaut had been awarded the grand prix at the Cannes
Festival in 1959:

> We won the day in having it acknowledged in principle that
> a film by Hitchcock, for example, is as important as a book
> by Aragon. Film *auteurs*, thanks to us, have finally entered
> the history of art.
>
> (Quoted in Bordwell and Thompson 1986: 373)

Second, the critical validation of Hollywood films served as part
of a critique of the then established French 'quality' tradition in
film-making. American and Italian film-making was seen as more
'realist' and also formally more open and inventive. This may be
taken to mean that Hollywood film-making was understood and
used within a generational, modernist project. It was a means of
killing off French 'fathers' in the cinema, in accordance with
Harold Bloom's ideas (1973, 1975) about the 'misreading' of
'father' figures in literature as a means of marking the originality
of the son(s).

The most remarkable formal qualities of *A bout de souffle* are
clearly alien to the style of classical Hollywood cinema. The film
is dedicated to Monogram Pictures, one of the smaller Hollywood companies known primarily for their low budget 'B-
movies'. But the low budget and the basic gangster-thriller story
are just about the only aspects which Godard's film shares with
its Monogram predecessors. It is the playful, inventive, and 'intellectual' form of the film that has brought it its historical (and
lasting) appeal to certain audiences.

The scene in which Belmondo pays tribute to Bogart, for
instance is hardly necessary for the unfolding of the plot. It is
primarily a meta-statement, which appeals to a supposed audience's interest in film history, in film aesthetics – in film-as-a-
medium. Its relevance for the plot is that it provides an idea
about the protagonist's motivation: he acts as he does not least

because he is imitating a certain American type of hero he knows from the movies.

There is, in other words, a striking lack of a more explicit psychological motivation in the film. It limits the display of emotions to an absolute minimum, concentrating on 'toughness' and occasional irritation more than anger. This is not only due to the acting style, but is also a result of directorial choices in the use of the camera, and in editing. One of the well-known formal characteristics of the New Wave films is the use of the (then new) light-weight, hand-held camera. This gives *A bout de souffle* a casual, improvised, or documentary look. The cinematographer, Coutard, followed the actors from a distance, seated in a wheelchair, while they strolled along the pavements of Paris, partly improvising the dialogue. The film thus contains relatively few close-ups and traditional shot-reverse-shot sequences. When, for instance, the main characters drive to Orly airport, where Patricia is to interview the American director, we see them only from the back seat of their car – although the neck is hardly the most expressive part of the body. Another example might be the final discussion between the two, after Patricia has told the police where they can find Michel, in which the pair hardly look at each other at all. Instead they mostly turn their backs to each other – and Michel wears his sunglasses indoors.

All of this means that the kind of emotional involvement invited by Hollywood's frequent use of emotionally charged close-ups and more or less intense shot-reverse-shot sequences is denied in *A bout de souffle*. Godard's film suggests that the audience use a more *distanciated* form of apprehension. This is also underlined in the editing style. While the film is full of long takes (especially in the conversations between Patricia and Michel), the cutting often seems abruptly 'insensitive' compared to Hollywood traditions at certain points, where emotional tension must be at a peak, or where some kind of recognition, afterthought etc. would be clearly marked in an average Hollywood film. One such point is obviously the crucial scene where Michel has shot the policeman: we do not see his emotional reaction to the incident – the film takes us directly to a long-distance shot of someone (presumably Michel) running across a meadow in the dusk. The extreme of discontinuous editing known as jump-cuts occurs frequently in the film, cutting certain dialogues, for instance – like the one between Patricia and her editor – in pieces. This blatantly calls the audience's attention to the film-maker and his creative work, and takes it away from the narrative, disrupting identification.

These elements of cool, formal play with the medium do, as I said, invite a distanciated form of reception; they tend to deny the kind of emotional investment in the characters and the narrative typical of Hollywood film aesthetics. But this is *not* to say that the film does not create an emotional impact. A Danish friend of mine told me how excited he and his friends were after seeing the film in 1960. They ran, staggering, down the streets of Copenhagen, with one hand covering an imaginary wound in their backs, imitating Michel's final run in the film. British colleagues too have told me about the strong and lasting impression the film made on them in the sixties – and how it still affects them.[2] My point is that this emotional impact must be regarded mostly as a result of some kind of intellectual 'processing' of the film's tragic presentation of an Existentialist view of 'the human condition'. It is not least the absolute lack of sentimentality that produces sentiment: the protagonist is – like those in Greek tragedies – in the hands of a merciless Fate once the crime is committed. The quite unnecessary, 'unpremeditated' killing of the policeman may also be seen as an intertextual reference to Mersault's more or less accidental shooting of a man unknown to him in Albert Camus' now classic Existentialist novel *L'Etranger* (1942). The lack of sentimentality both in this novel and in *A bout de souffle* serves to clarify that the stories are not about psychology so much as about philosophy, about a certain Existentialist problematic: the 'absurdity' of human existence, the lack of meaning, the world experienced as alien. It is this concretised vision of the condition of Modern Man more than any identification with the characters (which of course also occurs) that moves the film's typical audiences.

Michel's unmitigated toughness throughout the film is in a way finally legitimated by Patricia's betrayal. He is a 'stranger' also to her; there is no salvation in romance, in love. Any fulfilling relationship between them is impossible. Michel is on the run from the film's very start, and finally gets tired of running – tired of living: he more or less voluntarily lets himself get killed. The woman is in a sense 'guilty' (Michel calls her *dégueulasse*, meaning something like 'disgusting'), but as she responds by stroking her lips in the Bogart gesture Michel himself copied, she can't be very different: she too is fundamentally isolated, playing a part in a world beyond her control.

'America' – as a *sign* – is present in the film in many ways. The constantly restless Michel steals American cars, listens to American music, imitates American film stars, wants an American girl who works for an American newspaper, etc. He is a lower-class person, whose desire for American phenomena is a desire for metonymic representations of America, a common metaphor for Modernity, meaning to him something like 'power, independence, and abundance'. While in a sense being sympathetic to this desire, the film ultimately shows that it is profoundly futile.

But the pessimism of the story told is at the same time interestingly contradicted by the foregrounding of artistic inventiveness and control: the filmic text is at least a demonstration of human possibilities: 'art' triumphs where 'life' is hopeless. Both aspects of the film demand a 'distanciated' form of reception in order to be appreciated, and various formal elements tend, as argued above, to deny straightforward emotional involvement. The film was perfectly tailored for an audience of relatively young, postwar intellectuals, predominantly male, many from middle- or even lower-class backgrounds – those who were filling the universities in the 'student explosion' of the sixties.

BREATHLESS: ROCK AND ROLL MELODRAMA

The introductory part of McBride's *Breathless* is set in Las Vegas, the city which became the emblem of American postmodernism after Robert Venturi's book *Learning from Las Vegas* (1972). During the first couple of minutes – the title sequence – vital information about the protagonist is provided. And his difference from his French forerunner is obvious.

The first shot of Godard's film shows a softporn magazine page with a drawing of a very long-legged woman, while Michel's voice is heard reading from the paper. McBride's version starts with a pair of pointed shoes, with brass toe-caps, and the bluesy tune 'Bad Boy' being played while the hero Jesse sips beer: 'I'm just a bad boy (lalala . . .), all dressed up in fancy clothes. I ain't taking no troubles, to blow my bubbles away . . .' Jesse instructs a female friend to help him steal a car, then he is suddenly shown reading aloud from a comic magazine about the 'Silver Surfer':

> In all the galaxies, in all the endless reaches of space, I have found no planet more blessed than this one. And yet, in its uncontrollable insanity, the human race seeks to destroy this shining jewel, this blessed sphere, which men call earth. And trapped upon this world of madness, stand I, Silver Surfer.

Jesse comments approvingly, laughing, 'Yeah, you tell 'em, Surf Man, you tell 'em.'

This introduction of the male hero emphasises his fifties rock and roll style – and charm. His attention to his 'surface' is both echoed in his ironic-admiring identification with the 'Silver Surfer' and contradicted by it: the hero of this comic expresses himself in an excessive, melodramatic style (almost) overstating his moral quality – which seems to set him apart from (the rest of) humanity. The difference in moral quality between McBride's and Godard's heroes is also clear from the way the shooting of the policeman is related, and from the fact that Michel robs a former girlfriend, while such a scene is missing in *Breathless*. Jesse is sensitive and basically good morally; Michel is an amoral bastard. Jesse's adherence to the rock and roll stylistic codes of the fifties underlines his alienation in the otherwise contemporary Los Angeles in which most of the film is set. His fascination with the Silver Surfer is also connected with this image: it represents the kind of moral innocence which was often also associated with 'the fifties' in the nostalgic 'revival' of the period that took place from the late seventies. Later in the film, the Silver Surfer is referred to several times, and a 10- or 12-year-old boy calls the Surfer 'a jerk' since he doesn't know what is in his own best interest, but keeps getting into trouble for the sake of some stupid, righteous moral ideas.

All of this means that Jesse's toughness is as dated, if not *out*dated, as the rock and roll music he listens to and keeps bringing to his mind. He is an alien in the contemporary Los Angeles urban environment, not only stylistically, but also morally: he seems to be just about the only moral person around, even if he is also a small-time crook.

Jesse may thus be seen as constructed in a way that makes him resemble previous lone representatives of moral integrity in the Los Angeles area: the heroes of the hardboiled detective fiction of the thirties and forties, Philip Marlowe and others. It may be worth while to quote Raymond Chandler's classic statement here:

> In everything that can be called art there is a quality of redemption. It may be pure tragedy, if it is high tragedy, and it may be pity and irony, and it may be the raucous laughter of the strong man. But down these mean streets a man must go who is not himself mean, who is neither tarnished nor afraid.
>
> (Chandler 1964, quoted from Fløgstad 1976: 32)

Breathless is definitely not 'pure' or 'high' tragedy: it is a 'low' tragedy that invites both pity and irony. The pity is what sets it apart from *A bout de souffle* and instead ties it firmly to the *melodramatic* tradition in American film. This is evident both in characterisation and in various other excessively expressive elements in the film's style.

Jesse is a character who has a minimum of complexity. On the one hand he is a specialist in car-theft who robs an innocent man in the restroom of a restaurant and has killed a policeman. He is a criminal. On the other he is still, as stated above, basically a good guy, opposing a 'normality' which seems corrupted in many ways. His macho toughness is 'only a front', a shell, barely covering a sensitive core, full of strong emotions and vitality. His special affection for rock and roll – be it Jerry Lee Lewis' wild boogies or Elvis Presley's sentimental ballads – serves to express this 'true core' of his personality. Jesse is, in a way very different from Michel, offered as an object of identification for the males in the audience, and most probably – also through the display of his naked body – offered as an object of desire for the females (as well as a significant proportion of the males, no doubt).

Clearly, however, the audience are also offered moments of irony. One scene in particular may be given as an example. When Jesse learns from the television in Monica's apartment that the police have identified him as a cop-killer, he also notices that the neighbours are watching TV – and knows that the net is closing in on him. He then goes through a desperate 'inner battle' which is signified in the most typical excessive, melodramatic way. He sits on the bed, without a shirt, holding his head in both arms, walks restlessly on the floor, then turns his bare back to the camera, and gradually, as the music on the sound-track builds up, starts humming 'Suspicious Minds' (!). Still humming, he walks in rhythm to the bathroom door, and throws it open with a grandiose gesture. The song has now reached full volume, and Jesse sings along. Well inside, where Monica is taking a shower, he drops his trousers and opens the glass door to the shower, moving as if he were Elvis Presley in concert.

The scene is quite parallel, in the use of music build-up and excessive gestural acting, to the scene in King Vidor's film *Duel in the Sun* (1949) where Pearl (played by Jennifer Jones) goes through an internal battle between her 'good' and 'bad' sides. The difference is that the scene in the latter case was obviously intended to be taken very seriously by the audience. The scene described from *Breathless* offers an *ironic* reading to anyone who sees it (which means that it provides comic relief): it highlights the excessiveness of Jesse's macho style, by explicitly turning it into an act, a performance. At the same time, it demonstrates, still very clearly – almost didactically – how this style and the music that goes with it are used as a psychic *defence*.

Such moments of irony do not, however, alter the fact that an invitation to an emotional involvement is fundamental to the film. Nor do interesting elements of the 'postmodern' play with images which might be the topic for another essay on the film.[3] *Breathless* is on the whole a film built for a 'non-distanciated' form of reception, while still presenting a number of traits which invite reflection both during and after viewing.

This obviously also applies to the remarkably excessive and expressive end sequence described in the summary above. It offers a very strong mixture of sentiment, ironic humour, and dramatic tension which very clearly turns Jesse into a *symbol*, a symbol of what for lack of a better term one might call the Melodramatic Rock and Roll Man: an explosively vital bundle of sexual, romantic, and rebellious energies. *A bout de souffle* ends extremely pessimistically, the hero dying embittered and hating the woman who betrayed him to the police. *Breathless*, on the other hand, emphatically tells us that both Love and Resistance are possible (if extremely difficult), and thus actually has a 'happy ending'. The audience may leave the theatre feeling good: the guy they identified with was basically good and basically right, and there is hope that *they* will succeed where the hero, because of unfortunate circumstances, failed.

MELODRAMA, MODERNITY, AND THE MELANCHOLY MACHO

As mentioned at the very beginning of this chapter, Michel (and thus the film about him) pays tribute to Humphrey Bogart's star persona. A further discussion of *A bout de souffle* and *Breathless* could then concentrate on how their male heroes relate to Bogart's typical character.

Umberto Eco has talked about how all the 'clichés' in *Casablanca* produce a 'sense of déjà vu to such a degree that the addressee is ready to see in it what happened after it as well' (Eco 1979/1988: 453). But *Casablanca* does not simply assemble clichés already available, though it does that too; it also presents a particularly powerful version of what was *later* to become a cliché: Bogart's melancholy macho.

Casablanca is a melodramatic film which clearly centres on the issue of masculinity, since Humphrey Bogart's Rick character and his problems are the film's main focus. Rick is torn between two attitudes to life: that of the tough, cynical macho and that of the 'sentimentalist'. This conflict is – in a manner typical of classic melodrama – explicitly formulated by the police prefect Renault in an early scene, where he says that 'under that cynical shell, you're at heart a sentimentalist'. Rick does not object in any way to this statement, and the rest of the film demonstrates that it was quite correct. After seeing Ingrid Bergman – Ilse – again after many years, he turns to depressive drinking at night, expressing his emotions by gestural 'clichés', standardised signs equal in function to those of the classic melodrama: he bangs his fist against the table, later covers his face with his hands, and finally – after having hurt his Only Love by bitter, cynical accusations so that she leaves in tears – buries his head in his arms while the score underlines his sadness and the screen fades into black. It is a short, filmic version of a melodramatic *tableau*.

Rick later abandons his proclaimed principle, 'I stick my neck out for nobody': his more or less forced (produced by the female protagonist) recognition or acknowledgement of his emotional 'inside' makes him 'do the right thing', also morally. That is, he accepts his loss of the Woman, his Love and Soft Spot, to Victor Laszlo, the impeccably solid hero whom he helps escape – and instead enters what seems to be the beginning of a beautiful but quite unlikely friendship with Renault, the cynical police prefect.

The melodramatic structure is clearly seen in the opposition between the cynic Renault and the hero Laszlo, representing two types of masculinity. Laszlo gives no evidence of any form of weakness or confusion. He is simply the icon of moral correctness. Renault, on the other hand, is a corrupt cynic, an icon of moral spinelessness. Rick cannot be Laszlo, and will not be Renault. He's a regular guy, you see, one of us, and so he can only perform regular bravery, by emotionally confronting and eventually accepting the Loss of Love. This also opens him up to male friendship, and takes him out of the self-inflicted Loneliness in which he lives at the beginning of the film.

The character type in question is introduced at different times in different media. It was actually first developed in the twenties – in the hardboiled detective fiction which in the forties appeared on cinema screens as 'film noir' detective thrillers. In film, it more or less disappeared in the late fifties and reappeared in the seventies. If we turn to television, it is worth noting that Sonny Crockett of *Miami Vice* was probably the first prominent case of a typical melancholy macho in that medium.[4]

The melancholy macho may be more 'realistic' than older heroes in two ways. Firstly, the 'new' hero does not represent a neat singular moral or psychological principle (righteousness, villainy, toughness, etc.) but embodies a battle between two such principles: rigid toughness on the one hand, and 'soft' emotionality on the other. Thus a minimal representation of psychological complexity 'in' characters replaces the more pure interplay between opposing principles embodied in *different* characters. Secondly, 'realism' may be said to be increased in the sense that the psychic and moral conflicts represented in the texts with the new male heroes were experienced as more relevant to fundamental problems experienced by the audience outside of the cinema, as more adequate representations of what masculinity was all about.

In my view, we can still speak of melodrama in this connection, since central characteristics of this mode or 'super genre' are still clearly in place. Firstly, the basic *Manichaeism* of the melodrama is retained, since the heroes are basically portrayed as embodying two opposing principles, not as 'realistically' complex characters produced by specific psychological and social circumstances from childhood on, even if brief 'pointers' to such circumstances may be included. Secondly, stylised acting and mise-en-scène still tend *excessively* to exteriorise and thus clarify the nature of the conflict between the two forces or principles, as do various surrounding characters, who tend to work as projections of them. Thirdly, and this is particularly important to my later argument, the Hollywood presentations of the troubled male heroes allow (in the text) and invite (from the audience) the *emotionality* central to classic melodrama.

Since melodramatic signs, according to Peter Brooks (1976), are excessive representations of something unspeakable, underlying the surface of existence, they are also open to many interpretations. Bogart's persona in both *Casablanca* and the detective thrillers is a case in point. From a Marxist point of view, it may represent the frustrations and anxieties created by a morally corrupt capitalist society. From a psychoanalytically informed feminist point of view, it may represent a castration anxiety created by growing independence for women. Both of these views seem perfectly viable to me. Still, I would like to suggest a third interpretation which may to some extent be capable of subsuming the other two: the melancholy macho is a product of a situation in which a loss of objects for libidinal 'investment' - real persons or 'some abstraction which has taken the place of one, such as one's country, liberty, an ideal and so on' (Freud 1917/1984: 252) – tends to make the subject direct his libidinal energies inwards. This, according to Freud, is what characterises the condition known as *melancholia*. In search of an accessible, believable object, frustrated by repeated failures to establish solid 'external' object relations, he turns to himself. Unlike in mourning, 'the free libido' released by the object's death/disappearance is not 'displaced on to another object', but is 'withdrawn into the ego' (Freud 1917/1984: 258). Freud continues: 'There, however, it was not employed in any unspecified way, but served to establish an *identification* of the ego with the abandoned object' (258). This *narcissistic* incorporation of the lost object means that the love for the object is retained while the object itself is given up. And ambivalence in relation to the object comes into play: feelings of love and hate become self-love and self-torment.

Narcissistic melancholia – in non-pathological forms – thus offers an interesting set of rewards in a situation of frustrations on many levels, in many areas, not only in sexual relations proper. In Modernity, all that is solid melts into thin air. Consumption helps only momentarily. It cannot satisfy the desire for stable object relations which the Original Separation (from the mother) created, and which rapid socio-cultural developments increasingly deny us even the illusion of. Authorities and ideals crumble, and women can't be trusted simply to be there for you any more. The loss is irreparable. Only the blues remains: the joys of self-love, self-reproach, self-hate – which, in Freudian dialectics, are simultaneously the love for and punishment of the lost object.

From a certain perspective, Bogart's melancholy male character type is, then, a striking instance of how Hollywood's melodramas have been able to capture and pleasurably represent on cinema screens dilemmas, anxieties, and pleasures experienced by audiences in the majority of modernised/modernising societies. From a social and historical point of view, then, it is interesting that both Michel and Jesse differ significantly from the melancholy macho I have discussed above.

PAIN VERSUS PLEASURE

Both *A bout de souffle* and *Breathless* connect class, gender, and nationality in interesting ways. Godard's film tends to invert the nation-codes: the French hero is a lower-class male who loves anything American, including an American high-culture woman. In McBride's film, the hero is an American lower-class male, also representing slightly outdated low culture, who is in love with a French high-culture woman. At this point, *A bout de souffle* clearly works to question certain cultural clichés, while *Breathless* seems to take the same clichés for granted.

But the most important difference between the two films remains their difference in 'style': French modernism on the one hand, and the American melodramatic tradition on the other. *A bout de souffle* breaks with melodrama in more than one way. Its lack of focus on emotionality has already been noted. In addition, it is hard to detect Manichaean structures in the film, because neither Michel nor Patricia is 'good'. Of melodrama's central characteristics, only *stylisation* remains.

While the Godard film must certainly be said to have opened new vistas for the 'language' of film, one can hardly say the same for McBride's – even if the latter clearly makes inventive use of devices which would never have occurred, say, in a fifties Hollywood melodrama. From a formal point of view, then, the French film is obviously of greater 'cultural significance' than the American. But an evaluative comparison gets more difficult if the films are regarded as representations of the problems of Modern Masculinity. As noted above, Godard's film is almost completely without the emphasis on emotionality which marks the melodramatic tradition. *A bout de souffle* consequently loses to a great extent the specific merits of melodrama pointed out by Thomas Elsaesser in his seminal essay on melodrama in film:

> The persistence of melodrama might indicate the way in which popular culture has not only taken note of the fact that the losers are not always those who deserve it most, but has also resolutely refused to understand social change in other than private contexts and emotional terms. In this, there is obviously a healthy distrust of intellectualization and abstract social theory – insisting that other structures of experience (those of suffering, for instance) are more in keeping with reality.
>
> (Elsaesser 1973/1986: 282f.)

In line with this, one might have said that *Breathless* is (in a sense) 'deeper' in its treatment of the specific problematic I concentrate on here. *Breathless* not only *shows* emotionality, it also invites or directly works to engage the emotions of the audience too, as 'whole' human beings, not primarily as intellectuals. Thus, since it invites such identification, it is possible to regard it as a more provocative film *to self-conscious intellectuals* than *A bout de souffle* in relation to a central problematic in modern masculinity: the association of emotionality with 'softness' – with femininity. Modernist aesthetics – and its primary audiences – may allow an almost unlimited number of themes and 'devices'. Only *sentimentality* is absolutely forbidden and despised, in all kinds of texts, in all media. Certain emotions, such as 'tenderness', 'love', 'brokenheartedness', etc., are impossible to represent if they are not stylised, distanciated in some way. The whole argument around melodrama's 'excess' may thus be seen as built to 'save melodrama for the intellectuals'. This is also why older melodramas tend to be regarded as better than contemporary ones: it is easier to find stylisation in them. *Breathless*, on the other hand, may be less acceptable, except in its most openly excessive sequences.

But *Breathless* differs from the films that inspired *A bout de souffle* in that it does not really present us with a melancholy macho. If Bogart suffered from narcissistic melancholia, then Jesse must be said to be in a better shape: he's narcissistic only. He may hesitate to kill a rabbit, and he is sorry when he has shot a policeman. But his guilt doesn't really seem to bother him. Unless the media remind him of his crime and the fact that the police are after him, he lives totally devoted to the here-and-now and his egocentric, rather short-sighted Mexican project. He suffers, but less because of Loss than because he unfortunately has the Los Angeles police chasing him. To a post-1960s audience, more characterised by a degree of happy narcissism than the melancholy version of it, it is basically a pleasure to identify with this vital, good-natured rebel. He is not just recognisable, he is flattering.

If *Breathless* does away with Bogart's pain, *A bout de souffle* does away with his being 'at heart a sentimentalist'. The *audience* may of course suspect that Michel acts as he does because deep down inside, he is a sentimentalist, too. But the film does not show this. Instead, it takes the toughness of the 'shell' to an extreme, purifying it, presenting it as style only. Identifying with Michel brings no rewards for the audience. The kind of pure macho toughness he represents takes him to a death in bitterness which may be tragically heroic, but otherwise not very desirable. *A bout de souffle* is thus implicitly critical towards its hero. It does not flatter its typical male audiences – except by inviting them to a collective of intellectuals who can appreciate and interpret the stylised and meta-filmic recirculation of Hollywood signs.

REFERENCES

Bloom, Harold (1973) *The Anxiety of Influence*, London: Oxford University Press.
    (1975) *A Map of Misreading*, New York: Oxford University Press.
Bordwell, David and Thompson, Kristin (1986) *Film Art,* New York: Random House.
Brooks, Peter (1976) *The Melodramatic Imagination*, New York: Columbia University Press.
Chandler, Raymond (1964) 'The Simple Art of Murder', in his *Pearls are a Nuisance*, London: Penguin.
Eco, Umberto (1988) '*Casablanca*: Cult Movies and Intertextual Collage', in D. Lodge (ed.), *Modern Criticism and Theory*, London, New York: Longman House (first published 1979).

Elsaesser, Thomas (1973/1986) 'Tales of Sound and Fury: Observations on the Family Melodrama', in B. Grant (ed.), *Film Genre Reader*, Austin: University of Texas Press.

Fløgstad, Kjartan (1976) 'Den dialektiske detektiv' ['The Dialectical Detective'], *Basar* 1.

Freud, Sigmund (117/1984) 'Mourning and Melancholia', in: *Pelican Freud Library*, vol. 11, London, New York: Penguin.

Gripsrud, Jostein (1989) 'Masterson's Male Masterpiece: The Penetrating Story of a Norwegian Western (or Two)', in M. Skovmand (ed.), *Media Fictions* (The Dolphin no. 17), Aarhus: Aarhus University Press.

Grodal, Torben Kragh (1987) 'Melankoliens potens: *Miami Vice*' ['The Potency of Melancholia: *Miami Vice*], Kultur og Klasse 56, vol. 14, no. 4, Copenhagen.

NOTES

1 Since John Sturges' *The Magnificent Seven* (1960) was a remake of Akiro Kurosawa's *The Seven Samurai* (1954), which was in turn inspired by American westerns (and there may be other similar exchanges in film history), the term postmodern is problematic here. It seems more reasonable to me to regard these examples as instances of cultural exchange typical of *modernity's* internationalisation of media culture, not at all limited to film.

2 A Danish friend who grew up in a smaller city than Copenhagen has told me of more concrete, less philosophical attractions that the film was experienced as having by those then (and there) in adolescence: it was regarded as being sexually explicit, and there were rumours that someone urinated in a washbasin.

3 I am thinking, for instance, of the use of colour in the scenes from Las Vegas and the drive in the desert, and the use of the enormous murals in Venice, LA, in sequences towards the end of the film, where Jesse is chased by the police: it is sometimes hard to discern the film's 'reality' from the mural's 'fictions'. The use of the Buonaventura Hotel in downtown LA in a certain scene may also be taken as a self-reflexive sign meaning 'this is about postmodernism'.

4 An article on *Miami Vice* (Grodal 1987) has in fact been important as inspiration for the argument I am trying to develop here.
   The time-differences between the media are probably best understood as related to the degree of segmentation of their respective markets – i.e. audiences. Literary texts could be produced for smaller groups with more or less special tastes. As more capital-intensive productions, films – especially before the Second World War – would normally have to be directed at larger, more complex audiences. Television has until quite lately in principle been thought of as a medium which delivers to 'everyone'. If Sonny Crockett is the first melancholy macho hero in a TV show, this may be taken to reflect the fact that either television now increasingly 'targets' specific shows

at specific audiences or that the character type in question is now relevant, less marginal, to something in the neighbourhood of 'general audiences'. Both interpretations are plausible, and of course not mutually exclusive.

To be added here is the fact that the character type also appeared at different times in different countries, and across media and genres: Kjell Hallbing is a Norwegian writer better known as Louis Masterson, whose western novels have sold millions in more than ten countries. When he created his hero, Morgan Kane, in the mid-sixties, he was tired of the Zane Grey type of hero. He wanted something 'more realistic' (cf. Gripsrud 1989). The Morgan Kane character was unequivocally an unhappy man from the start, portrayed as a psychologically armoured, generally melancholy macho, who also constantly revealed fundamental frustration with his armour, his machismo. In other words, Hallbing produced a character who had more in common with Philip Marlowe than with Roy Rogers.

Chapter 6

More than just images: the whole picture

News in the multi-channel universe

Peter Larsen

From the very beginning of Norwegian television all national transmissions have been the responsibility of one single, publicly owned, broadcasting company – the NRK. But things are not the way they were. As we approach the turn of the century, one of the last public service monopolies in the world is coming to an end.

According to a bill passed by the Norwegian Parliament in 1990, a second national channel will be established in the fall of 1992. The new channel, TV2, will be a public institution, subject to the same kind of general regulation as the old monopoly, but unlike the NRK it will be allowed to carry commercials, and the consequences in terms of day-to-day programming policy are expected to be similar to those to be seen in the recently established second Danish national channel: the Norwegian TV2 will presumably concentrate its resources on the production of entertainment, sports, and news programmes, and its general output will be much less diversified than that of the NRK.

The days of the NRK monopoly are numbered: it has been crumbling for years, as the general deregulation of European television has also reached Norway. Inside the country, experiments with various forms of community television have led to the establishment of a number of smaller local stations in recent years. The most popular ones follow the pattern of international channels: they carry commercials and their output consists mainly of game shows, crime series, soaps, and sit-coms. Although this kind of programme policy is inconsistent with the terms of the original experiment, no decisive legal steps have as yet been taken to stop these stations.

From the outside, the NRK monopoly has been broken by

overspill from neighbouring Scandinavian public-service channels: in various regions of the country viewers have for decades
been able to receive Swedish, and in some cases even Danish
television. But more importantly, the number of households connected to cable networks increased dramatically during the 1980s,
as did the number of privately owned satellite dishes.

At the end of the 1980s 27 per cent of the Norwegian population had access to non-Norwegian transmissions, and the figure
is growing rapidly: according to an official survey, conducted by
the NRK research unit in the Spring of 1991, the so-called
Norwegian 'multi-channel universe' consists of 1,476,000 viewers,
or approximately 40 per cent of the total population.

Most viewers who belong to this 'multi-channel universe' have
access to Sweden's two public-service channels (Kanal 1 and
TV2), one Swedish commercial channel (TV4), one Scandinavian
commercial channel (TV3), and a Norwegian commercial channel
(TVNorge – a 'local' Oslo-based channel whose programmes are
transmitted to various other parts of the country as well). To
these options can be added a selection of (or in the case of
viewers owning satellite dishes: the whole range of) international
channels like SKY, SKY News, SUPER, MTV, CNN, BBC
Europe, TV5 Europe, RTL Plus, SAT1, and 3SAT.

CHOICE IN THE MULTI-CHANNEL UNIVERSE

Thus, access to a multitude of international TV channels has
become an everyday phenomenon for large groups of Norwegian
viewers – as it is for viewers all over Europe. For a fairly large
section of the Norwegian population television has finally become
what critics of the NRK have demanded for several years: a
question of choice.

Old viewing habits are, however, hard to break: as indicated
by a number of recent surveys, most viewers in the 'multi-channel
universe' still list the NRK as their first priority. First and foremost they use the new choice to increase their daily supply of
entertainment, fiction, and sports programmes: whenever the
NRK is fulfilling its public-service obligations by screening programmes intended for special-interest groups, they wander off to
other, more promising, pastures. And even when doing so, these
Norwegian viewers seldom stray very far from home: after NRK
their most common choices are TV3 and TVNorge, followed by

the two Swedish public-service channels. In other words, using the remote control, these viewers create their own, individual alternative to NRK, a kind of imaginary Scandinavian 'TV2' with a fixed menu consisting of a few popular types of programmes.

As far as the choice of *news programmes* is concerned, there is another consistent pattern. In this field viewers inhabiting the 'multi-channel universe' react like all other Norwegian viewers: they prefer to watch the daily news on NRK – just as viewers in the other Scandinavian countries stick to the news programmes transmitted by *their* national public-service channels.

The Scandinavian viewers' loyalty towards these programmes is not hard to understand. Unlike most of the other news services in the multi-channel universe, the national programmes are conducted in the viewers' native language, they give extensive coverage to national and even local events and issues which directly affect the social situation of the audience, and in most cases they also present and discuss major international events from a 'local' or 'national' point of view.

On the other hand the viewers' behaviour in this area is not totally unaffected by the possibilities offered by the recent expansion of the television universe. While news programmes in most international multi-channel environments are transmitted at regular intervals throughout the day – starting with extended breakfast news followed by shorter news updates each hour during daytime, and so forth – the Scandinavian channels have only recently begun to adjust themselves to this pattern, and the output is still quite limited, normally consisting of three daily news programmes: a short one in the late afternoon, a main programme in prime time, and another short one in the late evening. The differences in scheduling and extent are some of the reasons why the news coverage on various international channels has begun to attract the attention of some Scandinavian viewers, especially the younger ones.

This tendency is particularly evident in times of major international crises, as witnessed by the way in which Norwegian viewers reacted to the events in the Persian Gulf region in the early months of 1991. Many of the viewers in the multi-channel universe got into the habit of tuning in to CNN or SKY News several times during the day for quick 'updates', and even those who chose to stick with the Scandinavian commercial channels got an impression of how these international twenty-four-hour news services operate: TV3 replaced its own, very short, news programmes with continuous transmissions of SKY News before and after normal transmission hours, while TVNorge and a number of affiliated local stations chose to transmit the CNN service at various times during the day.

'More than just images: it's the whole picture', promises one CNN slogan. Norwegian newcomers to the multi-channel universe use the international twenty-four-hour news services not as an alternative but as a supplement to the information supplied by their own national news programmes, as a means of getting, if not 'the whole picture', then at least a 'fuller picture'. Whether CNN or SKY News actually provides the viewers with 'more than just images' is an open question. But whatever the answer, at least the viewers get a new *experience* and a new perspective on the news genre. They discover that there are in fact other ways of organising and presenting the news than the one chosen by their national public-service television.

NORWEGIAN PUBLIC-SERVICE NEWS VERSUS CNN

It is almost 7.30 p.m. TV sets all over Norway are turned on. On the blue screen there is a clock, a logo showing that the sets are tuned in on NRK, and a text stating that the programme starting at 7.30 is *Dagrevyen*, the prime-time news. Precisely five seconds before 7.30 an energetic voice is heard saying: 'Dette er NRK. Klokken er 19.30. Vi får nyheter' – i.e. 'This is the NRK. The time is 7.30. Now we shall have the news.' Then follows the familiar title sequence accompanied by a brisk tune. And, finally, the real programme starts.

The formula is well known. National news programmes all over the world are introduced in the same way: a screen message states the name of the channel, the title of the news programme, the time – and is then followed by a short sequence in which these few initial bits of information are repeated in images, spoken words, and music.

In spite of all repetitions such introductory sequences are in no way superfluous. The music and the spoken messages have the quite practical function of calling absent viewers back to the TV set for the evening's main news programme. But first and foremost such sequences serve as a kind of ritual punctuation mark: establishing a brief break in the television schedule, they emphasise the transition from one type of programme to another, and they prepare the viewers for the next programme – which, in turn, ends half an hour later with a shorter, similar sequence.

Viewers who choose to watch the news on a channel like CNN have a quite different experience. The CNN news does not 'begin' in any sense of the word, but is always there, twenty-four hours a day, regardless of whether the viewers are watching or not. The viewers are always breaking into the programme, so to speak, and on entry they usually find themselves *in medias res*, in that they are immediately thrown into the middle of a report, a series of headlines, or a sequence of commercials and trailers for coming events.

Although there is no formal, introductory sequence to 'open up' the CNN programme, there are various other types of 'guidance' at work. Normally a small logo in the corner of the screen will tell the viewers that they are tuned in to this particular channel, and at irregular intervals the continuous sequence of 'headlines' and news reports will be broken by short promos and trailers. To this should be added that the programme is constantly being interrupted by the anchorpersons, who in statements directly addressed to the viewers, stress the name of the channel, informing them what particular part of the total programme they are watching at the moment, and which parts will follow next.

Thus, compared to the practice of the national news programmes, the CNN guidance takes place 'inside' the programme, so to speak, and it has a different function: the intention is not to guide the viewers 'into' the programme but to help them find their bearings 'in' the programme. And the anchorperson's recurrent meta-statements also have another important function: like the promos and the trailers they are part of a constant negotiation between channel and audience, a negotiation aimed at persuading the viewers to *stay* with this particular channel.

The NRK daily news and the news provided by CNN represent two extremes in the present Norwegian multi-channel universe, two variations of one and the same television genre, an 'old' form versus a 'modern' one: on the one hand a traditional, and quite 'formal', national news programme produced by a public-service institution; on the other a relaxed, informal, continuous twenty-four-hour news service produced by a commercial, international media corporation.

To these differences could be added Raymond Williams' well-known dichotomy, *item* versus *flow*: the Norwegian news programme is constructed and presented as a self-contained entity, as an 'item', marked and separated from other major elements on the schedule of the national public-service channel. Like many of the other elements, this particular item consists of a series of smaller segments, but, in contrast to the general tendency in international television, these segments are highly organised, and appear in a predetermined sequence according to a fixed compositional pattern: 'headlines' are followed by 'stories', which in turn may be the subject of 'reports' and 'commentaries'; after the 'hard' news comes the 'soft' news; and everything is rounded off by the weather report.

The CNN programme, on the other hand, is an example of the never-ending 'flow' characteristic of most modern international commercial television systems. Most of the time, short segments, usually no more than two minutes long, follow after each other – 'headlines', 'updates', 'reports', and 'interviews' are mixed with commercials, promos, and trailers for coming attractions.

The immediate experience of the CNN flow is that of a fairly casual juxtaposition of interchangeable elements, but as new viewers are getting used to the format they discover that the various types of segments actually appear at fairly regular intervals in a relatively permanent order, and that even a few longer, more traditionally organised 'feature programmes' and special-interest 'magazines' are inserted into the flow from time to time. So, there is, after all, some kind of internal structure at work in the continuous flow, but it is fairly loose – merely a minimal, sketchy framework from which the actual programme can deviate at will. Furthermore, the importance and relevance of each flow segment is apparently constantly reconsidered during the broadcast: updates are suddenly interrupted by commercials, just as commercials and trailers are broken off by new updates, and so on.

MODES OF ADDRESS

The difference in formal organisation between the two types of news programmes discussed above is in itself an indication of some further differences, for instance differences with regard to general *mode of address* and presupposed *viewer position*. Obviously, the NRK programme is aimed at a stable position, at a viewer who is supposed to follow the whole sequence of segments, a viewer who has decided beforehand to watch a particular item appearing in a fixed time-slot on a fixed schedule; while, correspondingly, the implicit CNN-viewer is a person who is browsing through the channels, and who therefore has to be caught in passing, tempted to stay on.

Some further differences at this level may be explored by returning to the introductory sequence of the NRK daily news and more specifically to the spoken words: 'This is the NRK. Now we shall have the news.'

The statement is, undeniably, rather absurd – the NRK is, after all, still the only national television channel in Norway, and *Dagsrevyen* is one of the most popular of all its programmes: every day approximately 50 per cent of the potential Norwegian audience chooses to watch it – so there is really no need to stress either the channel identity or the nature of the programme to be shown.

However, the spoken statement has another, much more important, function: 'This is NRK' – certainly, but the word 'this' not only refers to the channel ('You are watching the NRK'), but is also a reflexive sign referring to the very voice that makes the statement: 'This [the voice you hear] is the NRK.' It is the institution itself which addresses its audience, or more precisely, this incorporeal voice speaks 'on behalf of' the institution, and 'represents' an immaterial, institutional 'subject' which is in fact unable to address the audience in any other way than in the form of a 'representation'.

With the phrase 'Vi får nyheter' – meaning something like 'Now we shall have the news' – the voice includes the viewers in the very institution it represents, or in other words, enacts a merging of the institution and the national community, and at the very same time delegates the institutional authority to somebody else, to yet another 'representation': for the next half hour 'we', the institution and the nation, will listen to somebody else, to 'our' people in the newsroom – who from now on, acting on 'our' behalf, will tell 'us' all 'we' need to know about the state of affairs in the world today.

According to traditional public-service ideology, news transmissions are one of the core functions of institutions like the NRK: in order to participate in the democratic decision process, citizens should have access to all relevant information on all crucial events affecting their social life and, moreover, this information should be presented in an objective, impartial, and fair manner. However, the very authority and reliability of such institutions are always contested. There is always the possibility that some groups of viewers might react with suspicion and doubt, that they will question the way in which the news has been selected and presented, thereby questioning the independence and impartiality of the institution as a whole. While the NRK as an institution is based on the idea of a unified and homogeneous national audience, there is always the risk that its actual audience will fall apart and divide itself along the lines of social conflicts existing within the national community.

Therefore, the contract between the institution and the national audience must be ritually renewed each day, the viewers must be addressed as citizens, and the institutional subject must guarantee that the anchorperson and the reporters appearing on the screen are its and the nation's legitimate representatives.

When this is done, when the word has been ritually passed on from the institutional voice to the anchorperson, the real programme can begin: after having read the 'headlines' and greeted the audience with a friendly 'Good evening', the anchorperson passes the word on again to various reporters and commentators. Like these other narrators the anchorperson works at the centre of the national institution, but they are also *the narrational centre* of the programme. Looking at the world from an Olympian point of view, the anchorperson selects and introduces the stories which are in turn being told by the other narrators; from time to time the anchorperson reappears in order to close the stories and link them to new ones until the moment comes when it is time to say: 'That is all for tonight. Goodbye!'

If one makes a distinction between the content of a news narrative and the way in which it is narrated, i.e. between news as 'story' and news as 'discourse', the formal structure in the Norwegian news programme can be described as follows. In terms of content the programme is a mere sequence of stories about the state of the world at the moment, but these stories are told by different narrators, mediated through different discourses which are in turn organised in a hierarchical structure. Within any single discourse other discourses may be inserted, for example in the form of 'quotations' from press statements, news conferences, interviews, and so on, but, more importantly, all discourses at this level are parts of the anchorperson's overarching discourse. Regardless of their internal relations, they are always in the last instance presented as 'quotations', subsumed and mediated by one single 'master discourse'.

The individual stories told during a given news programme are usually 'unfinished' reports on events in progress, and in many cases they are not related to each other at the level of content; but they always appear within one single closed and coherent discourse, mediated by one single narrational subject.

Watching the national news programme is a way of keeping oneself informed about the present state of the world, but for the NRK viewers it is also, and perhaps primarily, a way of participating in a daily ritual through which they reaffirm their position as members of the national community.

The relationship between viewers and a news programme like CNN News is not established by means of a ritual contract through which each individual viewer is subsumed under a national community. The CNN audience consists of individuals connected by the fact that they are television viewers tuned in to this particular channel, and as pointed out above, their relationship to the channel is subject to constant negotiation. Correspondingly, the anchorpersons occupy a different position from those of the NRK programme.

From one point of view, the CNN anchorpersons perform the same functions as their NRK counterparts. They are the central narrators in the programme, in charge of the general distribution of news stories within the never-ending flow; like their NRK colleagues they are constantly passing the word on, opening and closing other narrators' discourses, and so on. There is thus an evident narrational centre in the CNN flow, but this centre differs from the one described above in some important respects.

While the CNN anchorpersons clearly appear as the formal representatives of the channel, they are not endowed with any final institutional authority and consequently their discourse is different from the NRK 'master-discourse'. They are, like all other narrators in the flow, constantly being overruled: their discourse is broken off by commercials or by new, more interesting, stories which are inserted into the flow from a position outside their realm. Apparently most major narrational decisions are taken elsewhere, in another centre which is not directly represented in the narrative.

To sum up: although the NRK news programme consists of many different stories it is, at the level of discourse, presented as a self-contained item, as a 'work', and, more precisely, as a fairly traditional 'work': it is a highly organised narrative, told from a central Olympian position by a 'strong' narrator in complete control of the story universe. The CNN programme represents another way of telling: it is a continuous flow of loosely connected stories, mediated through a series of decentred discourses.

If we leave the level of narration for a moment and look at the way in which the two channels more concretely handle the available news material, some further differences immediately spring to mind, differences related to the institutional organisation of the channels in question and to their position within the total media environment.

With the appearance of channels like CNN and SKY News – channels operating in a competitive multi-channel environment and specialising in continuous, twenty-four-hour news coverage – there has been a pronounced shift of emphasis in the way in which 'news' is conceptualised. To bring the audience 'up-to-date' on recent events is certainly a major ambition of any news service, but the new channels' fierce competition for audience shares seems to have made the practice of 'updating' more or less synonymous with 'news'. This is not to say that 'overviews', 'analyses', presentations of 'background material', and so forth are totally absent from the never-ending flow, but, compared to the practice of the national news services, the position of these more traditional, journalistic sub-genres is clearly weakened in favour of the myopic 'updates', with their concentration on minimal alterations and developments.

Another equally significant feature is the fact that the twenty-four-hour news services compete not only with each other but with the total number of programmes available within the multi-channel environment at any given time. In order to catch the

attention of distracted viewers zapping their way across the channels, the news flow must first of all be *entertaining*: consequently,
special priority is given to stories with strong *visual* and/or
emotional qualities. 'Raw', *live* transmissions of spectacular
events are preferred to traditional, edited reports. Much energy
is invested in producing *scoops*, in being the first to bring striking
pictures from major events.

The practice of continual updating, the emphasis put upon live
coverage, the search for images with strong emotional impact –
all these features affect the more general, formal organisation of
the flow. One example is the position of the anchorperson, discussed above.

While the anchorperson in a traditional national news programme addresses the viewers from a superior, controlled position, the CNN anchorperson operates from a position much
closer to the audience, still representing the news service in
question, but also just another viewer, a person who, like the
viewers in front of the screen, attentively watches the images as
they are transmitted live from the field.

At the lower levels of the narrational hierarchy, one important
consequence is the development of a new relationship between
the reporter's discourse and the accompanying images. While the
verbal summary, the spoken story illustrated by available visual
material, is still the preferred form in traditional news coverage,
the CNN reporter's discourse is in many cases mere *interpretations of images*, commentaries subordinated to the demands of
the visual material.

The twenty-four-hour news services are in constant need of
material. And since there are usually a very limited number of
spectacular, visually entertaining events in progress at any given
time, 'updating' means *repetition*, as the same stories are told
over and over again with only minor alterations. Another solution to this problem is the use of *padding*. The regular interruptions of news flow by commercials, trailers, promos, and the like
are examples of this practice, as are the extensive live transmissions from political press conferences, committee hearings,
and so on: such transmissions are inexpensive, they can be used
to fill a substantial amount of programme time, and they can be
interrupted at will the moment more interesting material is
received from the crews in the field.

Even in this case the narrational coherence of the news programme is affected. The viewers are given direct access to the 'raw' material of the situation, and are thereby placed in a position similar to that of the reporters present in conference room, i.e. they are confronted with an unstructured mass of information and statements.

SIMILARITY AMIDST DIFFERENCE

During the preceding discussion, I focused on a series of formal differences between two types of news programmes currently available to Norwegian viewers in the multi-channel universe. But there are also some evident similarities to be taken into consideration.

Viewers with access to many television channels soon discover that choice in the field of entertainment and fiction is really a choice between various versions of 'the same, between slightly different variations of familiar international genres and formulas. Viewers who in the days of the Gulf War returned to their national news programmes after having watched the updates on channels like CNN or SKY News made a similar discovery. Most of the main stories about the war were identical from channel to channel, but this was only what could be expected in a situation of this kind. More surprising was the discovery that the channels in most cases also used the same *visual material*.

In an interview with *Le Monde* (10 February 1991), the French media researcher Marc Ferro used this specific experience as a point of departure for a more general statement concerning the production of television news: 'everyone sees the same pictures. Instead of several national newsreels putting out their own material simultaneously, there is now something like a supranational picture-producing system.'

As a description of contemporary news production this statement is not really to the point. It could at least be argued with some justification that there was nothing absolutely new about the way in which the events in the Gulf were covered by the various international and national news services. In the interview Marc Ferro is implicitly referring to the traditional production of cinema newsreels, but television news has from the very beginning been organised in a quite different way. 'National' production of visual material on major international events has never played any significant role in this area: national news institutions all over Europe have for several decades been using the services provided by 'a supranational picture-producing system' – a system consisting of the Eurovision news pool and a few major Anglo-American distributors like Visnews and WTN. What viewers usually experience as specific 'national' coverages of international events is in the majority of cases merely national reports read to the accompaniment of images produced elsewhere.

The coverage of the Gulf War may serve as an example of how international news has been produced and distributed for decades. But from the perspective of viewers like the Norwegian newcomers to the multi-channel universe, it was *experienced* as an indication of a new situation – because for such viewers the Gulf War represented the first major opportunity to compare public-service news with other forms of news presentation.

One result of this was a heated public debate in Norwegian newspapers concerning the NRK's position. From one point of view this debate was a mere repetition of those debates that occur at regular intervals wherever television news is organised within the framework of a public-service monopoly: once again the critics accused the NRK of being biased, of uncritically subscribing to Western points of view, and so on.

This is not the place to discuss whether this critique was justified or not. In the present context another aspect of the debate is more interesting, i.e. the fact that much of the critique was based on comparisons between the NRK and the international news services and was focused on the NRK's use of international *visual material*. The fact that NRK reporters were seen commenting on the same images which many of the viewers had seen several times during the day on other channels was interpreted as lack of institutional autonomy and authority. And some critics further interpreted this practice as an indication of a general movement on the part of the NRK news in terms of programme structure, a movement towards the model of the international news services.

The NRK's news coverage is dependent on the way in which the general international news system is structured, and because of the evident changes in the immediate environment, the institution is trying to adjust its news service to the new situation. But although the NRK news uses the same visual material as most other news services in the world, and although some of its news transmissions during the Gulf War tended towards being mere updates, there are still differences in the way in which this material is presented and interpreted.

In the concluding section I shall discuss some of these differences on the basis of a few examples.

COUNTDOWN TO GULF WAR: NRK VERSUS CNN

On 10 January 1991 the news services still talk about a 'crisis' in the Gulf and everybody hopes that a war can be prevented. It is one of the days 'in between', a day with no spectacular events. The day before, US Secretary of State James Baker has had unsuccessful talks with his Iraqi counterpart, Tariq Azis, in Geneva. The UN deadline is still five days ahead.

The main stories on all major news programmes are (i) the debate in the US Congress on legislative approval for using US military force in the Gulf; (ii) an improvised press conference at Geneva airport with James Baker before his journey to Saudi Arabia; (iii) discussions about the kind of peace initiative UN Secretary Perez de Cuellar might suggest during his coming visit to Baghdad. Some channels added a few stories concerning various European peace initiatives.

On this day, a large part of CNN's *News Hour* from 6 to 7 p.m. CET consists of live transmission from the US Congress debate. At the beginning of the second half-hour a congressman is abruptly interrupted in mid-sentence and after a series of commercials and trailers for forthcoming programmes the anchorman appears on the screen saying that the transmission will be resumed if interesting new developments should occur, but now it is time for a 'news update'.

The update unit lasts two minutes and consists of three segments. The newsreader starts with a summing up of the main positions presented in the Congress debate so far. In the transition from the live transmission to the news update segment the long Congress debate is being condensed into two ultra-short extracts from senators Mitchell's and Senator Warner's speeches, representing two opposed points-of-view. Next follows a clip showing James Baker entering a plane in Geneva and the information that he 'is in Saudia Arabia right now' and that he thinks there is 'still hope' for a peaceful solution to the crisis. The final clip shows UN secretary de Cuellar being interviewed by reporters in the UN lobby while the newsreader reports de Cuellar's travel schedule for the weekend.

The news update unit is followed by another two minute-unit: a report by Charles Jaco on the 'mood' of the US troops in Saudi Arabia. While the update segments have the same formal structure as the introductory headlines in traditional news programmes, this new segment is organised like a traditional report, i.e. it consists mainly of a spoken text and a few short interviews 'illustrated' by a series of more or less relevant images.

After two minutes of commercials, trailers,and promos the Gulf section is rounded off with a six-minute interview with an English expert. And the programme continues with a weather report followed by other international news.

The Gulf crisis section of NRK's *Dagsrevyen* lasts fourteen minutes and is thus somewhat longer than the corresponding CNN section. After the headlines come three larger segments: (i) a summary of the general situation illustrated by clips from the US Congress debate, the Baker press conference, and the interview with de Cuellar; (ii) a report on the closing of the British embassy in Baghdad, illustrated by clips shown half an hour before on the BBC *Six O'Clock News*; and (iii) a report on British troops rehearsing at night in Saudi Arabia, illustrated by clips that have been shown in the CNN report and in a corresponding report on the BBC.

In the initial summary some emphasis is put on a French peace initiative, but as far as the selection of stories is concerned the most significant difference between the NRK programme and the news coverage on CNN and BBC lies in a final section in which some 'local' aspects of the crisis are discussed: the themes are the situation facing a few Norwegians in the Gulf region and the possibility of establishing an UN Peace Corps in the region with Norwegian participation.

Thus there are both similarities and differences between the news presentation on the two channels: they both have the same main stories and they both use the same or similar visual material, but while this material in the CNN version accompanies the reading of very brief headlines, it is used as illustrations of more comprehensive reports and summaries on the NRK. Thus, from a formal point of view the NRK programme is still quite different from the CNN news and much closer to a programme like the BBC *Six O'Clock News*.

This example may further be used to draw attention to some characteristic features of the visual material transmitted by all the various news services.

In the business section of the BBC's *Breakfast News* a clip from James Baker's press conference the day before is presented in order to show how the New York stock exchange reacted to the news of the failed negotiations. At the bottom of the screen a figure shows the movement of the Dow Jones index: at the start of Baker's formal statement it is showing +40, but the moment he says the word 'regrettably', it begins to drop and after a few seconds it is down to −11.

As speech-act theorists have pointed out, words are acts, and some spoken statements may lead to consequences just as dramatic and far-reaching as those of the most spectacular physical acts. In the BBC's presentation a consequence of one such statement was visualised very convincingly.

Most of the main stories on the news programmes on 10 January concerned political statements, interventions aimed at changing the situation in the Gulf, but none of them had any spectacular consequences, at least none that could be visualised in such an entertaining way as Baker's statement the day before. And this is, after all, the case with most political statements.

On such a day, when all important news stories concern various forms of political negotiations and interventions, it is quite difficult to produce visually entertaining news programmes, and even the CNN returns to the practice favoured by the national news services: the stories do not 'happen' in the images, but have to be 'told' – in spoken texts which in turn are being fairly casually 'illustrated' with whatever images are at hand – with clips showing politicians being interviewed or arriving at conference rooms, and so on. Both the twenty-four-hour services and the national news services feel the need for alternative visual material to break the monotony of talking heads – at least this seems to be the reason why most news services on 10 January spent considerable transmission time showing British Embassy employees engaged in moving their belongings into waiting cars.

In this connection, a comparison with the practice of *Aktuellt*, the main news programme transmitted by one of the Swedish public-service channels, may be useful. Although the programme is clearly organised according to the model of the traditional national news programmes, it differs in some important respects, as some examples from 10 January show.

First of all, the crisis in the Gulf has a low priority in the programme. The main story of the evening is local, and in the international news section the Gulf events are presented in a fairly short segment. Much emphasis is put upon the French peace initiative, and there are brief reports on the US Congress debate and de Cuellar's travel plans. These reports are illustrated with some of the same material used by the other channels, but the clips are much fewer and in many cases stills of leading politicians are used at points where other channels would bring in clips from interviews and similar material.

Corresponding to the low priority given to visual news presentation, there is in this programme a strong emphasis on background material relevant to the understanding of the present situation. The Swedish UN ambassador who has negotiated with the Iraqi leader during the Iraq–Iran War is interviewed and gives an evaluation of de Cuellar's possibilities for reaching a solution during his stay in Baghdad; there is a report on de Cuellar's and Sadam Hussein's personal backgrounds, and so on.

Obviously, the difference between this programme and the NRK news has to do with the fact that the Swedish programme operates within a national duopoly and that it is placed fairly late in the evening schedule: it starts at 9 o'clock and reaches its audience at a time when most of the viewers have watched the early news on the other national channel. In other words, it addresses an audience who know the major headlines of the day and are up-to-date with the latest developments, and consequently it is free to concentrate on providing the viewers with various forms of background material.

The point is, however, that as the schedules of the national Scandinavian news services are being transformed according to the international pattern, and as the number of Scandinavian viewers with access to the multi-channel universe rises, all these news services are catering for audiences similar to that of the Swedish programme.

In this situation, the most likely result is that in order to maintain the present high audience shares, the national news services will go one step further in adjusting themselves to the international pattern; that they will change even the way in which news is edited and presented, i.e. that the movement towards more headline news, updates, visual entertainment, and so on which at the moment is only a tendency – and most pronounced in the short afternoon programmes – will be the dominant feature of the prime-time news.

Obviously, the national news services must accept that from now on they are operating in a multi-channel universe, and that an increasing number of their former loyal viewers will use the international twenty-four-hour services for updates and visual entertainment. But this new competition can be met in other ways than by transforming the national news services according to the international models and by competing with the twenty-four-hour news services in areas where they are quite clearly superior. As the Swedish programme suggests, a more reasonable solution would be to organise the national news services as *alternatives* to the other services, to meet the competition by concentrating on reports, background material, analyses, and so on, i.e. by emphasising precisely those forms of presentation which are the backbone of the traditional public-service programmes.

Chapter 7

Postwar Americanisation and the revitalisation of European culture

Søren Schou

After the Second World War the influence of American popular culture made itself felt in all Western European countries. The Americanisation which took place after 1945 was unprecedented in scope and effect, although the impact of American popular culture on Europe was not an entirely new phenomenon. The mass entertainment of the interwar years, if not made in the USA, had depended heavily on American models. European audiences looked to America, trying to copy the affluent lifestyle and urban sophistication of the American screen idols. Nevertheless, from 1945 onwards the process of Americanisation took a quantum leap.

In the immediate postwar years Western Europe consisted of a heterogeneous group of nations. Some had fought together with the Americans, while others had been adversaries; some had been occupied by the Germans, while a few had remained neutral. To some Europeans the Americans were liberators, to others they came as occupants. It might have been expected that these important differences would influence attitudes towards America, so that it would be possible to detect a more pronounced resistance to American culture in the former Nazi or Fascist countries than in the allied or liberated ones. Surprisingly, there is little evidence of this. The American way of life was generally and eagerly embraced, not only by allies, but also by former adversaries. The image of America, presented to Europeans through the mass media, extended its magic to all Western European countries and has continued to do so, regardless of the particular nation's role in the war.

'What's German culture? These days it's American culture – the same books, the same music, the same movies, even the same clothes. They've bought us wholesale and they have the nerve to sneer' (Willett 1989: 1). Such complaints about the homogenising influence of American culture have been common in the European debate over the last forty years. In my opinion, this widespread intellectual concern over postwar Americanisation points to some real problems concerning the question of national identity in the era of international mass communication. Nevertheless, the traditional anti-American stance taken by many European intellectuals has often seemed insensitive to the fact that the American influence *revitalised* European culture in numerous ways.

The general Americanisation of Western Europe is beyond the scope of this chapter. I shall confine myself to a discussion of Americanisation in my own country, Denmark, during the immediate postwar period. To some extent, the Danish development can be regarded as typical of widespread European trends, but it exhibits a number of features which can only be understood in the light of specific Danish cultural traditions.

AMERICANISATION

Americanisation is a simple word. What it refers to, however, is a complex process taking place on many levels at the same time. Even if we limit our perspective to the process of *cultural* Americanisation, the diversity of processes alluded to is staggering. The study of Americanisation is the study of the *transmission* of values, ideas, images, and myths from the USA to other parts of the world, but it deals with processes of *transformation* as well. From the viewpoint of the receiving country, the influence of the dominating power makes itself felt in many, often subtle, ways. The values, ideas, and so forth are rarely imported 'wholesale'. Instead, they interact in various ways with established cultural patterns in the receiving country. Thus, the original significance of a particular image or myth may be drastically changed, endowed with a new meaning when introduced into a new cultural environment.[1] The concept of 'cultural imperialism' is too crude, as it is insensitive to the process of accommodation taking place, unable to account for the intricate transformation of values and symbols when they appear in another cultural context.

Certainly, some aspect of Americanisation could and should be studied in export–import terms; it is possible, indeed desirable, to give the study of Americanisation a solid, empirical foundation by asking questions such as: how many American films were seen by Danish audiences during the period 1945–9? But when it comes to the significance of these films – *how* they were seen and interpreted by a Danish audience, or what *needs* they satisfied – such quantitative considerations are insufficient, and are only a springboard for the study of the process of Americanisation proper.

Another trap to be evaded is the concept of American culture as a monolithic structure. Immediately after the war, the popular culture of America was probably experienced by Europeans as homogeneous, characterised by common values and images emerging from one identifiable centre. Recurrent patterns do exist, of course, and prevailing European generalisations about what constituted the 'typical American' were not altogether unfounded. At the same time it must be emphasised that such stereotypes were simplifications. American culture was not, and is not today, an ideological or aesthetic monolith; conflicting trends exist, even within the mainstream of American culture. The ideals of *Gone with the Wind* are not identical with those of *The Grapes of Wrath*, to give just one obvious example from the period discussed here. Nor had Hollywood's particular brand of light family entertainment much in common with, say, the daring experiments carried out by jazz musicians at the same time. They articulate different experiences of America, but it is hardly likely that the general European public were aware of such differences during the late forties.

The longer story about the Americanisation of Denmark, leading up to the present, is beyond the scope of this chapter. In summary, however, it has been characterised by a growing awareness of the heterogeneity of American culture and American society. Concepts of the 'other' or the 'alternative' America, unknown to the generation of the first postwar years, caught much attention during the following decades. Of course the emergence of a number of sub-cultures from the fifties onwards helped undermine the generalised image of America, but this image was too simplistic in the first place, as it had glossed over the diversity already existing within American popular culture of the forties.

The evolution from a naive to a relatively sophisticated view

of American culture seems to me to be one of the more important trends of the last forty years. Eventually, the generalised
attitude to American culture typical of the late forties was transformed into a more *selective* appraisal of specific trends within
that culture. But confusingly enough, the rebellious students of
the sixties, influenced by the alternative USA, often considered
themselves 'anti-American' – an inappropriate term which
obscures the fact that many Europeans protesting against the war
in Vietnam were inspired by the ideals and artistic expressions of
the American youth culture. What was considered anti-American
should, then, rather be called anti-establishment. The solidarity
with black protest in the USA and the attempts to emulate the
culture of the Californian hippies both pointed to another
America than that of the Pentagon and the White House, but
the vital models still emerged from the USA. The concept of
anti-Americanism rested on assumptions about US culture as a
monolith – assumptions plainly contradicted by the protesters'
own 'Americanised' lifestyle.

1945: THE YEAR OF CHANGE

But this is carrying the story of Americanisation beyond the
period which I will be discussing in this chapter: the late forties.
My starting point will be the end of the Second World War,
where the impact of US culture on liberated Europe was strong.
It can be argued that the process of Americanisation had begun
much earlier. If widespread, positive images of America are
considered a vital part of the process of Americanisation, it is
possible to maintain that this process originated in the nineteenth
century. Images of the American Utopia were extremely powerful when 250,000 Danes emigrated to the USA between 1870
and 1914 in search of wealth and new opportunities. But negative
images of America as a money-obsessed, materialistic society
have a long tradition, too. The 'threat' of Americanisation, considered as the epitome of the moral and aesthetic collapse after
The First World War, had already been an important *topos* in
the Danish cultural debate during the twenties and thirties.[2]

Nevertheless, 1945 was *the* year of significant change in the
cultural relations between the United States and Western
Europe. The USA now acquired the status of a super power
dominating the liberated and defeated nations of Western

Europe. This domination does not in itself explain the surge of pro-Americanism so vividly experienced in countries like Denmark in the late forties. A number of historical examples could be given to show that the effect might have been quite the opposite: a nation, dominated by another, stronger nation, often rejects the values of the dominating nation. This is the case of the Baltic countries of today; but we need look no further than to the situation in Denmark during the German occupation. The domination of Nazi Germany certainly did not result in widespread pro-German attitudes in the vast majority of the Danish population.

Obviously, Germany and the United States established themselves in quite different ways. Germany exploited Denmark, while the USA helped modernise our agriculture and manufacturing industries through the Marshall Plan. This would account for the radically different ways in which we received the Germans and the Americans. But the widespread pro-Americanism of the first postwar years needs further explanation, as many other issues than economy in the narrow sense of the word were at stake.

Let me give a number of additional reasons why the process of cultural Americanisation became so successful – leading not only to gratitude towards the liberators, but to a lasting pro-American attitude among those who were young at the time.

First, the Americans were the bountiful relatives from abroad, and they had a seminal role to play in the inauguration or speeding-up of the process of modernisation in Western Europe. The halo of luxury and wealth surrounding the leading power in the Western hemisphere greatly contributed to the European fascination with America.

Second, the mass cultural agencies of Europe, exhausted or destroyed by war, were not able to deliver the goods to the mass audiences craving for entertainment and visions of a better life. Instead, these needs were taken care of by the American mass communications industry during these years. The dream pictures spread all over poverty-stricken Western Europe were almost exclusively American in origin or carbon copies of American products.

Third, the USA which huge European audiences came to know and long for in this way was not the real USA, but a glorified replica. It was a replica, however, based on values that seemed less crude to Europeans than the American mass entertainment of the years before the war. In order to assess the impact of American culture during the postwar years, it is essential to bear in mind that US public life and entertainment were still deeply influenced by the spiritual heritage of the New Deal period and the Roosevelt administration. And, in the words of Lary May, 'after the attack on Pearl Harbor, a similar progressive ethos continued to inspire a former isolationist country to carry its democratic élan into the battle against fascism and tyranny abroad' (May 1989: 3).

The goals of US domestic and foreign policy still seemed informed with this progressive ethos: for a while American political life was closer to progressive European concepts of the welfare state and democracy than it had been before – or was to be again for some time. Populism in its left-wing form was making itself felt not only in politics, but in American mass entertainment as well. To Europeans, the US had been a symbol of freedom since the birth of the nation. Now, it also appeared to many Europeans as a nation fighting for more egalitarian, maybe even social democratic, ideals.

All this was soon to change. The progressive ethos and the populist 'We the people'-rhetoric of the forties all but disappeared during the Eisenhower decade, with its cold war mentality and obsession with the red scare. But immediately after the war populism was still an important issue in American thinking and self-representation.

The American super power thus met us Europeans in its most 'Europeanised' form. It was the left-populist US we came to know, but also a USA which had in no way dispensed with its venerable image as a nation of and for the free; on the contrary, this image had in itself been strengthened by the victory over Nazi Germany.

Fourth, there is a final, and in my opinion decisive, reason why Americanisation lead to widespread pro-Americanism in the immediate postwar years. The USA we came to know was a USA represented through the media: a glorified, but also a very *convincing*, artistically persuasive image.

This point is often overlooked. At that time, in the mid-forties, American mass culture reached a period of artistic culmination, setting it apart from the previous and following decades. One of the reasons for this is that American mass culture had recently been greatly enriched by the considerable number of European artists who had emigrated to America as fugitives from Nazism. Many of these serious and creative artists had found work in the entertainment industry.

This is a story that can be told in various ways. It can be rendered with a tragic twist as a story of compromises, even of prostitution, when highbrow artists were forced to comply with the demands of popular culture. But there is another side to it: what the individual artist might consider a degrading experience was all to the benefit of the entertainment industry. The contributions by all these great artists helped transform American popular culture radically. Compromises were made, but it was not only the artistic *avant garde* that changed in the process, it was the entertainment industry as well.

The composer Kurt Weill, who made the transition from Bert Brecht to Broadway, is the classic example, but many others could be mentioned: film directors like Erich von Stroheim, Fritz Lang, and Billy Wilder – the sombre film noir, a considerable innovation in American film, had been developed largely by German or Austrian émigrés. Or film composers like Erich Wolfgang Korngold, a former Austrian *Wunderkind*. Creative artists became superior craftsmen, sometimes degrading themselves, but giving new life to the world of entertainment.

It was not only recent immigrants, but also American Jews and black artists who helped shape US entertainment in decisive ways during the forties. Jazz and film – the most important new art forms of the century – flourished. In particular, jazz went through a very daring phase of experiments and innovation without precedence in popular culture. (This process would eventually alienate jazz from the domain of popular culture, but that is another story.)

If this picture appears too idyllic, it must be admitted that the late forties established other and much more conservative trends as well in US popular culture. Those years also saw the last flowering of radio entertainment, lovingly depicted in Woody Allen's film *Radio Days*. Radio was slowly giving way to the new TV culture, but as far as content is concerned the two home media were not very innovative, celebrating 'time-honoured' values of domesticity and traditional sex roles. To many Americans, the postwar years were a period of restoration after the turmoils of war. They would tend to regard the inoffensive soap opera as the epitome of popular culture during this period, and they might find it difficult to recognise the picture offered above.

There is a reason for this divergence: the American popular culture presented to Europeans was not that of the home media, i.e. radio and TV. Images of cosy domesticity may have loomed large in the USA, but the kind of entertainment Europeans were confronted with was as a rule considerably more innovative. Eventually, the sit-coms and soap operas would find their way to European audiences, but in the forties the TV age had still not dawned on Europe, and the portrait of America presented abroad was still painted by the 'old new' media, the film and the record industry, enriched by the influx of artistic talent.

Besides, there is the 'time lag' to be considered. Many of the productions Europeans became acquainted with during the latter part of the forties originated in the war years. A large number of the most important film premières came from the American companies' huge wartime backlog. European audiences were presented with the cream of the business, and were spared many of the trivial efforts which would have been part of the imported repertory under normal circumstances.

In many ways, American popular culture of the forties – or rather the parts of it that Europeans became acquainted with – may be compared to the most vital periods of European culture, the most obvious parallel being the Elizabethan period. Several characteristics apply to both eras: vulgarity, certainly, but also diversity, a high degree of inventiveness, and vitality. The concentration of artistic talent in the USA during these years was indeed impressive. Everybody could easily make their own list of artists at their very peak in the forties, but let me just mention John Ford, Frank Capra, Billy Wilder, John Huston, Howard Hawks, Fred Astaire, Duke Ellington, Coleman Hawkins, Charlie Parker, Billie Holiday, Benny Goodman – to pick a few random names from a long list.

The artists mentioned here seem to me particularly interesting, as they are all located at an ambiguous point between high and popular culture. Somehow, a Capra or a Holiday do not seem to fit into the fixed categories of 'high' and 'popular' culture. The production and distribution of their work was entirely in the hands of the commercial mass media, but their work transcended this origin, as richly faceted and individual as any European œuvre of the period one would care to mention.

Evidently, the prevailing concept of popular culture adhered to by European intellectuals had proved to be false. There was no necessary, sinister connection between mass cultural modes of production on the one hand, and the levelling or trivialisation of artistic endeavour on the other. However, this was commonly claimed in European intellectual circles, even by expatriates like Adorno and Horkheimer, who were unable or unwilling to grasp the artistic merits of American popular culture of the period. Only the vulgarity of this 'Elizabethan' period had caught Adorno's and Horkheimer's attention when they wrote *Dialektik der Aufklärung* in their American exile, not the exhilarating sense of experiment that was also a sign of the times.

One could turn to George Orwell's well-known essay about 'good bad literature'[3] in order to characterise the merits of American culture in the forties. During those years, the mass media poured out a steady stream of what you might call 'good bad art', i.e. artistic products which in their outward appearance closely resemble pure trivia and have no pretensions to being considered elitist culture. The jazz records of tin-pan alley songs, the film noir, the song and dance films of Fred Astaire: they were 'bad art' only from a formal point of view, i.e. entertainment products made in accordance with the standards of the industry. But it was also '*good* bad art', engaging, vital, and inventive.

It would be a gross over-simplification to say that the popular culture of America consisted of 'good bad art', while the kind of art postwar Europe had to offer had the opposite characteristics. A lot of 'good good literature' was written in Europe during the late forties. I need only refer to the Existentialist writers dealing with the experience of war and the general awareness of a cultural breakdown in a more probing and introspective way than most American art.

Nevertheless, it is probably fair to say that as a rule the European art of the late forties was retrospective in outlook and undynamic in character, whereas the best part of American popular art was extrovert and vital, sometimes showing a degree of social awareness that makes the accusation of 'escapism', often directed towards all kinds of popular culture, seem inappropriate.

To sum up: the *decisive* cultural Americanisation of Europe – brought about during the immediate postwar years – took place in a specific context. US values appeared in a form more appealing to Europeans than ever before – and because of the cultural starvation of the war years, Europe was extraordinarily sympathetic to these values. Some kind of cultural Americanisation would probably have taken place in any case, but the specific constellation of American populism and high artistic standards in entertainment on the one hand and European postwar dreams of a more colourful and prosperous life on the other would in my opinion account for the spectacularly successful process of Americanisation.

The America that we Europeans came to know was the image brought to us by American popular culture. During the forties, very few Europeans would get a first-hand impression of the country. The USA most of us became acquainted with was the America that the Americans themselves *wanted* us to know.

As I have argued, this re-presentation was not monolithic. Writers like John Steinbeck and Richard Wright called attention to problematic aspects of life in the USA, and even Hollywood occasionally dealt with controversial issues of race and poverty. The mainstream of American popular culture, however, created a number of national stereotypes very flattering to the Americans themselves.

The many US films from the late forties and fifties about the Second World War may illustrate this. Howard Hawks' *Air Force* is as good an example as any. This film, from 1943, had its Danish première on 14 May 1945, only nine days after the German surrender. *Air Force* is a tribute to the American bombers fighting against the Japanese after Pearl Harbor. The story about a bomber crew is a powerful re-enactment of the American myth of the 'melting pot'. The captain of Irish origin, the Jew from the Bronx, and the farm boy from Milwaukee may be very different persons, but the common challenge teaches them how to function as a *team*, an American team. The non-hierarchic relations between officers and men and the atmosphere of unceremoniousness and dedication were totally different from German depictions of warfare and offered very persuasive images of social integration.

In other war films, American and European values were directly confronted, leaving little doubt concerning the superiority of The American Way of Life. The American appeared as the true guardian of democracy, serious about his ideals, but easy-going and friendly, often displaying a degree of self-irony.

The Europeans, on the other hand, whether French and British Allies or German enemies, were definitely old-fashioned in comparison, burdened by the long tradition of public-school drilling and obsolete ideals of class (the British), or atavistic remnants of pre-civilised barbary (the Germans). In other words, the whole of European civilisation was seen as belonging to the past. Intensely *present* was only the American with his fancy battle-dress exposing the body, not imprisoning it like the constricting German uniform.

VOICES OF WARNING FROM LEFT AND RIGHT

The impact of America certainly did not take place without warning voices in countries like Denmark. Concern about the Americanisation of Danish culture was a major issue in the cultural debate during the postwar years.

The two most important groups of intellectuals, the conservative existentialists of the so-called *Heretica* School (named after a cultural magazine), and the radical intelligentsia attached to another periodical, *Dialog*, had little in common. The *Heretica* School, trying to reconcile modern existentialist thinking with the traditions of the Danish rural past, was influenced by the apocalyptic modes of thought prevailing at this time throughout most of Europe. *Dialog*, on the other hand, adhered to the ideals of Socialism and cultural radicalism of the thirties.[4] Practically nothing united the *Heretica* and *Dialog* intellectuals – with the exception of a deep scepticism concerning the USA.

The two groups got on speaking terms later on, in the mid-fifties, when a new magazine, *Vindrosen*, was launched as a kind of compromise between them. It is interesting to see that only the idea of anti-Americanism – apart from their univocal denunciation of Nazism – formed some common ground between the former adversaries. The first programmatic editorial alluded to 'the puerile America', the only *topos* uniting the two traditions.[5]

The most stubborn resistance to the process of Americanisation emerged from the radical left and from the conservative intellectuals. In this respect, the Danish debate was typical of the discussions going on in other European countries, especially Britain.

In his study, *Towards a Cartography of Taste*, Dick Hebdige calls attention to a 'negative consensus' existing between radicals and conservatives in England, quite reminiscent of the 'negative consensus' between *Heretica* and *Dialog* in Denmark (Hebdige 1988). Writers as diverse as Evelyn Waugh, George Orwell, the Leavises, and Richard Hoggart were unanimous in regarding the American influence as a threat to British values. The consensus could only be negative, however, as Hebdige points out: 'Though there was never any agreement as to what exactly should be preserved from the pre-War world, there was never any doubt amongst these writers that clearly *something* should' (Hebdige 1988: 51).

Hebdige goes on to underline the differences: For Eliot and the Leavises it was minority (high) culture that needed protection. For Orwell and Hoggart it was the traditional working-class community that was threatened by the impact of inauthentic mass culture. There are similarities between Orwell and the Danish cultural radicals, regarding Americanisation as a threat to working-class ideals, on the one hand, and between Leavis and the Danish conservative intelligentsia, seeing American ideals as a challenge to traditional culture, on the other.

In his book *Looka Yonder!*, Duncan Webster gives a useful survey of the British debate on Americanisation during this period. In some ways, the situation in England was not strictly comparable to that of Denmark. The British population did not experience the Americans as romantic liberators coming from some exotic land, as they had already come to know them well during the war years. The GIs stationed in England were regarded with mixed feelings, and stereotypes of the materialistic and irreverent Americans were fairly widespread. More importantly, the British regarded the Americans as political *rivals* in a way the Danish population certainly did not. Or in Webster's words: 'If there had been 'covert hostility' to the GIs' affluence, this hardened into a more generalised anti-Americanism after the war due to a public resentment of the transformed power relations seen in Britain's loss of Empire and decline as a world power and America's increasingly dominant international role' (Webster 1988: 183–4).

The point that Hebdige and Webster try to make, however, is *not* that anti-Americanism was the prevailing attitude in the British population as a whole. Even the British, observing the rise of the new super power and seeing their own nation relegated to a position in the second rank, were fascinated with all things

American. Positive images of America persisted throughout the period, but they are not so easily documented as the warnings put into print by the articulate opponents of Americanisation. Pro-Americanism operated, as it were, out of sight of the discourse of Americanisation, being – in Hebdige's words – 'constructed and sustained underneath and in spite of the 'official' authorised discourses of school and State' (Hebdige 1988: 74).

AUTHORISED RESISTANCE, POPULAR ACCEPTANCE

The dichotomy between 'visible, authorised resistance' and 'invisible, popular acceptance' was much the same in postwar Denmark. The intellectual and artistic milieux around the *Heretica* and *Dialog* magazines are often considered *the* most important cultural movements of the late forties end early fifties. In their resistance to Americanisation, however, they were not representative of their time. While the Hereticans were concerned with the cultural past of agrarian Denmark and the radicals were attacking American imperialism, a new generation of Danes grew up, more familiar with American popular culture than with the contemporary high culture of their own country. This was a generation thriving on Americana, attending jazz concerts, reading American fiction and magazines, going to American films.

This cultural appetite certainly does not suggest that the new generation turned their backs on culture as such, and it would be quite misleading to characterise them as illiterate. The question is, then, what kind of cultural needs this growing import of US popular culture would fulfil, needs not catered for by Danish high culture. What did America mean to this generation? Why this infatuation with a nation very few had even visited?

One thing should be made clear from the outset: their image of America was not sophisticated, for it could not possibly be. At the time it was possible for adversaries to make sweeping statements about 'the puerile' USA, or for fans to accept all things American. The latter would tend to see the USA as *one* nation, where freedom was held in balance by the solidarity of the Roosevelt years.

The populist image had already been presented to us in the thirties in movies by Frank Capra and other directors (although they often dealt with the conflicts existing between these ideals and the real world). Now it was communicated in numerous ways. To cite just one small example: in the mid-forties, Frank Sinatra sang about 'The House I Live In',[6] the American House. The singer refers to the coexistence of things great and small in this house. He sings about 'the worker by my side' – an echo of the 'We the people' – rhetoric of the period. And he celebrates the American values in a way that goes straight to the heart:

The howdy and the hand-shake
The air of feeling free
But especially the people
That's America to me.

Populism and the folksy lifestyle of the small village were on the agenda. And yet the image of the USA combined populism with affluence. The rhetoric of the howdy and the hand-shake suggested the small, hard-working community of yesterday, but this image was enhanced by visions of the carefree consumer society with the Coke and the streamlined car. The paradoxes inherent in this double representation of American life may puzzle present-day observers of the period, but apparently contemporary audiences did not take offence. Cosy images coexisted with a display of wealth and luxury, worlds removed from the desolate reality of war-ridden Europe. Particularly impressive was the image, presented in films and magazines, of the new urban landscapes, the world of the metropolis, with all its promises of hedonism and easy living.[7]

Even the rural past of the westerns somehow seemed contemporary as well. It is one of the main points in Duncan Webster's book that the American populist tradition has accommodated itself to the changing times, never sinking into the nostalgic, unreachable past, but remaining vital to this day. In this respect it is quite different from the corresponding British tradition, the remembrance of old pastoral England. Even the American cowboy was somehow a contemporary figure, something that could not be said of the inhabitants of rural, feudal England.

In Denmark, and also in Britain, the resurrection of ancient national values as an attempt to oppose the process of Americanisation was doomed to fail, since the majority of the population did not long for the past. What they sighed for was an affluent society in the future. In this cultural context, the keepers of national traditions themselves seemed to embody the gloomy and desolate daily life of postwar Denmark.

The future was sought elsewhere by a young generation of Danes, fascinated by the image of America brought to them through the mass media. These dream pictures embodied a vision of a life without coupons, of an affluence and a 'now'-culture which they felt could become theirs eventually. To a whole generation, America achieved a fetishist value remaining relatively unaffected by the steady stream of less flattering information about the real USA that would flow during the following decades: the witch hunts of the McCarthy period, discrimination against black Americans, the Vietnam War and Watergate.

This generation had no qualms about their loyalty to the USA. It is my impression that the youngsters of the early postwar years – many of whom would later on have important roles to play in the shaping of modern Denmark – remained obstinately pro-American, infatuated with the America of their most impressionable years. *They* were not involved in the Vietnam demonstrations; the older generation were represented in the Vietnam movement only by former members of the *Heretica* and *Dialog* circles, that is to say by the minority of intellectuals on the right and left, who had 'always' been anti-American. To the large majority of their generation, the charisma of the liberators was still weaving its spell.

A final point I would like to make is that the impact of America after the war may have been increased by the fact that American popular culture was regarded as a threat by school authorities and the high-culture establishment. The Danish writer Tørk Haxthausen published the book *Opdragelse til terror* (*Seduction to Terror*) in 1955, in which he discussed the damaging effects of American comic books on children. This book, influenced by Frederic Wertham, is just one example of the concern over Americanisation of the period; many others could be given. The cries of alarm about the seduction of the innocent and adult warnings about the depraving influence of American films and comic books may well have had unintentional effects. It may be that young people tended to regard American popular culture as the proverbial forbidden fruit, a way of turning one's back on the establishment and of rebellious showing off, years before the real youth rebellion began.

If this is true, the situation was strange indeed: the process of Americanisation was eagerly accepted by young people from the smaller nation as a way of *resisting* authority. The success of

American culture was in that case partly due to the fact that it was interpreted by young people as a kind of anti-authoritarian revolt.

Whether this story of Americanisation should be considered a depressing one is a matter of personal opinion. The relative strengths of the nations being what they were, both politically and culturally, it was probably unavoidable that the impact of America should be strongly felt on a small country like Denmark. The USA was not only the larger, but also the more modern nation, and hidden behind the process of Americanisation another process was taking place: that of *modernisation*.

The US self-representation in magazines, books, and film appealed to most of us, obviously more so than our own national heritage. Why? There is a reason more profound than the explanations dealing with the artistic merits of American popular culture or the anti-authoritarian lure of the forbidden fruit. American films, magazines, and books told us about a life many of us were going to live, an urban or suburban life. In Denmark, daily existence was changing for many people as we left our agrarian past and approached a new status as an industrial nation. A new self-awareness was sought in order to come to terms with this changing world, new and more sophisticated ways of looking at life, new ways to communicate. The inspiration had to come from the most advanced industrial nation in the world.

American popular culture became a guide during this mental transformation; the American big city fiction helped us adjust to changing times. One could say that it was instrumental in bringing about the 'mental' modernisation of Denmark. But it should be emphasised that the modernisation occurred in a *specific*, American form not strictly inherent in the process of modernisation itself.

Maybe the correct key term for the process I have tried to describe would then indeed be modernisation. But the modernisation of postwar Denmark was closely interwoven with concepts and ideals deriving from another nation. To deplore the modernisation in itself would seem to me unprofitable and evasive. To explore the – American – *modality* of the process is an altogether more interesting activity.

REFERENCES

Christensen, P. K. (ed.) (1983) *Amerikanisering af det danske kulturliv i perioden 1945–58*, Aalborg: Aalborg Universitetsforlag.
Haxthausen T. (1955) *Opdragelse til terror*, Copenhagen: Fremad.
Hebdige, D. (1988) *Hiding in the Light*, London & New York: Routledge.
May, L. (ed.) (1989) *Recasting America. Culture and Politics in the Age of Cold War*, Chicago: University of Chicago Press.
Orwell, G. (1984) *The Collected Essays, Journals and Letters of George Orwell*, vol. 4, London: Penguin Books.
Webster, D. (1988) *Looka Yonder! The Imaginary America of Populist Culture*, London: Comedia/Routledge.
Willett, R. (1989) *The Americanisation of Germany, 1945–1949*, London: Routledge.

NOTES

1 A good illustration of the cultural transformation taking place was the Swedish reception of the so-called 'cool' jazz of the early fifties. Swedish musicians explored the affinities between this lyrical brand of jazz and their own musical heritage of ballads in strikingly original ways.
2 In the novels by Jacob Paludan, from *De vestlige Veje* (1922) to *Jørgen Stein* (1932–3), the materialism and soullessness of the American lifestyle was an important issue.
3 See George Orwell's 'Good Bad Books' (1945). Reprinted in Orwell (1984:37–41).
4 For the cultural magazines of the early postwar years, see Michael Bruun Anderson (ed.), *Dansk litteraturhistorie*, vol. 8, Copenhagen: Gyldendal, 1985: 105ff., 192.
5 *Vindrosen*, 1, Copenhagen: Gyldendal, 1954: 3–4.
6 The world-famous Danish *Heldentenor*, Lauritz Melchior also had a hit with this song.,
7 It would only be fair to point out that some important films of the period did not gloss over the contradictions in the facile and harmonising representation of America. The cosy world of the small town with its drugstore and white picket fences was indeed threatened by modernity, according to postwar films like Capra's *It's a Wonderful Life* and Wyler's *The Best Years of Our Lives* (both 1946). These films, exposing the incompatibility of populist and metropolitan values, testify to the fact that Hollywood entertainment of the period was no monolith.

Part III

Popular audiences and cultural quality

Chapter 8

Intertextuality and metafiction
Genre and narration in the television fiction of Dennis Potter

Ib Bondebjerg

THE FICTION-MACHINE OF TELEVISION: A CHANGING SCENE

The mainstream products of television fiction are heavily industrialised, especially when we talk about TV fiction from the commercial super powers (networks in the US, the large national semi-commercial stations in the larger European countries, and the transnational satellite channels). Viewed in an abstract cultural perspective, this seems to establish a firm genre contract between the television industry, the actual sender or producer of programmes, and the audience. However, neither the genres nor the reception of television fiction can be considered as a simple process of production according to a fixed format, or a stereotyped process of reception.

Genre contracts should rather be viewed as floating structures that are negotiated between industry, text, and audience in a specific socio-cultural setting, and as such subject to historical change. The industrialised production process creates structures and formats that cross national borders and socio-cultural divides: genre products form a possible framework for cultural and ideological mainstreaming. But they are also embedded in diverse formations of pleasure and play: they are the basic material from which cultural and psychological negotiations create different forms of reception-texts.

The fiction-machine of modern television is both a mythical, a narrative, and a poetic machine. But whereas traditional critics have often – from the standpoint of elite culture – tended to stress the legitimating, mythical, and conventional narrative form of television fiction, 'postmodern critical theory' tends to claim that the lines dividing elite culture, *avant garde* culture, and the so-called mainstream of mass culture are increasingly blurred: television creates a mixed culture where mainstream meets experiment, and the popular poetics merges with the forms of anti-narrative and meta-fiction.

Dennis Potter's television fiction reflects this situation very clearly. It is not just another version of the classical *avant garde*, now finally reaching television: rather his way of using television can be read as a symptom of a broader tendency in which mainstream and experiment are merging in a new way. The development of rock videos is an already fairly well-analysed example of the same phenomenon, which can also be found not only in European films, but in popular American cinema and American network shows. This phenomenon, then, is not just a European *avant garde* cultural trend, but a vital part of a more widespread cultural condition of the postmodern. However, we still need to distinguish between the more 'commercial' and the more 'critical' forms of popular postmodern aesthetics. Potter is an example of the latter.

Potter's television fiction is certainly an extraordinary example of a possible new tendency in television, but different critics such as Eco (1985), Grodal (1990) and Olson (1987) have traced similar tendencies in a broad range of popular, mainstream television narrative. For instance the TV series *Moonlighting* clearly works both on a heavily intertextual basis and on a meta-fictional level. Here the normal process of narrative decoding or constructing of the story and the normal ways of identification are bracketed by meta-fictional devices, playful references to the discourse, and intertextual repetition or deconstruction of classical genres and film. This does not necessarily give this construction a strong critical dimension, but it may also be seen as a way of legitimating ordinary fictional needs, for a new kind of audience who might otherwise feel they were being addressed as too naive.

The elimination of or play with this 'naive addressee of the first level' is discussed in a broader perspective by Eco (1985: 18), who sees a tendency now to address a 'sophisticated addressee at the second level' more explicitly. Olson (1987) follows the same tendency, with his notion of the matured audience, and the increased presence of meta-fictional devices in even commercial network television. He defines meta-television as a new form of popular postmodernism that can be found on at least three levels: *medium-reflexive structure*, *genre-reflexive structure*, and *text-*

reflexive structure. At the first level we find a growing audience awareness of the communication situation reflected at the diegetic level, and also an increasing number of inter-programme references. The second level points to an increased structural mixing, copying, quoting, and recycling of different genre cues within programmes, demanding schemata knowledge of a large variety of intertextual experience. The third level of meta-fiction can be characterised as the deliberate play with the basic narrative machinery of time, space, and style: a sort of play with the 'normal' construction of the story of classical narration.

The increased intertextual consciousness in the production and reception of television mainstream series and the use of a playful, meta-fictional dimension does not mean that (American) commercial television has become 'critical' or, as a whole, non-narrative. But it is most certainly a symptom of a new cultural situation, in which a kind of 'popular *avant garde*' is made possible. However, many of the meta-fictional and intertextual devices in popular postmodern television and film may be characterised as mere 'gimmicks' on a largely narrative background. Dennis Potter's television fiction clearly goes further: here the meta-fictional dimension and the intertextual clues are used to create a discussion of the fictional process in the relation between narratives and our lives, the processes of mind, body, emotions, and cognition in a narrative that has popular, realistic, modern, and postmodern features.

CULTURAL INDUSTRIES: THE CHANGING OF PARADIGMS

Andreas Huyssen has recently baptised the traditional Frankfurt paradigm 'the theory of The Great Divide' (Huyssen 1986: ix). He defines the great divide as a critical 'discourse that insists on the categorical distinction between high art and mass culture' (Huyssen 1986: viii). The theorists of the great divide, above all Adorno (Adorno 1972), dismiss mass culture from jazz to American TV drama as an industrialised and debased art form. Moreover, the theory of the great divide considers the audience of mass culture to be naive dupes, and thus lays the foundation for a rather paternalistic project of emancipation.

In the new, critical, postmodern paradigm, which has been formulated not only by Huyssen (1986) but also, among others, by Eco (1985), Hebdige (1988), and Collins (1989), this concept of both mass cultural products and of the audience has been changed. Huyssen defines the postmodern not as an aesthetic difference primarily between modernism and postmodernism, but as 'a new set of mutual relations and discursive configurations' in which modernism, *avant garde*, and mass culture come together. He elaborates on the hidden contradiction he sees in Adorno's writings, in which, after all, there are certain limitations to the reification that mass cultural products can inflict on the audiences. This resistance can only be related to a more active and open form of reception than that foreseen by the traditional, critical paradigm. And if this fact is established, the next step would logically be to admit that mass cultural products, on closer examination, reveal a greater multitude of discursive strategies and openings, which contradict the traditional image of conformity.

Much the same theme is discussed by Eco in his efforts to trace the relation between innovation and repetition in modernist and popular texts. He shows how the degree of intertextual dialogue, once supposed to be typical of experimental, *avant garde* art and a culturally sophisticated model reader, is now a broader phenomenon, part of a meta-fictional play in a number of widespread mass-media texts (Eco 1985: 171). Following this theme, Jim Collins' book on popular culture and postmodernism (Collins 1989) dismisses the notion of culture as a hierarchical master system that can somehow explain both production and reception (Collins 1989: xiii). This, however, should not lead to false notions of 'implosion' (Baudrillard 1985), in which narrative structures and coherent genre systems seem to vanish, and the overall meaning of anything is said to disappear. Stuart Hall has efficiently met this 'implosion-theory' with a more adequate 'explosion-theory' (Hall 1986). The coding of texts and audiences is as strong as ever, but the cultural codes are more plural, i.e. double-coded or multi-coded, and the connection between model texts and designed model readers is not the linear process from above assumed by classical critical theory.

Elaborating on this idea, Collins refers to Jencks' (1986) concept of 'imaginary museum' and the term 'bricolage', borrowed from French structuralism by Hebdige (1979), as a way of characterising a more active audience trying to make sense in a culture with a huge network of competing discourses and genres. According to the metaphor of the imaginary museum, the semiotic culture of the media more and more resembles not only a stock-piling of an ever-growing variety of products that are recycled in many ways, but also a crowded museum of people trying to make sense. There is an ongoing semiotic process where, on one hand, messages or arrangements of items from the museum are arranged in different ways to catch the attention of different audiences and individuals; on the other hand, the individual creates, selects, and actively tries to interpret the bombardment of various messages. The term bricolage in fact just underlines this last aspect of reception. As Collins puts it, ' . . . [in] cultures where no overarching, pan-cultural distinctions between official and unofficial, mainstream and *avant garde* are in effect, bricol-age becomes the inevitable response to semiotic overload' (Col-lins 1989: 145).

In a large number of empirical reception studies (Katz and Liebes 1986; Schrøder 1988; Morley 1980; Ang 1985; Jensen 1986), and in the revised cultural–semiotic perspective of Fiske (1987), a similar case is made for the semiotic power or even freedom of the audience, and the individual recipient, either to resist the power of media messages or to construct their own meanings. But although the empirical reception studies show a new audience concept at work which underlines the bricolage activity of the viewers and the differences in reception, it is important to point out that even though a centralised concept of control and uniformity may be abandoned, no subject is 'free' to construct meaning or to choose freely from the shelves of the imaginary museum (Jensen 1990). Texts work hard to construct their readers, and readers carry intertextual as well as cultural codes with them. So the selection and construction of meaning is of course strongly influenced by the intertextual and cultural codes already at work, by the textual signals, codes, and intertex-tual references set in motion by a particular text, and by the choices made possible at the different levels on which the imagin-ary museum can be nationally and transnationally organised.

POTTER, TELEVISION, AND THE CULTURAL INDUSTRY

Very few so-called 'serious' writers have decided to write primar-ily for television. Dennis Potter, however, is one of them: since 1965 he has been the author of at least 28 TV dramas, 3 original mini-series with other directors, and 4 adapted mini-series, and in his latest mini-series he is both author and director. His mini-series have been seen by millions of viewers, not only in Britain and the rest of Europe, but also in the USA. An American critic recently named him the most resourceful innovator in British screen drama (Fuller 1989: 31). Although his plays and mini-series have not made the leap from the BBC and the European public-service culture to commercial, American network television, they have been aired on PBS channels. But even though Potter has not been shown on network television in the US, the outstanding success of David Lynch's new crime mini-series *Twin Peaks* clearly indicates that the line between experiment and commercial television can be crossed.

However, Potter has also engaged in a close encounter with the Hollywood cinematic apparatus, the mainstream cultural industry par excellence. He wrote the script for Michael Apted's 1983 film *Gorky Park*, a film with an intriguing, political thriller plot. As an author Potter thus has first-hand knowledge of the classical narrative tradition of the Hollywood thriller, which forms the background of the intertextual and meta-fictional play with crime fiction narration clichés in, for instance, his maze-like mini-series *The Singing Detective 1–6* (1986).

A transformation in the opposite direction is seen in Herbert Ross' American film version from 1981 of Potter's original six-part mini-series *Pennies from Heaven* (1978), the 'Hollywood-isation' of which tends to transform a sharp piece of social criticism and meta-fictional play with televisual and popular codes into mainstream musical and comedy. These examples show Potter's deliberate attempts to cross 'the great divide' between high culture and mass culture. He is afraid neither of embarking on the commercial vessel of Hollywood nor of using or referring to the products of television mass culture in his mini-series and plays. It is as if his Welsh, Socialist working-class background gives him a certain 'disdain for high art and a belief in the notion of a democratic culture' (Fuller 1989: 31). In many ways Potter's forms of television narration can be viewed as a daring experiment in the mixing of modernist and popular discourses in a sort of critical postmodernism or popular *avant garde* dialogue.

Potter constantly challenges his audience, not only by attacking the dogmas of naturalism and realism or the logic of classical narratives, but also by a multi-layered twisting of discourses, plot-lines, and intertextual references and genre frames. Although his cooperation with Hollywood shows a more straight-forward and narrative Potter, and although he has created clear-cut realist narratives, for instance his four-hour mini-series *Christabel* (1988), he is mainly characterised as a television narrator by his constant efforts to visualise the flow of a postmodern consciousness, saturated with popular culture and mass media. The mixture of fiction and reality that is often staged in his television fiction is thus a symptom of a postmodern condition, a world of what seems to be a 'hyper-reality' and communication based on 'floating signifiers'. The world and the mind are represented as a staged media-scene where both the protagonists in Potter's fiction and in the end the audience may wonder who is the author and master of the narrative. However, as we shall see, Potter is not a postmodernist in the uncritical or Baudrillard sense of the word: his communication has substance and meaning beneath the chaotic surface.

Since Potter wrote his first piece of television fiction in 1965 – *Vote, Vote, Vote for Nigel Barton* – he has clearly been looking for a new kind of non-naturalist and non-realist TV fiction, and has also moved from single plays towards serialised fiction. Already in his speech at the Edinburgh International Television Festival in 1977, he defined his strategy in opposition to the dominating realist form of TV fiction and the naive belief in fact or the trust in the direct relationship between the word and the world, the image and the represented. He did not dismiss naturalism and realism, but clearly wanted to create a new sort of television fiction that could also be seen as an intertextual play with all the formats and genres on the television screen and a meta-fictional play with the frame itself:

> Most television ends up offering its viewers a means of orientating themselves towards the generally received notions of 'reality'. The best naturalist or realist drama, of the Garnett, Loach–Allen school for instance, breaks out of this cosy habit by the vigour, clarity and originality and depth of its perceptions of a more comprehensive reality. The best non-naturalist drama, in its very structures, *disorientates* the viewer smack in the middle of the orientation process which television perpetually uses. It disrupts the patterns that are endemic to television and upsets and exposes the narrative styles of so

many of the other allegedly non-fiction programmes. It shows the frame in the picture, when most television is busy showing the picture in the frame.

(Potter 1977: 37)

Potter has given another explanation of the dream-like, non-narrative technique of visual montage that he mostly uses:

All writers are aiming at a sort of realism, but naturalism assumes we sense the world out there to be exactly as it is – and I know that not to be the case. If they really examine themselves, most people know that their own aspirations, moods, memories, regrets and hopes are so tangled up with the alleged reality of the out there that it is actually interpenetrated by those feelings. Naturalism leads you to believe that you are just a creation of all the imperatives of the world – whereas the non-naturalistic dramatization of the inside of your head is more likely to remind you of the shreds of your own sovereignty.

(quoted in Fuller 1989: 32)

In consequence of this, he explains *Christabel* and his occasional return to the documentary or naturalistic discourse as 'a deeper need . . . to do a piece of naturalistic, chronological narrative as an act of writerly hygiene, just as you might wash your brain under the tap' (quoted in Fuller 1989: 33).

It seems that this brainwash – another metaphor for the psychoanalytical reading and deconstruction of narratives and identities taking place in all his works, not least *The Singing Detective* – has set free an even more radical TV writer lately. In his latest four-part mini-series, *Blackeyes* (1990), dealing with feminism and male desire in the construction of the feminine, he has developed his multi-layered soundtrack and visual montage of different narrative plots even further. It is told through the mind of not only one, but several writers. In this mini-series, of which Potter is both scriptwriter and director for the first time, he has surpassed himself and others. As Dunkley puts it,

Potter is so far ahead of the field in his use of television, that his story scarcely matters any more . . . this drama has a slighter narrative than *The Singing Detective*, but Potter is now using television as James Joyce used the novel and Van

Gogh used painting: as a multi-layered medium of intense self-expression.

(Dunkley 1990)

However, this might also indicate a new and radical *avant garde* position, a narrative process where discursive non-logic has killed any story-logic, and where a potential mass audience may be lost in Potter's television maze. *Blackeyes* is clearly a step away from a more direct positive dialogue with popular culture and genres, as it seems to deal even more subtly than before with the very construction of fiction, reality, and roles: a very advanced play with frames and a very complex sort of deconstruction, without the break into straight genre-pastiche of the two earlier mini-series.

NARRATION AND POPULAR POSTMODERNISM.

If the reception process of narrative fiction in a postmodern media culture can be seen as a kind of imaginary museum-work or bricolage, then the same can be said about the production of television fiction – of which Potter's is a very prominent example. The intertextual bricolage work and the loving deconstruction in the course of the narrative process of carefully selected genre codes is very intense in both *Pennies from Heaven* and *The Singing Detective*. One good example of this is that in both narratives popular songs are used to create a lyrical underlining of the narrative and at the same time a kind of punctuation or Verfremdung of the narrative process. The songs create an atmosphere of historical time in the stories, i.e. they have a referential sign function, and they are also realistically legit-imated by the occupation of the protagonist in the two narratives. In *Pennies from Heaven* he is a salesman of sheet-music, and in *The Singing Detective*, as the title indicates, one of the levels of the narrative makes Marlow (*sic!*) a part-time crooner.

But the songs also point to the imaginary or symbolic layers of the narrative and work to create overloaded semiotic junctions in the text. This happens in a fairly simple way in *Pennies from Heaven*, where the conflict between the dull everyday life of the Depression and the dreams of a better life is expressed in the confrontation of the songs and the narrative, and in the way in which the singing goes from background music to the voice of

the characters. Alternatively it can be done in a more complicated way, as in *The Singing Detective*, where the songs have
the same function as in *Pennies from Heaven*, but also glue the
fragmented narrative discourses together in a more symbolic way,
providing the viewer with a set of meta-fictional clues to the
narrative and psychological puzzle.

A good example can be found in part 3 of *The Singing Detective*, 'Lovely Days', where the Mills Brothers version of 'Paper
Doll' forms the background of a scene where a fatal separation
between Marlow's father and mother is taking place in a flash-
back. This song, dealing with the image of 'flirty guys', and thus
hinting that it is adultery by the mother that causes the separation, is sung first as a background-song; then by Marlow as the
grown-up singing detective, searching backwards in his own life;
then by the father, who was left behind; and finally by a group
of soldiers in the train, taking the mother and Marlow as a boy
to London and away from the father. This popular and rather
direct song is thus clearly used to get us to move up and down the
narrative layers. Simultaneously the development of an Oedipal
conflict is explained by the combination of narrative, visual symbols and the song.

In *Pennies from Heaven* the songs also clearly function on both
a narrative and a symbolic level. The realistic worlds portrayed
in this mini-series are, on the one hand, the depressing lower-
middle-class, suburban London culture during the crisis between
the two world wars, and on the other, life in rural provincial
England. The protagonist, Arthur, a salesman in sheet-music,
travels between these two worlds, and we follow his more and
more fatal love story with a (at the beginning!) very innocent
schoolteacher. The morals and daily life of greater London and
provincial England are contrasted, but what the two characters
have in common is the way they relate to or use popular culture
to dream about another life. For the female schoolteacher it is
fairy tales; for Arthur it is the popular songs of the period. The
worlds of the songs and the fairy tales are used metaphorically
to contrast and comment on the realistic world, and at the same
time they function as a distanciation mechanism or a sort of
meta-fictional device.

In a way the different forms of popular culture are given a
religious or Utopian dimension, as the title of this mini-series
indicates: they point to the hidden meaning of life, to the good

ideals and the kind of love and good life that cannot be found in reality. But at the same time, of course, they are seen as commercial speculations and as unrealistic dream worlds: they are meant to give pennies, profit, to live on unfulfilled dreams, but they nevertheless come from 'heaven': popular culture has taken over the role of the old religious songs, as it is directly thematised in the figure of the tramp, who contrasts the fate of Arthur.

The meeting point between the realistic narrative and the dream world of popular culture is visualised in several symbolic ways: a special colouring of the scenes, the transformation of realistic space using, for instance, oblique angles, the use of double exposure, the movement between filmic and graphic techniques and the use of different popular genres that are suddenly inserted into the narrative. The titles of the individual parts are lines from popular songs: (1) 'Down Sunny Side Lane', (2) 'The Sweetest Thing', (3) 'Easy Come, Easy Go', (4) 'Better Think Twice', (5) 'Painting the Clouds', and (6) 'Says My Heart'. Also in the painted pictures used during the opening credit-sequences of each part we move around in a world changing between idyllic suburban houses, fairy-tale worlds, symbolic, mythological worlds and pictures of the city in either decay or below a slightly rosy sky. In this way popular codes meet with realistic codes and modernist codes, merging into a kind of very complex postmodern fiction machine. Also the ending of the series is characteristically ambiguous: Arthur is framed for a murder which the tramp has actually committed, and is hanged, but appears again to tell the audience that of course we have to have a happy ending as well!

Although the foregrounding of songs is a well-known phenomenon in the Hollywood musical, and also has a popular history in drama and opera, the use of songs in Potter's series, where we also find sequences that directly use the musical genre, is clearly a Verfremdung effect. The use of songs is therefore just a general symptom of the overall narrative structure of the text, or rather the way in which the narrative is made excessive and points to itself. The Metz/Baudry (Metz 1982) definition of the classical narrative film and the position of the spectator characterises it as a discourse concealing the marks of enunciation, a discourse disguised as story, a discourse in which the viewing subject is allowed a privileged but totally controlled position as voyeur. The television narrative of Dennis Potter is clearly a break with this alleged invisible narrative contract between the classical narrative genres and the audience.

Metz's psychological–semiotic theory of narrative cinema, supported by the Lacanian differentiation between the real, the imaginary, and the symbolic order, is a powerful theory of narrative reception, and it cannot just be dismissed, since it touches upon the more subconscious or emotional processes behind visual narratives. However, this view tends to overlook the more active and conscious processes taking place in the decoding of narratives. This has been demonstrated very convincingly by David Bordwell (Bordwell 1985) in relation to filmic narrative, and it is even more necessary to keep in mind when analysing narrative structures of television.

Where traditional semiotic theory talks about narrative in a textual, structural sense, Bordwell, from a cognitive point of view, defines a new term 'narration' as 'the process whereby the film's syuzhet [usually translated as 'plot'] and style interact in the course of cueing and channelling the spectator's construction of the fabula' (Bordwell 1985: 53). The concept of the invisible narrative contract of the classical narratives is probably only valid at a very superficial level, and the theory is based on a sort of underestimation of the mass audience of cinema and TV.

In dealing with narration as a dynamic process, as suggested by Bordwell (Bordwell 1985: 30), it is then necessary to see narration as a kind of cueing of the viewer, rather than a firmly constructed position, a cueing which gives the viewer a certain amount of freedom and a set of variable options for processing and decoding the narrative, depending on the narrative forms of the text in question. As regards the more subconscious perspective, this must also be understood as an important, active part of this process. In Potter's TV narration, subconscious/psychoanalytical cues and symbols are spread all over the narrative. So here a visual positioning of the viewer in a puzzle of visual stream-of-consciousness mingles with a very conscious cueing of the viewer through intertextual frames and competing narrative lines and discourses.

As mentioned above, this break with the concept of the passive viewer of Metz' theory of film-enunciation and reception is even more necessary when we analyse television narratives. Whereas the cinematic apparatus to a larger degree consists of closed texts, and so to speak places the viewer in a special viewing position, creating a sealed-off 'fictive' space, television should rather be considered a channel inside everyday cultural practices. One of the reasons for the explosion of meanings in postmodern culture is precisely that an enormous flow of television forms – fiction, fact, and 'faction' alike – are now floating freely into the family sphere. The semiotic overload, the fusion and mixture of cultures, audiences, genres, and so on, is clearly a result of the way in which television has been occupying the communicative centre of most cultures over the last twenty years.

This 'semiotic glut' creates a gradually more knowledgeable audience and a diversified intertextual scene, which displays, on the one hand, a more meta-fictional form of popular mainstream fiction, and, on the other, a space for a poetic and experimental dimension in TV series and TV narration. *The Singing Detective* is an example of this latter type of double- and multi-coded television fiction: the mixing of mainstream and *avant garde*, of modernism and postmodernism, of genre-signals belonging to both the narrative and non-narrative traditions.

POPULAR *AVANT GARDE* TV: THE SINGING DETECTIVE

The Singing Detective is an example of a narration, in Bordwell's sense of the word, where the viewer will have to go to extremes in his use of schemata to construct the fabula. There is no straightforward linear and causal chain of events, and as far as agents are concerned, they seem to slide into each other's identities. Rather than narrative progress we see repetition, recycling of themes and visual segments: an associative web, eventually leading us towards a story. The syuzhet and the style both show signs of excess. The core of the narration in fact becomes the construction itself: the meta-fictional effect is precisely that as we try to construct the fabula, we are all the time forced back to the system of construction, and to a system of competing syuzhets or plots, and styles attached to these competing plots.

At one level, this is just the result of the intertextual frame and double narrative-line borrowed from the detective genre: we follow a detection process and are at the same time conducting our own investigation in order to construct the story of this detection. The opening sequences of *The Singing Detective* take place in the narrative and stylistic traditions of film noir and the hardboiled detective story. I shall call this level *the crime plot*. In the crime plot we follow a detective, named Marlow (as in Chandler's novels, but without the 'e') involved in a rather hopeless spy story, which is visualised in scattered parts all the way through the narrative. This narrative, however, is also framed by a meta-fictional dimension that is linked to a second level, which I shall clall *the therapeutic plot*. In this plot the author of a novel, also called *The Singing Detective* lies paralysed by a skin disease in a London hospital, and at one level of this therapeutic plot, Marlow, because that is also the author's name, is rewriting his novel as a film, and we are then witnessing this lower- or upper-level visualisation process seen as the crime plot. But of course the whole six-part mini-series we are watching can also be seen as a sort of representation of the whole lot of feverish and partly imaginary projections taking place in the head of the protagonist, the author.

The therapeutic plot, which is more and more heavily intertwined with the crime plot (in which the author represents himself in several characters, one of them the detective), clearly works to make the viewer construct a sort of psychoanalytical fabula. That is, a story of a skin disease which is the symptom of a set of basic repressions, gradually leading us back to a version of the primal scene: his mother's adultery and her death by suicide, jumping from a bridge. And as already mentioned, this incident is heavily related to a basic and unresolved Oedipal triangular conflict lying at the bottom of the whole narrative. Note, for instance, that the crime plot moves between three places: an apartment where paid-for sex takes place and two restaurants, named Skinscapes and Laguna. Contempt for women, skin disease, and water are thus symbolically connected in the narrative space. At a third level of the narrative we therefore find another syuzhet/plot and style, the *socialisation plot*, which, intertwined with the crime plot and the therapeutic plot, traces the life of the author/detective and the voice-over narrator back to his childhood in a poor, working-class, mining district.

What happens on the aesthetic and narrative level is basically that these three systems of narration are combined into both competing and interrelated discourses in the narrative decoding and constructing – in the mind of the protagonist and eventually in that of the viewer. The narration requires a very active processing on the part of the viewer, activating all kinds of schemata, and also foregrounding a number of stylistic schemata because of the very explicit way styles and forms of narrative cueings are used together with intertextual references. The process of detection taking place in the crime plot gives us a number of clues that point to clues in the socialisation plot, which are then gradually worked through in the therapeutic plot. At the centre of all the narratives we find the figure of the author/detective in different forms, and the two ultimate detectives are of course the viewer and the super-narrator behind it all, Dennis Potter.

At the fourth level of the narrative process we therefore find the *meta-fictional plot*. This plot constructs a fabula about how fabulas are constructed. We are actually witnessing a fiction theory in practice, relating the different layers of action, cognition, reflection, and emotion working together in the mind and the body and in fiction to each other. Thus, inside this fictional world, created by a feverish and paralysed ego, and created by a real-life television author, Dennis Potter, who himself suffers from the same skin disease as his protagonist, we see how so-called reality is mixed with so-called fiction. Not only does one plot mirror the other and challenge the viewer to combine them, but all the time characters and events from the different narrative frames feel the same or perform the same acts and eventually cross the walls of the different narrative spaces or address each other from discourses that are represented as separate.

Actually, in the last sequence of part 6, two minor characters from the crime plot enter the hospital and the socialisation plot to confront the author of the novel/film with the fact that they have such minor roles, no names, and are just supposed to do all the dirty work. They literally try to shoot the author, who is only just saved by his own detective-figure, his own fictional alter ego – who then suddenly eliminates the author instead of the characters who rebel against their roles. However, the next day the author is resurrected and well, and leaves the hospital!

The medium-reflexive dimension is thus very strong in *The Singing Detective*, but not just as a playful gimmick. It points to a much more direct discussion of the function of fantasy and fiction in our lives and in society. One of the symbolic scenes that keeps recurring is a scene from the socialisation plot where Marlow as a boy climbs a tree in a forest. In this way he might be said to be trying to escape from his problems, but his action is also an expression of the need to overlook and control chaos. In the tree he converses with God and himself, working through his problems, and he clearly expresses the wish to be a detective. The tree then also allows us to see a connection between the imaginary and the symbolic order, the process whereby we try to use our 'narrative desire' (Brooks 1985) to construct stories – our own and larger ones.

Detective fiction is a powerful model for this narrative desire, but even though Potter uses this form positively, as an image of all narrative constructions in search of the understanding of basic traumas, he also treats popular fiction as a possible shield or diversion. This is shown, for instance, in the dialogues between the psychiatrist and Marlow, where his detective stories are used as clues to the 'hidden story'.

The fourth part, 'Clues', thematises the way in which Marlow is constantly rewriting and transforming his life and basic problems through different narrative processes. His wife attacks his use of detective stories: 'Write about real things in a realistic way – real people, real joys, real sorrows – not the silly detective stories. Something more relevant.' But Marlow replies: 'Solutions – all solutions and no clues, that's what the idiots want. That is what they understand by the bloody novel – I'd rather have it the other way around. All clues and no solutions. That's the way the world is. Lots of clues and no solutions' (Potter 1986: 140). Of course this is contradicted by his own eager construction and decoding of narratives, and by the role narrative structures play even in a postmodern culture, where narrative structures are supposed to disappear: we all try – when confronted with fiction – to construct the story, to find meaning, and if it is not there, we tend to read it in.

However, this particular dialogue can also be seen as part of an ongoing dialogue in the text and between the different plots and styles of The Singing Detective as a discourse where high culture/avant garde meet with mass culture. As a writer and as a person Marlow is haunted by psychological and cultural guilt and an enormous inferiority complex. Through the therapeutic plot and the socialisation plot this is linked to the feeling that he is an informer, that he himself is actually the guilty one, the true criminal, hiding behind the mask of the hardboiled detective and the skin disease. In a way, then, the whole narrative project of The Singing Detective, and in fact much of the rest of Potter's television fiction, can be seen as a sort of critical deconstruction of the popular narrative text. In the last part of the story all the popular texts and intertextual references evaporate into thin air, and we are firmly back on the track of social realism. The text, then, is not a wide open narrative, like many of the commercial TV serials, but a kind of narrative where in the end a clear solution and a hierarchy between the discourses are established. The aims of the text are psychological insight and emancipation, and the ideology seems to point in a critical direction. But it is not a high-culture accusation of the popular text that is put on the agenda. Rather it is a criticism aimed at the institutionalised forms of socialisation in connection with which the popular text can be seen both as a clue and as a form of diversion, not a solution in itself.

Potter is able to speak through both the *avant garde* channel of narration and the popular channel of narration, creating a very dialectic sort of 'stereo effect'. If, for instance, we take a closer look at the intertextual signals and frames in *The Singing Detective*, we find within the crime plot not only the hardboiled genre but also elements of the classical detective story, where the intellectual reflection process dominates over action, and we also find elements of more psychological crime fiction, where the focus on the emotions of both criminal and detective is essential. In the therapeutic plot we also find a wide range of intertextual references. First of all the melodramatic form and style is clearly at work across the different plot-lines, but we also find extensive use of social realism, especially in the socialisation plot. But all the time the text may suddenly turn into a symbolic or radical text, using a modernist montage technique and editing, a stream of images like a spider web that make patterns of a non-narrative kind. This is the case, for instance, whenever we approach the visual representation or memorising of the primal scene, the death of the mother or other aspects of the socialisation plot and its hidden fabula. Finally it must not be forgotten that the use of comedy and satire is widespread in the text: the sudden cuts from the symbolic or deeply troubling scenes to extremes of morbid humour is a very important part of the aesthetic construction of the text.

Potter has learnt from the postmodern condition not to respect the discourse of the great divide, but rather to respect narration processes and viewer constructions taking place on both sides or across the divide. He is thus undermining the elitist side of the *avant garde* project without losing the critical dimension, and without surrendering to easy notions of postmodern commercialism and nonsense.

MODEL VIEWERS AND ACTUAL VIEWERS: POTTER AND THE AUDIENCE

There is no qualitative, empirical reception analysis available to tell us how different viewers evaluate and decode Potter's television fiction. And it is in fact very difficult to get empirical data on these kinds of very complex decoding processes and fiction formats dealing with a variety of intertextual references and subconscious mechanisms. But we have some quantitative evidence of the average Potter-viewer in the UK and Denmark. In Denmark we only have data on the reception of *Pennies from Heaven* (1990), whereas we have UK data on *Christabel* (1988), *Blackeyes* (1989), and the repeat of *Pennies from Heaven* (1990). Unfortunately neither of the countries has data on *The Singing Detective* in the official broadcasting research units.

The Danish figures show that *Pennies from Heaven*, which was broadcast fairly late in the evening, had an average audience of 3.5 per cent of the possible audience, or approximately 150,000 viewers. On an evaluation scale from 1 to 5, with 5 as the maximum, the average evaluation is 3.64. These figures clearly show that this mini-series has not reached what you would call a mass audience in television terms. But it is still a mass audience compared to book-readers and cinema- and theatre-goers, at least in Danish terms, and the evaluation of the programme is above average. The typical Potter-viewer in Denmark is fairly well educated, lives in the greater Copenhagen area, and is more likely to be self-employed, a senior citizen, or a manual worker than a civil servant, a student, or an apprentice, and is likely to be over thirty. However, it is clear from the figures that although we are talking about relatively small figures, we have a very differentiated group of viewers. It is not a mass audience, but on the other hand it is not an elite audience by composition.

The average audience in the UK for the three mini-series is of course much higher in absolute figures: *Pennies*, 2.7 million, *Blackeyes*, 5.5 million, and *Christabel*, 5.6 million. The percentage figures are also much higher than in Denmark (at least for the last two mini-series): roughly around 10 per cent of the total population. So here we are talking about a mass audience. The evaluation of all three series, expressed as an average appreciation index, is above average, with *Christabel* at the top: on an index scale with 100 as the maximum, the three series score as follows: 76 (*Pennies*), 51 (*Blackeyes*) and 79 (*Christabel*). *Blackeyes* thus receives the lowest evaluation of the three, while the naturalistic drama *Christabel* is the highest rated of the three. Female viewers dominate at approximately 55 per cent, except in the case of *Blackeyes*, where we have 55 per cent male viewers (perhaps because of the juicy sex-scenes!). The average viewer for *Christabel* and *Pennies* is clearly a person over 35, whereas *Blackeyes* interestingly enough has a much younger viewer profile: people aged twenty-five to thirty-four. The average social composition of the audience for all three series together is AB (higher and lower managerial, professional or administrative groups), 17 per cent; C1 (skilled supervisory non-manual and lower non-manual groups), 24 per cent; C2 (skilled manual workers), 26 per cent; and finally DE (residual groups such as state pensioners and casual workers), 33 per cent.

One cannot draw the conclusion from these empirical data that Potter is a commercial success, as one might from the ratings system in American network television. But certainly these figures show that Potter's television fiction does cross the line between the two sides of a former very sharp, great divide between high culture and low culture. His fiction represents a sort of semi-popular *avant garde* on a television screen that was once much more divided between very popular and pretty straightforward commercial naratives and very high-cultured TV drama – he is a critical postmodernist in practice.

REFERENCES

Adorno, T. W. (1972) *Kritiske modeller* (*Critical models*), Copenhagen: Rhodos.

Ang, I. (1985) *Watching Dallas*, London: Methuen.

Baudrillard, J. (1985) 'The Ecstasy of Communication', in H. Foster (ed.), *Postmodern Culture*, London: Pluto Press.

Bondebjerg, I. (1988) 'Popular Fiction, Narrative and the Melodramatic Epic', in M. Skovmand (ed.), *Media Fictions*, Aarhus: Aarhus University Press.

Bordwell, D. (1985) *Narration in the Fiction Film*, London: Methuen.

Brooks, P. (1985) *Reading for the Plot*, New York: Vintage Books.

Collins, J. (1989) *Uncommon Cultures*, London: Routledge.

Dunkley, C. (1990) 'A Funny Sort of Feminist', *Financial Times* (date unknown).

Eco, U. (1985) 'Innovation and Repetition: Between Modern and Post-Modern Aesthetics', *Daedalus* 114. 4.

(1986) *Faith in Fakes.Essays*, London: Secker & Warburg.

Ellis, J. (1982) *Visible Fictions*, London: Routledge & Kegan Paul.

Fiske, J. (1987) *Television Culture*, London: Methuen.

Fuller, G. (1989) 'Dennis Potter', *American Film*, March.

Grodal, T. (1990) 'Framing, Intertext and Metatext', in P. Dahlgren, K. B. Jensen and S. Kjørup (eds.), *Strategier för TV-analys*, Stockholm: Department of Journalism, Media and Communication.

Hall, S. (1986) 'On Postmodernism and Articulation. An Interview with Stuart Hall', *Journal of Communication Inquiry*, 2.

Harvey, D. (1989) *The Condition of Postmodernity*, Oxford: Blackwell.

Hebdige, D. (1979) *Subculture: The Meaning of Style*, London: Methuen.

(1988) *Hiding in the Light*, London: Methuen.

Huyssen, A. (1986) *After the Great Divide*, London: Macmillan.

Jameson, F. (1979) 'Reification and Utopia in Mass Culture', *Social Text*, Winter.

Jencks, C. (1986) *What is Postmodernism?* London: St Martin's Press.

Jensen, K. B. (1986) *Making Sense of the News*, Aarhus: Aarhus University Press.

(1990) 'Reception as Flow. The "New Television Viewer" Revisited', stencilled paper, University of Copenhagen.

Katz, E. and Liebes, T. (1986) 'Patterns of Involvement in Television Fiction', *European Journal of Communication* 1. 2.

Metz, C. (1982) *The Imaginary Signifier*, London: Macmillan.

Morley, D. (1980) *The 'Nationwide' Audience*, London: British Film Institute.

Olson, S. R. (1987) 'Meta-Television: Popular Postmodernism', *Critical Studies in Mass Communication* 4. 4.

Potter, D. (1977) 'Realism and Non-Naturalism', *Official Programme of the Edinburgh International Television Festival*.

(1986) *The Singing Detective*, London: Penguin.

Schrøder, K. C. (1988) 'The Pleasure of *Dynasty*', in P. Drummond and R. Paterson (eds), *Television and its Audience*, London: British Film Institute.

Chapter 9

Semiotics by instinct
'Cult film' as a signifying practice between audience and film

Anne Jerslev

On 7 February 1979 Howard Hawks' film *The Big Sleep* reopened at a major art cinema in Copenhagen. An expectant mumble was heard in the crowded audience before the lights went out; I felt like a member of a theatre's audience just before the curtain rises: an experience one mostly gets secondhand nowadays, watching films about theatre. I felt like a connoisseur among other connoisseurs. It seemed that all of us had watched *The Big Sleep* at least once before. We knew when the highlights were coming and it seemed to us that they were performed in that very same moment just for us. Every now and then, from somewhere in the rows a few lines would be cited that Bogart and Bacall were to sneer politely at each other on the screen seconds later. And right after the famous café-scene where the two of them are testing each other verbally via horse metaphors, a great many people in the audience applauded loudly. When the film was over everybody applauded vehemently and whistled as if to get the actors back on stage.

CULT FILMS AS DECONSTRUCTION

This bit of memory describes precisely a historically specific construction of a cult event in relation to cinema and a certain film. One might also say that it describes the putting into existence of a cult film. I am going to use this memory as a point of departure for a discussion of the very concept of *cult film. And* I am going to discuss the meaning resulting from the clash between an audience and a 'cult film' to come, a signifying practice that I shall call a *cult event* or *cult culture.*

I find this specific clash interesting for two reasons, both as a
cultural practice and as a sort of textual staging. In the first
place, it may be read as signifying postmodern culture in a wider
sense. I use the concept postmodern here merely to indicate a
mode of comprehension that transgresses modernity's hierarch-
ised construction of meaning: the cult event speaks of a cultural
practice that invalidates already fixed cultural codes, and constructs a certain relation between the filmic texts and their audiences on grounds of a perceptual cognition structured as an
'intertextual encyclopedia'; Umberto Eco (1984, 1985) uses this
concept to describe the extensive visual consciousness of a
modern audience that structures perception and cognition into a
pattern of pleasurable repetition. Second, the cult event is
interesting because its discursive practice can to a certain extent
be regarded as a symbolisation of the structural codes of contemporary media reception, both in the cinema and in front of the
TV set.

In the first of two articles on cult films in the Swedish film
journal *Chaplin*, critic Olle Sjögren writes that

> The concept of cult film has turned into a public relations
> device in Sweden. But underneath the term hides an inter-
> nationally widespread movement of heretics, constantly fight-
> ing against pompous orthodoxy, morally as well as aesthet-
> ically.

> (Sjögren 1988 – my translation)

Sjögren's statement represents a widespread understanding of the
cult film genre as constituting a sub-cultural movement, circulating in another cultural and institutional environment than the
cinema of popular culture. But I would suggest that it has now
become necessary to revise or to expand the use of the concept,
as we approach the end of the century. I shall argue below
that 'cult film' has lost part of the specific sub-cultural meaning
traditionally attached to it. The problem is not that film marketing has usurped the concept, but rather that: when any film can
be marketed commercially as a cult film – i.e. labelled a cult
film before it has even been shown in a cinema – then the public
relation business has labelled a tidal change in media culture.
I'm not arguing that cult film is a concept deprived of any meaning, but rather than indicating a certain genre it may be con-
veniently attached to a certain mode of reception. In view of the

amount of private video recorders that allow for screenings of the horror and splatterlike part of what Sjögren calls the aesthetics of heretics, and in the light of the continuing blurring over at least two decades of any certainty about art being the site of moral or aesthetic truth in contemporary culture, I find it difficult to understand cult films as merely subversive and consequently oppositional to popular media fiction.

Speaking of cult films and cult events I am primarily – and this is exactly my point – referring to a circulating and interdependent structure of meaning, involving an audience and a film. I am considering the cult event as an ancestral form of a more widespread culture of reception around 1990, thus representating a sort of cultural mentality to be found in the visual texts and then transformed and developed into a specific cult discourse by the cinema audience.

It is by focusing both on the aesthetic and the narrative similarities between contemporary fiction films and on the fact that, generally speaking, the audience around 1990 has changed in a crucial way in comparison with that of the 1970s, that the concept of cult film may be given a new significance. This is what interests me in this chapter. At the same time it is evident that films which deal with the lives and opinions of outsiders or in other ways address specific groups of spectators may still be part of sub-cultural activities.

In my previous description of the *Big Sleep* event, I focused on a specific circulation of meaning between cinema audience and film. The condition for this interaction is first of all a distance of time, in several ways: as 1970s spectators we were watching a film made in 1946, but at the same time (1979) we were spectators on an opening night, as if the film had been made that same year. We knew the film by heart, and yet we were in anticipation, as if we were going to watch a much-discussed film that had finally reached the country. The result of these clashes and contradictions of time was that we became highly aware of the viewing situation and of ourselves being constructed as spectators. Considering German theorist Gunther Salje's definition of the spectators' position vis-à-vis the film as 'das stumm-passive sich-fallen lassen' (Salje 1977: 273); or Christian Metz' reference to 'the spectator's solitude in the cinema' and his statement that the cinema audience does not, like the theatre audience, constitute 'a true "audience", a temporary collectivity'

(Metz 1982: 64), the cult event calls for theoretical concepts that are able to account for and to emphasise the ambiguity of the setting and the circulation of meaning.

But the circulation between audience and film also signifies an emotional distance, because of the fact that we know the film, though some of us probably better than others. Consequently, we do not merely or necessarily participate by identifying with the narrative development or the history of Bacall or Bogart. Because we know the story, we immerse ourselves in it. Rather, because we know the story, the pleasure of watching is derived from a position of sovereignty where hypothesis-making becomes a play-act, and the question 'What happens next?' is asked from a position of playful mastery, because we already know the answer. While the 'stereotyped frames' unfold in front of our eyes and ears – this is what Eco terms the stereotyped pattern of situations and narrative segments in genre films – we hasten devotedly towards the next beloved sequence before it has actually been projected. It is thus segmented and separated from the previous as well as the following scene, and this is why the virtuous repetition of the same few sentences is followed by applause and whistling.

The historical distance between film and audience even prolongs the intertextual references prospectively: not only is the spectator familiar with *The Big Sleep*, but this film points towards other and more recent films: other Marlowe interpretations, film noir remakes, other and more recent secondary texts: extra-textual media gossip about the characters who were also lovers in real life, and so on.

I will now move on to a 'classic' example of a film cult event. But first let me summarise: what quite obviously happened in the Copenhagen cinema may be interpreted as a textual deconstruction, a dismantling of the text as a coherent signifying system. But this deconstructive effort is made possible only because the film itself offers it as a possible way of reading: because the film itself is not as discursively coherent as it seems; because even a dozen viewings does not prevent the spectator from a feeling of confusion, of never quite understanding what has really happened and who really killed whom; and also because the film changes its story and narrative mode halfway through, from film noir to a love story.[1] Altogether, the pleasure of repetition, the historical distance as well as the incoherent narrative make up a signifying practice that can be labelled a cult event: the cult event transforms the film into a cult film and positions the spectators as a cult audience.

So the concept of repetition is central to this retheorising of the term cult film: one of the characteristics of the *Rocky Horror Picture Show* audience, as I am going to demonstrate, was that they had literally seen the film dozens of times. But repetition may also be theorised as a feeling of déjà vu, put into play by the aesthetically conscious intertextual circulation that is characteristic of contemporary media fiction. Both kinds of repetition make deconstruction a possible mode of reception. So in order to understand the specificity of the contemporary culture of media reception, it is crucial to conceptualise intertextual deconstruction.[2]

What happened in the Copenhagen cinema happens, of course, more evidently when one is watching a 'real' cult film, for example an 'outlaw' film or a 'midnight movie': some of the best-covered events, theoretically as well as journalistically, are the notorious screenings of Jim Sharman's and Richard O'Brien's *The Rocky Horror Picture Show* (1975). What takes place ritualistically is, for example, that

> Throughout the showing of the film fans call for camera cuts and character action. They ask questions of the characters, respond to the characters' comments, and add lines to the film's dialogue. The fans also 'help' the characters – by providing flashlights to show the way to Brad and Janet as they trudge through the dark, rainy night, for example. In addition, the audience adds its own special effects, such as hurling toasts when a toast is proposed in the film, and squirting one another with water pistols in the rain sequence.
>
> (Austin 1981: 46)

The internationally distributed, ritual performances of *The Rocky Horror Picture Show* audience are well analysed – ever since the film gained its status as a cult film after it had been scheduled in a small Greenwich Village cinema, from April 1976 until four or five years later. Jonathan Rosenbaum states (Hoberman and Rosenbaum 1983) that in the beginning the audience formed a sub-cultural group of sexual minorities. But after the midnight shows had become famous they were not only squeezed into the cultural hegemony by the mass media, but were also attended

eagerly by students, chasing the possibility of establishing themselves as a new *avant garde* of the cinema and thus filling the
cultural gap after the sixties nouvelle vague audience.[3] Here,
however, I am not interested in discussing whether the cult event
might be understood as a sub-cultural manifestation or not, but
rather in examining the specific discourse of the cult event.[4]

What seems to be the heart of the matter in the cult culture
is the deconstruction (either obvious or less obvious, but always
playful) of the film text's position of superiority; of the text
unfolding itself in front of the reader, thus placing and constructing a position of reading for the spectator.[5] This deconstructive
discourse is called 'radical bricolage' by Corrigan (1986). The
textual discourse is put into play by means of the spectators
pretending to be directors of and actors in the film at the same
time. The cult event may be understood at the same time as a
construction of and as a travelling through a fictional universe.

THE LITERATURE OF CULT FILMS – THE AVERAGE UNDERSTANDING

The concept of cult film, as I have theorised it, is not to be
understood as some fixed structure of meaning inherent in the
film text. It is not a genre concept, unless one goes along with
Andrew Tudor's very interesting and polemical theorising of
genre as a reception concept: 'Genre is what we collectively
believe it to be' (Tudor 1976:127). Cult film is fundamentally an
event. A cult film is only brought into existence in so far as one
talks of a certain interaction between a text and an audience.
On the other hand, this specific relationship is made possible by
certain textual arrangements and historical circumstances.

The existing literature on cult films has, however, aimed at
anchoring the understanding of the concept by focusing entirely
on aesthetic and thematic structures inherent in the films. As a
result of this a great deal of the literature consists of collections
of film abstracts and film commentaries, although with different
analytical points of view (Heinzlmeier, Menningen, and Schulz
1983, Hahn and Jansen 1985, Peary 1981, 1983, 1989).

Austin (1981) is the only author to have made a systematic,
quantitative study of a cult audience's behaviour of repetition
(*The Rocky Horror Picture Show* audience). Rosenbaum analyses
the audience of the same film (Hoberman and Rosenbaum 1983)

qualitatively, referring among other things to interviews with famous 'regulars', the ever-present fans.

There seems to be something very paradoxical in these collections of cult films, in the very fact that they are placed in a collection, because 'cult film' is basically a historical conceptualisation of a film. What may be regarded as and inscribed as a cult film at a certain period, in one country, may go completely unnoticed somewhere else or at another time. Only the passing of time makes repetition possible. And repetition places the film as not-new in relation to the spectator.

Critics who do not just collect titles seem to agree that what characterises cult films and the cult event are: firstly the screening hour: late at night, often at weekends; second low budgets and poor distribution, which place the films outside mainstream circuits. (Paradoxically this excludes a lot of the titles in the collections.) So there seems to be a common agreement in understanding the cult audience as oppositional to mass culture. Third, cult films are regarded as representations of the life of outcasts. This is the reason why there are similarities between what Chute (1983) names Outlaw Cinema and Hoberman and Rosenbaum (1983) Midnight Movies, and cult films. Finally most of the literature mentions the importance of the repetitive and creative audience behaviour when talking about cult films.

Cult films eventually become commercially successful. On the other hand one will also find in the literature of cult movies the assertion that cult films are not part of the industry's middle-of-the-road production. So Hahn and Jansen (1985) stress that cult films are blockbusters, but that not all blockbusters are cult films. Thus the undercurrent of the literature's statements is the conception of cult films as a sort of film art's trash-aesthetics and of the audience as the cinema's *avant garde*, fascinated by other films than the masses and being spectators in quite another way.

My objections to the authors who make cult film collections are, first, that they relate the concept to counterproduction – thus making reference to intellectuals and researchers who will be able to study popular culture and yet conceptualising this culture as 'camp', as Susan Sontag puts it. Second, 'cult film' becomes some sort of reversed sign of quality, signifying difference: an anthology of cult films is an anthology of films that are noteworthy, not for being art-movies, from an aesthetic point of view, but because they have been able to rise above the common denominator's darkness of commercial mainstream, gaining an audience that for this very reason love to watch them over and over again. Thirdly, I take issue with the anthologies' lack of interest in audience reception and patterns of audience behaviour. Analysis of the contextual setting of the film as an event is of the utmost importance in defining a film as a cult film, and conversely, the concept has no significance without reception analysis. And of course, audience behaviour must be the only reason for collecting films like *Blow-Up*, *Casablanca*, and *2001: A Space Odyssey* (Hahn and Jansen 1985) in the same anthology of *Kultfilme*.

In short: as I see it, the anthologies lack a historical and relative conceptualisation of cult films, and they fail to provide essential reflection on culturally determined signifying practices and signifying production.

CULT FILMS AND INTERTEXTUALITY

Now, if the literature mentioned above collects cult texts (films and stars) on the grounds of some vague notion of similarities between them as outlaw films – because of themes, production conditions, distribution, and/or audience composition – and if it is a common notion that cult films as cultural events are raised above economic calculations; if, on the one hand, the main argument is that either an audience's attachment to certain thematic positions or a place in a specific textual circuit makes a film a cult film – then, Umberto Eco argues, on the other hand, by using Michael Curtiz's *Casablanca* from 1942 as an example, what makes a film into a cult object comes from certain aesthetic or structural devices and a certain definition of quality. Consequently, he finds that there are films which are 'born in order to become cult objects' (Eco 1984: 209). Eco's article is interesting because he is taking a precise analytical point of view in relation to this spectator–text interaction, arguing what kind of textual structures invite a cult culture's spectator position. What makes a film into a cult object, he argues, an object so dearly beloved that repetitions constitute the act of viewing, is precisely its deconstructive address:

> In order to transform a work into a cult object one must be able to break, dislocate, unhinge it so that one can remember

only parts of it, irrespective of their original relationship with
the whole.

(Eco 1984: 198)

Thus *Casablanca* is not fascinating because it invites its audience
to identify with the narrative puzzle: will Victor be safe and will
Ilse go with him?, nor with the story of love between Ilse and
Rick: a story of two persons who were meant for each other,
but on whom Fate or world history played another trick. Yet,
in a sense these prototypical schemata are the reason for the
film's appeal. *Casablanca* is loved because the archetypical configurations

> indicate a preestablished and frequently reappearing narrative
> situation, cited or in some way recycled by innumerable other
> texts and provoking in the addressee a sort of intense emotion
> accompanied by the vague feeling of a déjà vu that everybody
> yearns to see again.
>
> (Eco 1984: 200)

In Eco's opinion, it is the large collections of archetypes, narrative traces, scattered into a, generically speaking, quite incoherent narrative that make up for the emotional appeal. And in
that sense he endows the cult object with a certain quality mark:
'Two clichés make us laugh but a hundred clichés move us' (Eco
1984: 209). The cult object is structured intertextually, or rather
reverberates into the realm of the unconscious, conceptualised
as a visual encyclopedia, 'the treasure of the collective imagination', as Eco calls it elsewhere (Eco 1985). But the intertextual
traces are not obvious in *Casablanca* as they are in contemporary
films. The quotation marks are not underlined, and the loss of
coherence is hidden underneath the story.

This visual or 'encyclopedic expertise' is an actual cultural and
cognitive fact; and this is why all new cult films relate to this
structure of culture and mind:

> What Casablanca does unconsciously, other movies will do
> with extreme textual awareness, assuming also that the
> addressee is equally aware of their purposes. These are 'post-
> modern' movies where the quotation of the topos is recognized
> as the only way to cope with the burden of our filmic encyclo-
> pedic expertise.
>
> (Eco 1984: 209)

A modern cult film is merely one huge collection of quotations, no matter whether, intertextually, it points forwards: *Casablanca* refers to 'Play it again, Sam', or backwards: 'Play it again, Sam' refers to *Casablanca*. The pleasure of watching the film is activated from the joy of recognition and the knowing expectation of what is to come, made possible by the intertextual references, subtle and yet so directly spoken; and/or the countless feelings of déjà vu, because nothing is spoken that has not been represented in some disguise before. In other words: all texts may be understood as variations, referring intertextually to one another and reverberating inside the spectator.

Taking Eco's point of departure one can easily characterise, for example, David Lynch's *Blue Velvet* as a contemporary cult film. It can be theorised as a 'postmodern movie', in Eco's terminology, in so far as the intertextual and intermedial references are its only mode of representation (its intertextual references are primarily to the œuvre of Alfred Hitchcock; its intermedial references are both to the common knowledge that actress Isabella Rossellini is the beautiful face of the beauty firm Lancôme's advertisements and to media gossip about Dennis Hopper's desperate private life).

Nevertheless, if as a spectator one is not able to catch the more or less evident references to *Rear Window* or *Vertigo*, to the Batman series of the fifties, to Brian de Palma's *Dressed to Kill* and to *The Rocky Horror Picture Show*, one can at least address and be addressed by the archetypical characters of the film: the Good and the Bad, the Child and the Adult, the Law and the Outlaw, and so on. Or one can be addressed by the familiar genres: the suspense and the horror film, and their classical scenarios: the lift, the dark staircase, the mutilated body.

Blue Velvet can be labelled postmodern by the fact that it exposes its own quotation marks so clearly. The blue, waving velvet curtain that opens and closes the film – a film quotation itself – underlines the very conscious and calculated construction of the film, stating its meta-textual presence. Finally there is an abundance of punchlines in the film ('That's for me to know and you to find out', 'Bud – King of Beers', 'Touch me! Hit me!', 'I close my eyes, then I drift away' – the Roy Orbison song that the awful Frank's perverted friend Ben mimes). These fragments of texts are framed by sketches, incoherently narrativised, to tell a story of a severed ear and a mysterious woman, Dorothy, the riddle of whom it is the project of the main male protagonist to solve. Perhaps![6] *Blue Velvet* thus fits very precisely into Eco's theorising about the concept of cult film, as he distils from a number of films their structural similarities: they are at once popular films and meta-films, referring to their own structuration.

But contemporary discussions of the dissolution of classic narrative discourses may imply that Eco's definition of a cult film is suitable for a wide range of films: that, by conceptualising cult film, Eco theorises fiction film in a wider sense as well as structures of a historically specific mode of reception. Here I am talking about a certain intertextual codification of and address to perception and experience. This is necessarily the case with contemporary screenings of *Casablanca*.

Eco himself seems to consider this historicisation by introducing the concept of Cult Culture. After having demonstrated intertextuality in Steven Spielberg's film *E.T.*, he remarks that

> The required expertise is not only intercinematic, it is intermedia, in the sense that the addressee must know not only other movies but all the mass media gossip about movies. This third example presupposes a *'Casablanca universe' in which cult has become the normal way of enjoying movies.* Thus in this case we witness an instance of metacult, or cult about cult: a Cult Culture.
>
> (Eco 1984: 210, my italics)

This cult cultural discourse, then, which addresses the fiction deconstructively, talkatively, more or less yellingly and more or less theatrically, is not something special. It is not to be understood as a sub-cultural discourse, but signifies a more widespread cultural setting, cutting the film text loose from its attachment to the screen in front of the spectator. For the film is always defined intertextually. And so are perception and reception.

The contemporary audience may thus be conceptualised as an audience of *semiotics by instinct*. And cult culture may be understood as a deconstructive and repetitive discourse, put into action by the possibility of activating intertextual codes, or in other words, references to the visual encyclopedia. In speaking about a meta-semiotic culture, one will necessarily have to address the unconscious in textual metaphors!

Seen through the magnifying glass of history, the low-budget film *The Rocky Horror Picture Show* is a classic example of this cult culture. The spectators' playing with the film – their deconstructive game – is made possible by repetition. The audience destroy the common opposition between temporal presence and temporal distance, and between actor (representer) and character (represented), that distinguishes theatre and cinema (see Metz 1982); and they replace the voyeuristic desire that constitutes cinema, so to speak, with a performance where voyeuristic and exhibitionistic pleasure are inseparable. And again, the cult culture is made possible by the fact that *The Rocky Horror Picture Show*, as a cult text, is structured as an intertextual collage. Its narrative oscillates consciously between different genres that are also constantly being interrupted by song and dance acts. It quotes innumerable other Hollywood films, for example *King Kong*, *Sunset Boulevard*, *Dr Strangelove*, and *Frankenstein's Bride* (see Rosenbaum, in Hoberman and Rosenbaum 1983). And the cult event itself, the performance in the cinema, consists of an endless chain of signifiers: a famous New York 'regular' plays the actor Tim Curry, who plays Frank-n-Furter. After a few years of screenings another 'regular' played the famous first 'regular', who plays Tim Curry, who plays Frank-n-Furter, and so on. And when Tim Curry announced his presence at a show in one New York cinema, he was, according to Rosenbaum, refused admission with the explanation that he was the third Tim Curry to arrive that day.

Finally, *The Rocky Horror Picture Show* performance appears in other films around 1980: in a sequence in Alan Parker's film *Fame*, two of the characters join a screening of *The Rocky Horror Picture Show* (Parker had Sal Piro, one of the famous 'regulars', as a consultant on the sequence). And thus the chain of signifiers continued as an audience watching *Fame* in a cinema in Florida rose to their feet and performed a *Rocky Horror* dance ('time-warped') that the cult audience in the represented film *Fame* dance in front of the screen together with the fictive characters of *The Rocky Horror Picture Show*![7]

RECEPTION OF MEDIA FICTION IS CULT CULTURE

If the concept of cult culture is to be understood more generally as a way of theorising the contemporary reception of media fiction, then cult cultures are constituted not only in the darkness of the cinema, but also in the twilight in front of the TV set, and around the video recorder.

Schrøder (1989) refers to an audience performance in a Los Angeles gay night club that seems very similar to that of an original sub-cultural cult audience. Only here the audience are watching *Dynasty* on a wall of several TV monitors – playfully, as Schrøder puts it, deconstructing the fictional text talkatively in exactly the same way as *The Rocky Horror Picture Show* audience.

Similarly, adolescent cultural practices around the video recorder may lend themselves to description in cult culture terms. Consider the following extract from an interview in 1987 with two adolescent boys (Peter and Michael) about their experiences with video films:[8]

Interviewer: 'Now, could you tell me why it is fun to watch the movies together with your friends?'
Peter: 'Yeah, you know, it's like with Michael, I don't think that his parents would like us to sit and scan forwards and backwards all the time. We scan to see . . . to see the funny parts.'
Michael: 'When you're with your Dad and Mum, right, they laugh y'know. It's not like with your pals, it's like . . . I think it's a lot more fun!'
Peter: 'We were hysterical, weren't we? . . . it was so funny!'
Michael: 'The night before I was laughing for a while with my Mum and Dad. You just laughed at the scene and then it finished and then it wasn't fun anymore. But when I'm with Peter, it was a scream. I was laughing for five minutes. It's like, no matter what happens, we were just screaming away. When Peter starts laughing, I start as well. And when I start laughing, Peter does. And it just goes on and on. No matter what happens we start laughing . . . But then, there were no grown-ups at home!'

There seems to be a lot going on between the two boys and their film and, of course in a less direct way, between the boys and their parents. The interesting thing here is that what structures the two boys' scanning of the tape forwards and backwards with the remote control unit is an instinctive and deconstructive reading, a dissolution of the textual layers of meaning into a kind of bodily rejection of the film's address and positioning of the subject. And equally, part of the deconstructive reading is a rite of repetition as the boys rewind to the same pleasurable segment over and over again. Contrary to the previous examples of cult culture, this small boys' audience does not refer to the fictional text in a dialogic way. Part of their pleasurable reading comes from their very obvious creation of an interpretative community by means of their control over the remote control unit – and thus by means of their changing the script and creating a reading position of their own. Moreover, on a more general level, the difference between cinema and video is that the boys may watch the video film once, but their favourite spots several times. The cinema audience watch both the film and their favourite sequences the same number of times. The boys are decomposing narrative time, whereas the cinema audience – either because they have literally seen the film before or because of the intertextually created impression of déjà vu – decompose narrative space.

Much visual fiction today, films as well as TV serials, on account of their textual construction, carry the possibility of constituting and thus participating in a cult culture. And structurally the contemporary reception mode approaches the cult culture of *The Rocky Horror Picture Show*.

I have already mentioned David Lynch's *Blue Velvet* as an example of an intertextual collage. His *Wild at Heart* is evidently structured meta-textually in the same way, carrying with it film history in an even more explicit way. The same goes for TV fiction, as Olson (1987) has demonstrated, talking about popular TV fiction as self-reflexive meta-television, 'putting readers in a powerful position and saluting them for their sophistication' (Olson 1987: 284). In other words, the encyclopedic expertise is activated through the meta-televisual address to a skilled TV viewer (Olson uses, among other examples, the highly self-reflexive TV serial *Moonlighting*). On the other hand, this TV-viewer often uses these skills for channel switching, thus playing with the very act of television watching – something which is particularly characteristic of youth audiences, who deconstruct any text, not just those which invite a deconstructive reading.

The 1970s cult culture of *The Rocky Horror Picture Show*, which was quickly extended from sub-cultural or minority groups to a wider youth audience, can thus, as a historical phenomenon and discursive practice, be regarded as a culturally as well as a geographically specific and limited media event. It arises locally, outside mainstream culture, but not directly in opposition to it.

Nowadays, I would suggest, it may be meaningful to conceptualise cult film in another manner. In the wider sense outlined above, it broadens the understanding of historically specific structures of media reception in relation to popular films and TV fiction as a whole. Cult culture focuses on the general invalidation of unambiguous codes. Whether (part of) the fiction is watched once or several times; whether it addresses its spectator with immense intertextual awareness, as is the case with *Blue Velvet*, *Twin Peaks* or *Moonlighting*; or whether, as a genre variation, it inspires the feeling of déjà vu, as with *Casablanca* or *The Big Sleep*, the contemporary audience partake in a semiotic discourse, a 'dialogue' with a present fictional text, placed in a different way from being presently unpresent (Metz 1982). Similarly, the spectators inscribe the characters into this discourse as if they were 'real' persons. And vice versa: the spectators inscribe themselves as actors in a story and a script that they write themselves. The audience play 'reality' as if it were theatre and the film as a reality that they consciously know as being represented.

In a sense the cult event refers to a signifying practice that transgresses – or at least is not similar to – postmodernism's founding concept of the circulating signifiers. On the contrary this audience discourse may be conceptualised as a way of making sense of important basic experiences of our 'optical empire' (Chambers 1986) – i.e. the experience of being a spectator as an everyday experience. In the discourse of cult culture there is a constant testing of and repetition of being (part of an) audience. Regarded as a historically specific phenomenon, cult culture transforms the spectators into an audience. If the spectator is inscribed as a subject in relation to classic Hollywood narratives, one may, by contrast, from the point of view of cult culture, speak of 'the subject' being inscribed as a member of an audience in and through the cult event. The contemporary cult audience are adults and without illusions. They are definitely aware of what they are going to get. The fictional spell and movement of innocent days is replaced by a more or less undisguised direction of repression of excess and boredom.

REFERENCES

Austin, B. A. (1981) 'Portrait of a Cult Film Audience: The Rocky Horror Picture show', *Journal of Communication* 31.

Chambers, I. (1986) *Popular Culture. The Metropolitan Experience*, London: Methuen.

Chute, D. (1983) 'Outlaw Cinema', *Film Comment*, 19. 5.

Corrigan, T. (1986) 'Film and the Culture of Cult', *Wide Angle* 8. 3–4.

Culler, J. (1981) *The Pursuit of Signs. Semiotics, Literature, Deconstruction*, London: Routledge & Kegan Paul.

Eco, U. (1984) 'Casablanca: Cult Movie and Intertextual Collage', in U. Eco, *Travels in Hyperreality*, Picador, 1986.
  (1985) 'Innovation and Repetition. Between Modern and Postmodern Aesthetics', *Daedalus*, 114. 4.

Elsaesser, T. (1986) 'American Graffiti und neuer deutscher Film – Filmemacher zwischen avantgarde und postmoderne', in A. Huyssen und K. R. Scherpe (eds), *Postmoderne. Zeichen eines kulturellen Wandels*, Rowohlt.

Ellis, J. (1982) *Visible Fictions*, London: Routledge & Kegan Paul.

Hahn, R. M. and Jansen, V. (1985) *Kultfilme*, München: Wilhelm Heyne Verlag.

Heinzlmeier, A., Menningen, J., and Schulz, B. (1983) *Kultfilme*, Hamburg: Hoffman und Campe.

Hoberman, J. and Rosenbaum, J. (1983) *Midnight Movies*, New York: Harper & Row.

Jerslev, A. (1991) *David Lynch i vore øjne*, Copenhagen: Frydenlund.

Kuhn, A. (1985) *The Power of the Image*, London: Routledge & Kegan Paul.

Lahti, M. (1988) 'Subjects in Search for the (Con)text – Intertextuality and the Spectator Subject', in Lähi Kuva, *Issues in Nordic Film Studies*: 1–2.

Lash, S. (1988) 'Discourse or Figure? Postmodernism as a "Regime of Signification"', *Theory, Culture & Society* 5: 2–3.

Metz, C. (1982) *Psychoanalysis and Cinema. The Imaginary Signifier*, London: Macmillan.

Olson, S. R. (1987) 'Meta-television: Popular Postmodernism', *Critical Studies in Mass Communication* 4.

Peary, D. (1981) *Cult Movies*, New York: Delta Books.
  (1983): *Cult Movies 2*, New York: Delta Books.
  (1989): *Cult Movies 3*, London: Sidgwick & Jackson.

Salje, G. (1977) 'Psychoanalytische Aspekte der Film- und Fernsehanalyse', in Thomas Leithäuser *et al.*, *Entwurf zu einer Theorie des Alltagsbewusstseins*, Frankfurt am Main: Suhrkamp.

Schrøder, K. C. (1989) 'The Playful Audience. The Continuity of the Popular Cultural Tradition in America', in Michael Skovmand (ed.), *Media Fictions*, Aarhus, Denmark: Aarhus University Press.

Sjögren, O. (1988) 'Underjordingarnas leende', *Chaplin* 219, vol. 30, no. 6.
  (1989) 'Underjordingarna sticker upp', *Chaplin* 220, vol. 31, no. 1.

Studlar, G. (1989) 'Midnight S/Excess. Cult Figurations of "Femininity" and the Perverse', *Journal of Popular Film & Television* 17. 1.

Tudor, A. (1976) 'Genre and Critical Methodology', in Bill Nichols (ed.), *Movies and Methods*, Berkeley, Los Angeles: University of California Press.

NOTES

1 In her book *The Power of the Image*, Annette Kuhn (1985) analyses among other things the narrative of *The Big Sleep* and the secondary story of Bogart's and Bacall's love affair.
2 When I use the concept of intertextuality in the following I am, on the one hand, talking about the obvious matter that all fictional texts, consciously or not, quote other texts. On the other hand, the concept of intertextuality theorises the more complex cultural sense in which the spectator's reception of a (filmic, for example) text is structured by, altogether made possible by, the filmic discourses that the audience have already met as well as other extra-media discourses (cf. Culler 1981, and for a discussion of film reception and intertextuality, Lahti 1988).
3 The cult audience respond in a both passionate and unpretentious way to their film, and this is why their spontaneous and at the same time choreographed behaviour vis-à-vis the film forms a contrast to the self-conscious intellectual behaviour that has characterised much of the sixties *avant garde* audience of art films. But these were 'discursive' films, contrary to the eighties 'figural', to borrow terms from Lash (1988), who for his part borrows this somewhat awkward opposition between modernist and postmodernist aesthetics from Lyotard.
4 Gaylyn Studlar's (1989) definition of a cult film is much the same in her very interesting article 'Midnight S/Excess. Cult Figurations of "Femininity" and the Perverse', in which she discusses in what way gender and sexuality are put into play in three cult films. Her theoretical point of departure is that 'the midnight movie frequently embraces perversion as an outlaw sexuality, a revolutionary excess of desire unhinged from accepted values and celebrated as social deviance'. But nevertheless she concludes her discussion of the sexually ambiguous characters of the transvestite Divine (in the John Waters film), the bisexual Frank-n-Furter (in *The Rocky Horror Picture Show*) and the androgynous couple Margaret and Jimmy (in *Liquid Sky*) by stating, firstly, that they do not transgress the culturally defined linking of femininity to perversion and secondly, that gender definitions are not too seriously questioned.
5 I am talking on another level from the Lacanian inspired psychosemiotic film theory to which my arguments indirectly refer. This film theory is definitely a theory neither of an actual audience nor of audience reception. But as a theory of the inscription of subjectivity in and through address in relation to the cinema, it is worth noting that this film theory conceptualises classic Hollywood films and thus classic narratives. So this theory is also a theory of popular films, not of *avant garde* films. In the light of other more recent narratives, other aesthetic devices and a different audience behaviour, empirically

speaking, the psychosemiotic theory's historicity needs to be questioned (as it is by Thomas Elsaesser, for example (1986).

6 For an extended analysis of *Blue Velvet*, see Jerslev (1991).

7 Just as Elsaesser (1986) states theoretically that the audience are no longer offered the psychic mechanism of identification by the film's address, it seems, on an empirical level, not to be by means of identificational mechanisms that the audience's costuming is initiated. The cult audience do not identify – they imitate playfully.

8 This quotation is taken from a more extensive interview that I conducted with two schoolboys aged thirteen or fourteen in the Summer of 1987 as part of a research project on youth and media reception. I am, of course, aware that I am jumping from the public to the private sphere, and that many differences of space and audience exist between these two spheres (see Ellis 1982). Here, however, I am interested in the similarities between the discourse of these boys, my description of cult culture, and reception theory's conceptualisation of TV spectators as an audience.

Chapter 10

Cultural quality: search for a phantom?

A reception perspective on judgements of cultural value[1]

Kim Christian Schrøder

> Nothing is more distinctive, more distinguished, than the capacity to confer aesthetic status on objects that are banal or even 'common'.
>
> (Pierre Bourdieu, 1984)

'QUALITY OF TV IS A MYSTERY'

It has long been common practice in intellectual circles in Europe to distinguish sharply between the creativity that finds expression within the recognised institutions of aesthetic endeavour and the mass-produced cultural commodities that are spewed out for mindless consumption by the cultural industry.

There is an equally long critical tradition in which the question of quality is completely irrelevant when the role of popular culture, and especially television culture, in modern society is being discussed – for the simple reason that most critics believe that commercial popular culture is by nature of low or no quality.

In terms of cultural policy, therefore, the respectable objective for intellectuals has always been to induce the popular audience to abandon their low taste, and to try to win this audience for the true qualities of legitimate art. This is the attitude on which most of the European 'public-service' broadcasting institutions were founded. In the words of former BBC Director-General Charles Curran in 1971:

> We must not allow ourselves to slip into the despairing attitude of seeing ourselves as casting pearls before swine. That would be the most arrogant folly. The course of wisdom is for us to

see ourselves as casting our pearls before people who have
been taught by us to appreciate their value.

(Quoted in Smith 1974: 190)

Within the terms of this elitist attitude, any discussion of the
'quality' of, say, an American TV serial would be absurd. And
this sort of paternalism is by no means just a voice from the
past: one of the anonymous contributors to *Quality in Television*
(1989) finds that the obligation of public-service television not
only to inform and entertain, but also to educate, is a cultural
boon that should not be abolished:

> People love being educated, if they find themselves undergoing
> the experience. But they will seldom actually *choose* to be
> educated. It will thus be a thousand pities if the broadcasters
> find that, increasingly, they have to follow the dictates of what
> people think they want rather than of what they will in fact
> enjoy.
>
> (*Quality in Television* 1989: 32)

In the American television culture – although devoted fans of
the TV medium are readily stigmatised as 'couch potatoes' by
cultural critics – the terms of the cultural debate are less arrogant
and permit an ongoing discussion of the relative quality of popular TV programmes, for instance in the various award ceremonies
(Peabody, Emmy) which annually distinguish quality products
from the general fare of the TV menu.

As these awards show, in addition to the common bottom-line
morality there is a genuine concern with quality in the TV industry, although the ceremonies can also be seen as one of the ways
in which this industry attempts to discredit those apocalyptic
visions of the modern TV culture which appear from time to
time (Postman 1984).

In connection with the awarding of the 1987 Peabody prizes
Les Brown, himself a member of the award committee, lashes
out against the upper echelons of the US TV industry because
of the haphazard manner in which it succeeds, once in a while,
in producing quality programming:

> I find it curious that people who spend their lives striving to
> afford cars and clothing of the very best quality, and who
> pride themselves on knowing the finest wines, are unable to
> say what constitutes quality in their own field, TV program-

ming. Quality of life they understand; quality of television is a mystery.

(Brown 1987)

Brown himself is careful to avoid the dual pitfalls of elitism and populism, as he rejects both highbrow 'uplifting' TV and the attitude which equates quality with popularity (something TV executives 'would not dream of doing with restaurants'). He ends up by opting for a basic notion of creative craftsmanship which ignores the specific moral or ideological, as well as the aesthetic, properties of the programme. Quality, he says,

> grows out of a profound respect for the integrity of the work by those in charge, without an eye to the ratings. Quality's only special cost is a fierce loving attention to detail.

(Brown 1987)

Not until the mid-1980s was the question of commercial quality allowed inside the confines of European academia. Boyd-Bowman (1985) in her discussion of Feuer, Kerr, and Vahimagi (eds), *MTM: 'Quality Television'* (1984) notes how the appearance of this book signalled 'the return to the realm of critical respectability of that long unfashionable concept: quality' (Boyd-Bowman 1985: 75).

This new addition to the critical discussion is not occasioned, however, by a general re-evaluation of the products of the cultural industry, but by a handful of outstanding programmes (notably *Hill Street Blues*) from one unique production company (MTM) which function almost as the exception that proves the rule of commercial American television. By labelling MTM-programmes 'at once artistic and industrial' (Feuer *et al.* 1984: x) the analysis clearly presupposes a frame of understanding in which the artistic is almost by nature at odds with the industrial.

Boyd-Bowman describes how 'the concept of quality has been shunned in structuralist and post-structuralist writing on culture'. This, however, has not prevented the existence of an almost unanimous consensus as to what does and what does not constitute quality in the cultural marketplace; after all, 'questions of value sneak into the most rigorous formalist discourses on film and television' (Boyd-Bowman 1985: 86).

Thus, in the ongoing public criticism of television fiction, 'quality' has consequently come to be associated with certain single plays or mini-series of indisputable 'greatness', such as *Brides-head Revisited* or *The Jewel in the Crown* (both of them, incidentally, produced for commercial networks). Such specimens of quality programming, which are neither politically potent in contemporary society nor aesthetically challenging, have been subtly included in 'a canon, which is perceived to be independent of personal taste' (Brunsdon 1990: 86).

In the British cultural debate, the reluctance of progressive intellectuals to touch a concept so laden with bourgeois ideology as 'quality' disappeared almost overnight when in 1988 the Thatcher government presented its White Paper, *Broadcasting in the 1990s: Competition, Choice and Quality*, which suddenly made it necessary to defend the scant occurrence of quality programming hitherto taken for granted – with no particular enthusiasm – under the old broadcasting system.

Analysts like Brunsdon (1990) are therefore primarily orientated towards the urgency of formulating a response to the Conservative challenge, as she realises how 'the "progressive" forces . . . are severely handicapped in this debate by their eschewal of any interrogation of what is, and could be, meant by "quality" in a discussion of television' (Brunsdon 1990: 67).

In accordance with this aim she, and other intellectual contributors to the debate (for example Mulgan 1990; Mepham 1990), even as they develop elements of a theoretically informed general argument about cultural quality, focus on the British policy implications of their analysis. They therefore situate their discussion around the quality of 'the overall provision rather than individual programmes' (Brunsdon 1990:77) and the likelihood of achieving variety and diversity under deregulated and market-based as opposed to public-service-orientated broadcasting systems.

The objective of this chapter is different: I readily endorse the intention to promote variety and diversity, but, as Mulgan (1990) observes, 'the abstract idea of diversity leaves unanswered questions of how good or bad the diverse programmes or channels are' (Mulgan 1990: 27). What I am going to outline in the following pages is a general theoretical framework for attributing value to specific fictional television programmes on the basis of taste-related audience readings of the programmes in question. The long-term political thrust for education and cultural practices of such an approach may turn out to be no less significant than the above-mentioned more deliberate attempts to intervene on the political scene.

REHABILITATING POPULAR CULTURE: THREE AMERICAN EXPONENTS

In America the tendency among heretical scholars has been not so much to concern themselves with the possible rare exception to the general mindless output from the cultural industry as to see quality as a property which is closely related to the audience experience, and which may therefore have a more general application to popular culture as a whole. This should not be taken in the sense of all products being of equal quality, but as a proposal that the final verdict of quality should be related to the actual experience of the various segments of the heterogeneous audience.

In his analysis of a despised genre like television melodrama, Thorburn (1976) suggests that the popular audience are

> impressive . . . in [their] genuine sophistication, [their] deep familiarity with the history and conventions of genre. For so literate an audience, the smallest departure from conventional expectations can become meaningful, and this creates endless chances for surprise and nuanced variation, even for thematic subtlety.
>
> (Thorburn 1976: 539)

Thus reappraising the aesthetic skills of the popular audience Thorburn recommends that the critical community revise its disparaging conceptualisation of what goes on in front of the prime-time screen: audience familiarity with the genres of television 'may lead them to perceive as complex aesthetic conventions what the traditional high culture sees only as simple stereotypes' (1976: 532).

Leslie Fiedler, writing about popular literature at about the same time, approaches the problem of cultural quality from a different angle. His perspective is radically iconoclastic, leading him to launch irreverent attacks on the origins, characteristics, and cultural consequences of good taste, such as the indignity and hypocrisy of 'having to condescend publicly to works we privately relish' (Fiedler 1975: 42).

The means through which this has been achieved is a set of

absolute criteria of discrimination, for instance the easy rule-of-thumb that 'there is an inverse relationship between literary merit and market-place success' (1975: 29). Similarly, the guardians of good taste have imposed their – allegedly universal and timeless – formal-aesthetic requirements on the general public, driving these requirements to an extreme where 'obscurity or at least high density and opacity tended to become . . . the accepted hallmarks of High Art' (1975: 37).

Fiedler also points out the political irony of the position of Marxist cultural critics: in spite of their faith in the potential of the working class, they have been as keen as anyone to denounce popular taste as vulgar and to defend elitist notions of art, maintaining that

> it is possible through education to purify the taste of the betrayed masses, to deliver them from their bondage to horror, porn and sentimentality by showing them the 'truth'. In practice this view amounts to the belief that the people can and should be unbrainwashed . . . into recognizing what is really, *really* good for them.
>
> (Fiedler 1975: 30)

Fiedler's analysis is unashamedly partisan and his message is a defiant one: whatever the guardians of taste call bad, he re-evaluates as good; what they see as seduction into indifferent acquiescence, he recategorises as disrespectful and irredeemable. In this sense his claims for popular culture are as absolute and universal as the established critics' claims for Art: there is no hint of the possibility that tastes may differ, that because people are brought up in different communities and educated differently, one person may come to love what another loathes, and vice versa.

The effect of *all* art at its peak moments, says Fiedler, is to 'cause the audience to get out of control, "out of their heads"' (1975: 41). Thus, in addition to a fundamental requirement of creative craftmanship, Fiedler ends up by advocating an approach to cultural quality which 'will if not quite abandon, at least drastically downgrade both Ethics and Aesthetics in favor of Ecstatics' (1975: 41).

Essentially this recommendation points in the same direction as does Thorburn's analysis: the direction of the audience, although with a different emphasis: while Thorburn stresses the audience's capacity for sophisticated aesthetic discrimination, Fiedler stresses the temporary release of the audience from rationality through the medium of the text.

Yet a third road to the rehabilitation of popular culture and its audience is taken by Schudson (1987), whose argument is more cautious and more meticulously scholarly than Fiedler's, but no less provocative if followed through to its logical conclusion.

For Schudson the observable tendency towards a new validation of popular culture raises a fundamental question: 'What rationale remains for distinguishing "high" or "elite" culture from popular culture?' (Schudson 1987: 52), which is essentially identical with the question of how one can distinguish cultural quality from its opposite.

Schudson sees the new validation of popular culture as a result of research findings within the fields of textual production, textual analysis, and textual reception, findings which have blurred the sharp distinctions between the worthwhile and the worthless.

First, in production studies it has been demonstrated how *all* cultural products are dependent on organisational and economic pressures (Hirsch 1981). Generally, high culture and low culture alike are produced with a view to commercial profitability and artistic integrity. The balance of the two concerns may vary, 'but commercial motive is rarely absent in the production of high culture, and respect for artistic integrity often has a place in the production of popular culture' (Schudson 1987: 54).

Second, in textual studies there has been an increasing awareness of the need to study the popular genres and to admit them into the curriculum, although the purpose of analysing these texts has more often than not been to demonstrate their aesthetic poverty and their ideological containment of the readers.

Under the influence of anthropological analyses of rituals, performances, and games in non-Western societies, however, scholars have also begun to analyse even the most trivial genres of the cultural industry as a potential vehicle of escape from the rationality and conformity of the everyday world, and as a medium for exploring cultural identities and the possibility of social change (see Turner 1977; Newcomb 1984).

Recently Olson (1987) has argued along aesthetic lines that quality of TV is a property which comes about more naturally as the relatively new medium and its audience grow to maturity.

Writing about 'meta-television', which is both medium-reflexive, genre-reflexive, and text-reflexive – and supporting his analysis with numerous programme examples – Olson sees television as a medium 'putting readers in a powerful position and saluting them for their sophistication. If self-reflexivity is one test of artistic maturity, there can be no doubt that television has matured' (Olson 1987: 284).

Third, the validity of these textual reorientations has been confirmed in recent empirical reception studies of romantic novels (Radway 1984), prime-time soap operas (Liebes 1984; Liebes and Katz 1986; Schrøder 1988a and 1989), and television commercials (Nava and Nava 1990), which have also confirmed the cultural connoisseurship of the popular audience. As Gripsrud puts it:

> the goal of [qualitative approaches to audience research] – often achieved – has been to empirically demonstrate that the complexity and even sophistication of popular audiences' reception of popular texts may well contradict the generally condescending condemnation of such texts by bearers of official 'good' taste.
>
> (Gripsrud 1989: 3)

Simultaneously, as Schudson sees it, most modern art has failed to live up to its traditional ethical obligations: although art claims to provide 'an enlargement of the individual's vision of what the human condition is and can be', it is not at all clear how this function 'can be connected to many of the leading experiments in art, music, and literature in our time. Many of these developments seem to focus on the formal properties of art, music and literature themselves' (Schudson 1987: 63).

In this situation one solution could be simply to abandon the attempt to define a meaningful concept of cultural quality, to let ourselves be flooded by a 'postmodern' cultural relativity where 'judgments of quality do not have pride of place and may not have much of a place at all' (1987: 64). Another alternative, which Schudson proposes with little enthusiasm, consists in exploring how 'the quality of art lies in how it is received, or in how it is created within the context of reception, rather than in some quality intrinsic to the art object itself' (1987: 59).

TASTE CULTURES AND THE QUALITY OF TASTE

On the basis of recent empirical reception research and in the light of Schudson's argument it seems clear to me that a viable concept of cultural quality as regards fiction must be based on the manner in which audience members make sense of the text, on the process of interpretation that depends in every respect on the sociosemiotic system at the individuals' disposal (see Fiske 1988; Schrøder 1988b).

The text itself has no existence, no life, and therefore no quality until it is deciphered by an individual and triggers the meaning potential carried by this individual. Whatever criteria one wishes to set up for quality, therefore, must be applied not to the text itself, but to the readings actualised by the text in audience members – readings which are multiple and hetero-geneous, be they 'preferred', 'aberrant', or both. It is a primary concern of this chapter to approach a definition of quality that does not carry an a priori bias against any such readings.

This should not be construed to imply that meaning production by audiences is random, or that audience members are 'sover-eign' to produce the meanings they choose. In hierarchical societ-ies culture, and textual readings, are necessarily patterned along class (and other[2]) lines, although the patterns may be harder to discern and have fuzzier edges today than they did fifty years ago.

Some of the recent positivist work on taste cultures (Lewis 1981) has tended to over-emphasise the blurring of traditional correlations between social class and cultural taste. In Lewis' definition,

> taste cultures consist of values and choices of cultural content
> that reflect these values . . . Distinct, recognizable taste cul-
> tures form because choices of content are not random, but
> patterned.
>
> (Lewis 1981: 205)

For Lewis, however, the characteristic mechanism behind the patterning is no longer social class, as research into media exposure patterns in the last thirty years 'has often found only very loose correlations between cultural preferences and class level' (1981: 206), so that 'taste cultures' are 'not correlative with social class'.[3]

As Lewis does not attempt to outline an alternative patterning mechanism behind the taste cultures, it becomes difficult to see his position as different from that which regards tastes as close to arbitrary: a result of idiosyncratic preference, despite his protestations to the contrary.

This position – which is merely based on studies of selective exposure to various media, not on an examination of the audience's perceptual processing of cultural material – is flatly rejected by Bourdieu in his preface to the English edition of *Distinction. A Social Critique of the Judgment of Taste* (Bourdieu 1984). Here he specifically proposes 'a model of the relationship between the universe of economic and social conditions and the universe of life-styles' (1984: xi), and he explicitly contradicts the belief that class is no longer the base of distinctive cultural tastes: that 'cultural differences are withering away into a common culture' (1984: 561). The rest of his book provides an impressive substantiation of the view that at the highest level of generalisation the crucial struggle in the cultural field is that going on between the 'aesthetic disposition', or 'pure taste', and the 'popular aesthetic', or 'barbarous taste', which correspond to the cultural practices of the dominant and dominated classes, respectively.

Bourdieu argues that there exists a fundamental correspondence between the socially recognised hierarchy of the arts and the social hierarchy of consumers which 'predisposes tastes to function as a marker of "class"' (1984: 2). Class members, broadly speaking, share schemes of perception and appreciation which Bourdieu terms 'habitus', a system of socially founded dispositions which ensure the continued reproduction of the social and cultural hierarchy along class lines.

The Bourdieu typology virtually regards 'pure' and 'barbarous' taste as polar opposites: while the former cherishes analytical detachment from the cultural object, the latter indulges in the immediacy of involvement; where the former relishes avantgardist formal experimentation, the latter only tolerates formal innovation that does not imperil comprehensibility; where the former serves the primary function, through the display of aesthetic erudition, of conferring distinction on the individual beholder, the latter has as its primary objective participation in a collective event.

As Bourdieu observes, it is not really possible 'to describe the "pure" gaze without also describing the naive gaze which it defines itself against, and vice versa' (1984: 32). In spite of this reciprocity, however, the two tastes are by no means equal in society's cultural landscape: '. . . the working-class "aesthetic" is a dominated "aesthetic" which is constantly obliged to define itself in terms of the dominant aesthetic' (1984: 41).

Nevertheless, as Bourdieu defines the two class cultures he does almost the opposite, thereby perhaps showing his own latent preference for the popular aesthetic.[4] The 'aesthetic disposition' is throughout defined negatively in relation to the 'popular aesthetic', as

> a systematic refusal of all that is 'human', . . . the passions, emotions and feelings which *ordinary* people put into their *ordinary* experience . . . Rejecting the 'human' clearly means rejecting what is *generic*, i.e. *common*, 'easy' and immediately accessible, starting with everything that reduces the aesthetic animal to pure and simple animality, to palpable pleasure and sensual desire.
>
> (Bourdieu 1984: 32)

> [The aesthete always] introduces a distance, a gap . . . vis-à-vis 'first-degree' perception, by displacing the interest from the 'content', characters, plot, etc., to the form, to the specifically artistic effects which are only appreciated relationally, through a comparison with other works which is incompatible with immersion in the singularity of the work immediately given.
>
> (1984: 34)

The popular aesthetic, on the other hand – already to some extent defined by implication in these quotations – is characterised by somewhat healthier properties: It shows

> a desire to enter into the game, identifying with the characters' joys and sufferings, worrying about their fate, . . . living their life, . . . a sort of deliberate 'naivety', ingenuousness, good-natured credulity . . . which tends to accept formal experiments and specifically artistic effects only to the extent that they can be forgotten and do not get in the way of the substance of the work . . . Popular entertainment secures the spectator's participation in the show and collective participation in the festivity which it occasions.
>
> (1984: 33–4)

So there are two major taste cultures. Why not just leave it at that, then? Well, because the historical genesis and development of these taste cultures have served a specific oppressive function, most pervasively through the educational system, serving the purpose of bourgeois domination of the cultural realm:

> The members of the working class . . . can neither ignore the high-art aesthetic, which denounces their own 'aesthetic', nor abandon their socially conditioned inclinations . . . still less proclaim them and legitimate them.
>
> (1984: 41)

In some cases, with confident and outspoken members of the dominated classes, one finds the sort of honest contradiction which dares to state the personal preference in the face of legitimate art. But a more general effect of 'pure' taste's claim to absolute and universal validity is to create the self-protective hypocrisy of people who know 'what is the right thing to say or do or, still better, not to say' (1984: 41).

Consequently, for cultural researchers working within Bourdieu's sociology of culture who like to think of themselves as contributing to a process of cultural democratisation, the rehabilitation of popular taste should present itself as an obvious task to take up. Bourdieu himself is very emphatic on this point, insisting that the denial of the qualities inherent in the popular aesthetic

> implies an affirmation of the superiority of those who can be satisfied with the sublimated, refined, disinterested, gratuitous, distinguished pleasures forever closed to the profane. That is why art and cultural consumption are predisposed, consciously and deliberately or not, to fulfill a social function of legitimating social differences.
>
> (1984: 7)

CULTURAL QUALITY: A RECEPTION-BASED APPROACH

As I see it, therefore, the task consists in abandoning the traditional, universal idea of quality. 'Quality' should no longer be seen as an absolute concept that can be applied impartially to any cultural product.

In its stead we have to formulate a set of criteria of quality which can accommodate the obvious relativity of cultural taste in a hierarchical society, that is, criteria which are neither prejudiced against popular taste nor characterised by cultural populism.

Valid verdicts about cultural quality must be based on the audience experience, or reading, of the popular text, and we must be prepared to find, to accept, and to respect a variety of verdicts; from a taste perspective, 'quality' can no longer be seen as a concept with universal application, but always as quality *for someone*.

Thanks to recent reception research we now know what Thorburn only hypothesised a decade ago: that

> outsiders from the high culture who visit TV melodrama [and other genres of popular culture, one might add] occasionally in order to issue their tedious reports about our cultural malaise are simply not seeing what the TV audience sees.
>
> (Thorburn 1976: 540)

The research done on soap opera audiences[5] confirms, and raises to a more general level, Bourdieu's axiom about high art: that 'a work of art has meaning and interest only for someone who possesses the cultural competence, that is, the code, into which it is encoded' (Bourdieu 1984: 2).

The insights of reception studies confirm the cultural connoisseurship, in the widest sense, of ordinary people, and make it absurd to deny the seal of approval from the popular texts that are capable of actualising such connoisseurship. They also make it unnecessary to go along indiscriminately with all the features of the popular aesthetic as described by Bourdieu. In particular, the total exclusion from the popular pleasure of *aesthetic appreciation* seems to be unwarranted in popular cultural practice,[6] as long as aesthetic experimentation does not lead to obscurity of meaning.

With this proviso it is clear that popular audiences are fully capable of reading texts playfully, of engaging in hermeneutic puzzles while keeping them at arm's length, and of appreciating 'work that challenges form, breaks or becomes self-conscious about formula, blurs the boundaries of genres, or seems to surpass the limits of meaning possible within a genre' – and other characteristics of quality which Schudson finds to be central to

aesthetic evaluation (Schudson 1987: 59), and which he is afraid
to lose as a result of the new validation of popular culture.

Nevertheless, in order to credit the central concern of the
popular audience, namely their desire for involvement and their
deep-rooted demand for participation, I suggest that – in addition
to shifting the site of cultural judgement from textual content to
audience reception – it is necessary to add to the two traditional
criteria of quality, Ethics and Aesthetics, a third criterion of
Ecstatics (cf. Fiedler above).

In plain terms, then, judgement about a TV programme's
quality should depend on what the various audiences get out of
it. If one of these audiences gets nothing from it (typically,
the case of *avant garde* TV drama watched by a working-class
audience), it is meaningless to tell these people that the programme has great quality. If, on the other hand, one of these
audiences gets a great experience from a programme (typically,
the case of a soap opera watched by the same working-class
audience), the question of the programme's lack of conformity to
the formal-aesthetic criteria of quality becomes less significant.[7]

In terms of practical criticism[8] the determination of quality, as
I define it, requires us to *ask of audience readings* of a text
whether these readings testify to:

(1) an *ethical* dimension: can the text be seen to have triggered
an enlargement of the individual viewer's vision of what the
human condition, in its multiple manifestations along lines of
class, race, gender, age, etc., is and can be? Can the text be
seen to have actualised the individual viewer's meaning potential
to explore alternatives to entrenched and oppressive ways of
seeing?

Thus a TV serial like *Dynasty* has ethical quality for the female
Danish viewer whom the Claudia character gets to reflect on
mental illness, normality, and deviance; for the female viewer
who reads the relationship between Blake and Krystle so as to
discover a potential course for her own life; and for those viewers
whose tolerance for homosexuality is increased by watching the
stress and pains of Stephen Carrington's struggle with his sexual
identity.

(2) an *aesthetic* dimension: to what extent does the text appear
to have made audiences aware of its constructedness, the creative
agency behind it: generic features, narrative structure, visual
imagery, point of view, montage, etc. – so as to make them

resist the temptation simply to immerse themselves in the visual representation as 'second nature'? To what extent can the text be seen to have invited audience members to be 'players' in the fiction?

Thus, again, a TV serial like *Dynasty* has aesthetic quality for the male American viewer who distinguishes between 'character' and 'actant role' with a clear awareness of the mechanisms of drama and narrative; for the female viewer who, associating from a Bolivian treasure-hunt scene, spontaneously comments on the generic similarity of this 'ingredient' to the then popular *Raiders of the Lost Ark*; and for those viewers who commute, so to speak, between immersion in and distance from the fictional content, because of their intimate familiarity with the generic conventions of the serial.

(3) an *ecstatic* dimension: to what extent has the text 'tingled the imagination of those who received it', to what extent has it caused 'the audience to get out of control, "out of their heads"'? To what extent has the text released us 'temporarily from the limits of rationality, the boundaries of ego and the burden of consciousness' (Fiedler 1975: 41)?

The mere fact of the 'addiction' of millions of viewers to *Dynasty* testifies to the ecstatic qualities of this serial. So does the reaction of the individual American male viewer whose awareness of *Dynasty*'s fictionality does not prevent him from intermittent self-forgetting involvement in the serial: 'I don't know what it is about it but you just, you end up . . . it pulls you in, like you're almost right there. You feel . . . you can feel it.' Similarly, a female Danish addict reports how 'On Sundays when I get out of bed I look forward to *Dynasty* so much I can hardly wait. It's as if, then one can clean the house before noon and things like that and then be looking forward to the hour when it begins.'

Any fictional text which actualises readings that substantially include all three dimensions must be regarded as possessing cultural quality *for the viewers in question*.

Any fictional text which actualises readings that include less than three of these dimensions must be regarded as possessing lower, little, or no quality *for the readers in question*. As to the role of the Ecstatic criterion, this means that it is a necessary but not a sufficient criterion of quality that the text *means* something to someone and *moves* someone.

While it should be fairly evident that in terms of ideological hegemony the requirements set up for the ethical and aesthetic dimensions have a counterhegemonic, liberating aim, it is probably necessary to dwell a little bit more on this perspective with respect to the ecstatic dimension.

It could be argued (and often has been in the fora where I have presented this argument) that it is politically dangerous to accord to Ecstatics any essential role in the definition of cultural quality. After the experiences of the 1930s, people warn, cultural quality and ecstacy should be kept in watertight compartments.

However, this is a way of reasoning which vastly exaggerates the potential of the media – and indeed any individual media text – for bringing about political and social revolutions, and a virtual return to the mass seduction thesis which continues to appeal to our apocalyptic imagination, without being in touch with the real processes that lead to fundamental social change. When all of the three criteria are observed, the stamp of quality will never have to be conferred on cultural works which confirm or reinforce the ideological hegemony of an oppressive social order.

On the other hand, it is clear that the ecstatic energy evoked by cultural objects does have a potential impact on social processes of change, but the direction in which this energy is released is largely determined outside the immediate media context, in the general conditions of socialisation and structures of feeling created as men and women make sense of their lives – to some extent assisted by their consumption of newspapers, books, television drama, etc.

Robert Weimann (1987), analysing from a materialist perspective the Elizabethan audience's enjoyment of Shakespearian drama, points to the vital role of fun, release, and reckless enjoyment for the challenge to authority represented by Shakespearian drama:

> any criticism, and especially a politically committed criticism, would as a matter of course condemn itself to a grim kind of puritanism if the sheer element of fun, release, reckless enjoyment were ever minimized or, even, by implication, theoretically ostracized. This is not to say that, for instance, the Brechtian concept of *Spass* (fun, pleasure) is, functionally, beyond ideology; the point is it cannot exclusively be defined

in terms of ideological structures and categories, any more than other forms of corporeal activity, such as eating, laughing, smiling, and sneezing can be reduced to ideological gestures of subversion or rehearsal.

one of the ways by which the Elizabethan theatre appropriated power was to challenge the representation of authority by an alternative authority of theatrical representation which derived at least part of its strength from vitalizing and mobilizing a new space for *Spass*, with all its irreverent and equalizing implications in the social process.

(Weimann 1987: 272)

Also when the analytical interest is directed towards less venerable cultural products than Shakespearian drama, no process of true political and cultural liberation can do without the 'ecstatic' energy released by the fictional representation in the popular audience.

POPULISM AND DIVERSITY

Some readers may find themselves speculating whether the suggested criteria will 'work' in a practical sense, when it comes to the day-to-day determination of the quality of tomorrow's new TV series or single play. The answer is that they won't – because they were never intended as a cultural tool that could be implemented as an instant arbiter of quality; as Mepham puts it, 'there is no arithmetic of quality' (Mepham 1990: 68).

To use the criteria in practice would require, first, the patience to wait for the answer for as long as it takes to carry out a complicated piece of post factum reception research about the programme in question, and, secondly, a willingness to go along with the political and cultural priorities that motivated the scholar to propose these criteria in the first place.

The ultimate objective in presenting the above criteria has been to *open a discussion* about the relationship between cultural value and cultural taste, and to challenge the established conceptualisations of quality that continue to dominate both the public debate about cultural issues and, not least, the aesthetic socialisation of the next generation at all levels of the educational system.

Some readers may feel that in being willing to award for some viewer groups the seal of quality to the 'mindless' serial genre of soap opera, this chapter is preaching the most vulgar form of populism, sacrificing all that can be uplifting on TV to the dictates of popular taste. But, although it *could* be argued that soap opera is television's 'great laboratory of modern everyday life' (Mepham 1990: 67), the above criteria do not force anyone differently inclined to embrace this genre as great art.

The only logical conclusion following from the criteria is simply that in a cultural democracy *all* tastes are legitimate and should be catered to, through a cultural policy of variety and diversity. Whether such objectives are more likely to be achieved under one economic and social organisation of broadcasting than another is a difficult question, the answer to which falls beyond the scope of the last few paragraphs of an essay about quality and taste.

But even if the criteria *were* populist, i.e. biased in favour of the taste of ordinary people, that should lead to serious concern only if we continued to conceive of ordinary viewers as cultural dupes happily applauding the most mindless and escapist TV fare. To the extent that ordinary people are becoming, or coming to be seen as, aesthetically resourceful players in their cultural environment, a bit of populism might be quite an attractive proposition, a tribute – long overdue – to that majority of the population who have for years tolerated and paid for the consequences of paternalistic cultural elitism.

REFERENCES

Allen, R. (1985) *Speaking of Soap Opera*, Chapel Hill, NC: University of North Carolina Press.
Bourdieu, P. (1984) *Distinction. A Social Critique of the Judgement of Taste*, London: Routledge (French edn 1979).
Boyd-Bowman, S. (1985) 'The MTM Phenomenon. The Company, the Book, the Programmes', *Screen* 26. 6.
Brown, J. D. and Schulze, L. (1990) 'The Effects of Race, Gender, and Fandom on Audience Interpretations of Madonna's Music Videos', *Journal of Communication* 40. 2: 88–102.
Brown, L. (1987) 'A Quantity of Quality', *Channels*, June.
Brunsdon, C. (1983) 'Notes on Soap Opera', in E. A. Kaplan (ed.), *Regarding Television*, London: British Film Institute.
   (1990) 'Problems with Quality', *Screen* 31. 1, Spring.
Feuer, J., Kerr, P., and Vahimagi, T. (1984) *MTM: 'Quality Television'*, London: British Film Institute.

Fiedler, L. (1975) 'Towards a Definition of Popular Literature', in C. W. E. Bigsby (ed.), *Superculture. American Popular Culture and Europe*, London: Paul Elek.

Fiske, J. (1988) 'Meaningful Moments', *Critical Studies in Mass Communication* 5. 2: 246–51.

Frow, J. (1987) 'Accounting for Tastes. Some Problems in Bourdieu's Sociology of Culture', *Cultural Studies* 1: 59–73.

Gripsrud, J. (1989) 'Genres and Qualities. Preliminary Notes on Hierarchies of Texts and Tastes', paper given at the IXth Nordic Conference for Mass Communication Research, Borgholm, Sweden, August (Danish version: *MedieKultur* 14, 1991).

Hirsch, P. M. (1981) 'Institutional Functions of Elite and Mass Media', in E. Katz and T. Szecsko (eds), *Mass Media and Social Change*, London, Beverly Hills: Sage.

Hjort, A. (1986) 'When Women Watch TV. How Danish Women Perceive the American Series *Dallas* and the Danish Series *Daughters of the War*', Media Research Department, Danish Broadcasting Corporation.

Hobson, D. (1982) *Crossroads. The Drama of a Soap Opera*, London: Methuen.

Lewis, G. H. (1981) 'Taste Cultures and their Composition', in E. Katz and T. Szecsko (eds), *Mass Media and Social Change*, London, Beverly Hills: Sage.

Liebes, T. (1984) 'Ethnocriticism. Israelis of Moroccan Ethnicity Negotiate the Meaning of "Dallas"', *Studies in Visual Communication* 10. 3.

Liebes, T. and Katz, E. (1986) 'Patterns of Involvement in Television Fiction', *European Journal of Communication* 1. 2.

Livingstone, S. (1988) 'Why People Watch Soap Opera. An Analysis of the Explanations of British Viewers', *European Journal of Communication* 3. 1.

Mepham, J. (1990) 'The Ethics of Quality in Television', in G. Mulgan (ed.), *The Question of Quality*, London: British Film Institute.

Mulgan, G. (1990) 'Television's Holy Grail. Seven Types of Quality', in G. Mulgan (ed.), *The Question of Quality*, London: British Film Institute.

Nava, M. and Nava, O. (1990) 'Discriminating or Duped? Young People as Consumers of Advertising/Art', *Magazine of Cultural Studies* 1. 1, March.

Neuman, W. R. (1982) 'Television and American Culture. The Mass Medium and the Pluralistic Audience', *Public Opinion Quarterly* 46: 471–87.

Newcomb, H. (1984) 'On the Dialogic Aspects of Mass Communication', *Critical Studies in Mass Communication* 1. 1.

Olson, S. R. (1987) 'Meta-Television: Popular Postmodernism', *Critical Studies in Mass Communication* 4: 284–300.

Postman, N. (1984) *Amusing Ourselves to Death*, London: Methuen.

Quality in Television (1989), London: John Libbey/Broadcasting Research Unit.

Radway, J. (1984) *Reading the Romance. Women, Patriarchy, and Popular Literature*, Chapel Hill: University of North Carolina Press.
Schrøder, K. C. (1988a) 'The Pleasure of DYNASTY', in P. Drummond and R. Paterson (eds), *Television and its Audience. International Research Perspectives*, London: British Film Institute.
—— (1988b) 'DYNASTY in Denmark. Towards a Social Semiotic of the Television Audience', *Nordicom Review* no. 1, 1988.
—— (1989) 'The Playful Audience. The Continuity of the Popular Cultural Tradition in America', in M. Skovmand (ed.), *Media Fictions*, Aarhus: Aarhus University Press.
Schudson, M. (1987) 'The New Validation of Popular Culture. Sense and Sentimentality in Academia', *Critical Studies in Mass Communication* 4. 1.
Smith, A. (1974) *British Broadcasting*, London: David & Charles.
Thorburn, D. (1976) 'Television Melodrama', in H. Newcomb (ed.), *Television. The Critical View*, Oxford: Oxford University Press.
Turner, V. (1977) 'Process, System and Symbol. A New Anthropological Synthesis', *Daedalus* 106. 3.
Weimann, R. (1987) 'Towards a Literary Theory of Ideology: Mimesis, Representation, Authority', in J. E. Howard and M. F. O'Connor (eds), *Shakespeare Reproduced. The Text in History and Ideology*, London: Methuen.

NOTES

1 This chapter is a revised version of a paper presented to the Third International Television Studies Conference, London, July 1988.
2 For the sake of theoretical coherence and expositional clarity, this chapter confines itself to the class/culture relationship. However, its general argument applies equally to the taste differences originating in gender, racial, ethnic, age, and other social categories (see Brown and Schulze 1990).
3 Other research, however, continues to find a clear correlation between social class and cultural preferences: see, for example, Neuman (1982).
4 Frow (1987) is very critical of this aspect of Bourdieu's work: he finds that its 'implicit supposition that one class stands in a more "natural", less mediated relation to experience than do other classes is a romantic obfuscation' (Frow 1987: 64).
   However, one need not go along with this misconception of Bourdieu's in order to use his categories analytically: it is possible to regard the 'popular aesthetic' as valid without also regarding it as 'natural'.
5 The argument in the following pages draws on the soap opera studies of a range of scholars, without requiring a detailed knowledge of them by the reader: Brunsdon (1983), Hobson (1982), Allen (1985), Livingstone (1988), Liebes (1984), Liebes and Katz (1986), Schrøder (1989), Hjort (1986), and many others.
6 As Frow (1987) points out, Bourdieu has a tendency to distinguish

much too rigidly between form and content, and to attribute them too easily to pure and barbarous taste, respectively – thus failing to appreciate working-class aesthetic connoisseurship.

7 In the same vein, Mepham (1990), whose vision of quality has many affinities with mine, insists that any talk of quality is meaningless if the concept is not anchored in people's everyday life concerns: 'Quality, whether we are talking about the quality of TV programming, of books, of football matches or of people, can only ever be given meaning by being connected with the purposes that give these things a place in people's lives, the values which they serve' (Mepham 1990: 56).

8 The concrete analytical examples used to support the argument in the following are drawn from the material collected in the Dynasty Project: a cross-cultural, empirical, qualitative analysis of the experience of a *Dynasty* episode among 16 Danish and 25 American viewers (see Schrøder 1988a and 1989).

Index